Long Island Sounds
2009
An Anthology of Poetry
From Maspeth to Montauk
and Beyond

Edited By
Tammy Nuzzo-Morgan
with
Edmund Miller
Allen Planz
and
Peter Thabit-Jones

1st Associate Editor:
J R (Judy) Turek

Associate Editors:
Lynn Cohen
Barbara Reiher-Meyers
Barbara Hoffman

Assistant Editors:
Justin Slone
Cassie DeMario

The North Sea Poetry Scene Press
Southampton, NY, USA

Featuring Works by:

Hassanal Abdullah * Bart Allen * Michael Ambrose * Debby Andreas * Philip Asaph * Susan Astor * David B. Axelrod * Sybil Bank * Bob Barci * Stanley H. Barkan * Diane Barker * Bill Batcher * Leslie Brooke Bell * Linda Benninghoff * Byron Beynon * Janice Bishop * Cliff Bleidner * Andrew Boerum * Sharon Bourke * Mel Brake * Thomas Brinson * Richard Bronson * Michael J. Bugeja * Margaret Garry Burke * Fred Byrnes * Louisa Calio * Paula Camacho * Vincent James Carbone * Edgar Carlson * B J Cassidy * Fran Castan * Sultan Catto * Jay Chollick * Clarity * Vince Clemente * Jonathan Cohen * Lynn E. Cohen * Lorraine Conlin * Victoria Cooper * Yolanda Coulaz * Lisa Cowley * Walt Dawydiak * Cassandra DeMario * Joan Digby * John Digby * Camillo DiMaria * Arthur Dobrin * Kathaleen Donnelly * Walter Donway * John Dotson * Peter V. Dugan * Robert Dunn * Desmond Egan * Carolyn Emerson * Duane Esposito * Sasha Ettinger * Graham Everett * Gil Fagiani * Pat Falk * Johanne Farmer * Kathryn M. Fazio * Harvey Feinstein * Thomas Fink & Maya Diablo Mason * Adam Fisher * Diane Frank * Ray Freed * James Friel * Celeste Gainey * Christine Gelineau * Gail Goldstein * Kirpal Gordon * Roberta Gould * Leonard Greco * Geraldine Green * Russ Green * George Guida * Chao Guo-Hui * Russ Hampel * Billy Hands * Barbara Hantman * Patrice Hasbrook * Meredith Hasemann-Cortes * Deborah Hauser * MC Healey * George Held * Frane L. Helner * Gladys L. Henderson * William Heyen * Joan Higuchi * Barbara Hoffman * Martha Hollander * Tony Iovino * Lisa James * Mike Jenkins * Evelyn Kandel * Rita Katz * Bobbie Kaufman * Nancy Keating * Kate Kelly * Ann Kenna * Teri Kennedy * X. J. Kennedy * Kay Kidde * Alan King * Brendan Kirk * Denise Kolanovic * Beverly E. Kotch * Lynn Kozma * Belinda Kremer * Mindy Kronenberg * Herbert Kuhner * Phillip Levine * Maria Lisella * Wes Magee * Rita Malhotra * Mankh * Maria Manobianco * Joan Marg * Maria Matthiessen * JB McGeever * Sandy McIntosh * Tom McManus * D. H. Melhem * Robin Metz * Edmund Miller * Jessie Miller * Greg Moglia * Eliza Jo Morgan * Annabelle Moseley * Gloria g. Murray * Melanie Myers * Paddy Noble * George H. Northrup * Barbara Novack * Tammy Nuzzo-Morgan * Thaddeus O'Neil * Linda Opyr * Alicia Ostriker * Jim Papa * Joanne Pateman * Simon Perchik * Russell Cameron Perry * Nancy Picone * Susan Pilewski * Allen Planz * Anthony Policano * Philip J. Postiglione * Kelly Powell * Elaine Preston * Tara Propper * JoAnn Proscia * Dominick Quartuccio * Barbara Reiher-Meyers * Marie Emmons Wayne Reinstein * Phil Reinstein * Tom Romeo * Ruth Sabath Rosenthal * Andrea Rowen * Paul Rubin * Alexander Russo * Thaddeus Rutkowski * Wendy Salinger * Darren Sardelli * Robert J. Savino * Steven Schmidt * Mary McGrath Schwartz * Ron Scott * Alan Semerdjian * Jackie Sheeler * Neil Shepard * John L. Silver * Cathy Silverstein * Hal Sirowitz * Marcia Slatkin * Justin Slone * Callie Jean Slusser * Barbara Southard * Cassian Maria Spiridon * Ed Stever * Carole Stone * Mario Suško * Douglas G. Swezey * Patti Tana * Gayl Teller * Peter Thabit-Jones * Aeronwy Thomas * Juanita Torrence-Thompson * Edilberto González Trejos * Jack Tricarico * Martin Tucker * J R Turek * Kempton B. Van Hoff * Kausalya Venkateswaran * Pramila Venkateswaran * George Vulturescu * Lois V. Walker * George Wallace * Richard Walsh * Muriel Harris Weinstein * Daniel Weissbort * Mark Wells * Maxwell Corydon Wheat, Jr. * Claire Nicholas White * Jamie White * Sandy Wicker * Ginger Williams * John A. Williams * Robert Windorf * Jack Barrett Wohl * Walter C. Wojcik III * J. Barrett (Bear) Wolf

International Standard Book Number: 0-9762795-8-4
13 Digit International Standard Book Number: 978-0-9762795-8-7
Library of Congress Control Number: 2009927106

Manufactured in the United States of America

The North Sea Poetry Scene Press
33 Woods Lane
Southampton, NY 11968
Thenorthseapoetryscene@hotmail.com

www.lipoetryarchivalcenter.com

Editor's Note

I would like to dedicate this volume of poetry to Aeronwy Ellis Thomas, whose spirit and sweetness will be greatly missed, to Vince Clemente who made the connection between Peter Thabit-Jones and me, and to Allen Planz, without whom I would not be where I am today in my poetry life.

This volume represents the fifth year of our annual anthology. In it, we have 212 poets: 157 from Long Island, 4 from Upstate NY, 24 from NYC, 10 from other states in the Union and 17 from other countries: Canada, China, England, Germany, India, Ireland, Panama, Romania, and Wales. We have English, Esperanto. French, German, Romanian, Spanish, and Tamil languages in our anthology this year. We also have a very well-written, wonderful-to-read essay by the esteemed Long Island historian and Suffolk County's first Poet Laureate, George Wallace. I hope you will take the time to read this piece as it gives a voice to the riches of Long Island's literary history.

Please read the biographies; they are not only interesting, but a peek into these poets' lives. They are a tease as to whom each is, a hint to what fullness is hidden from the world behind their words. We are indeed given a gift when we are given their poems to read, as the poems are little nuggets of them.

I would like to thank my three Guest Editors: Dr. Edmund Miller, Allen Planz, and Peter Thabit-Jones. It was an honor to work with these great men.

I would also like to thank my staff editors: J R Turek, Lynn Cohen, Barbara Reiher-Meyers, Barbara Hoffman, Justin Slone, and Cassie DeMario for their work on our annual anthology.

To the poets who allowed me to publish your work I say, "Thank you!" I also ask that you please read the other poets' work in this anthology, as it shows the good company you keep. I have assembled established poets with novice poets, giving the reader a wide spectrum of poetry.

Lastly, I would like to thank my family: Joey, Vinny, and Eliza Jo for putting up with my countless hours at the computer and on the phone getting this anthology published this year as every year. I love you all so very much!

Tammy Nuzzo-Morgan
Suffolk County's 1st Female Poet Laureate
2009 - 2011

Introduction

As a born and bred Long Islander, who spent twenty years away from home before coming back to the region in 1988, I can say that since returning I've come to realize that those of us in support of poetry on Long Island are carrying a torch passed on to us by three centuries of great writers whose lives were touched by their experiences on Long Island.

That includes not only the long-recognized cadre of "dead white men," as today's scholarly community likes to put it, but representatives of Native American, African-American, and Women writers. We've got it all -- Pulitzer prize winners, US Poets Laureate, and best selling authors...not to mention the humble, the unknown, the forgotten, and a huckster or two.

From the 18th and 19th centuries, the agricultural roots of our region produced some of the most important names in America's early literary days, beginning, of course, with America's "Good Gray Poet," Walt Whitman. Also of interest from that era are John Howard Payne, author of Home Sweet Home; Samuel Occum; and Jupiter Hammon, the first published African-American poet in America. And you can't forget the rustic "Poet Laria" Bloodgood Cutter, a favorite target of Mark Twain's sharp tongue; or the "Wild West" writer Prentice Mulford.

A more genteel tradition began to arise during the mid-nineteenth century, as the region was discovered by Manhattanites. There's the estimable William Cullen Bryant, of course, but colorful, sometimes forgotten, poets of that era include the "Laureate of the Rod And Gun" Isaac McLellan and "Genteel Poet" R. H. Stoddard. Their literary output is supplemented by that of such important figures as the African-Native American Olivia Ward Bush-Banks, Olive A. Wadsworth, Bliss Carman, and early twentieth century figures George Sterling and John Hall Wheelock.

Then, too, there are figures from the glamorous Gold Coast era of the early 20th century, featuring Book of the Month tastemaker Christopher Morley and ultimate novelist F. Scott Fitzgerald. Dorothy Parker, Ring Lardner, Mabel Wagnalls Jones, and children's novelists Frances Hodgson Burnett, Marjorie Flack, and Margaret Wise Brown also deserve a nod.

And as the century moved forward, a number of modernist authors were touched by their Long Island experience -- particularly Djuna Barnes, Paul Bowles and objectivists like Louis Zukofsky and George Oppen.

Then there's the Hamptons writers, like Frank O'Hara, James Schuyler and second generation New York School writers Ron Padgett and Alice Notley -- and Beat writers, especially Jack Kerouac but also Allen Ginsberg and Peter Orlovsky.

A number of expatriates -- from Europe mainly, but also Asia -- have called the region home, including some of the 20th century's great literary names -- including W. H. Auden, Andre Breton, David Burliuk, and Antoine de St Exupery. Meanwhile, the tradition of light verse which may be traced from Bloodgood Cutter through Dorothy Parker found new fruition among colorful figures in their own right, like Woody Guthrie, Joe Gould, and Si Tanhauser.

Finally, the contemporary era, with its influx of a well-educated residential suburban population -- and writing programs at our growing academic communities -- has resulted in the presence in our midst of such notables as H. R. Hays, David Ignatow, Louis Simpson, Jorge Andrade, May Swenson, Amiri Baraka...and the emergence from our towns and villages of such figures as William Heyen, Marvin Bell, Louise Gluck, and Colette Inez.

When you consider the breadth and scope of the field of writers that represents, there's good reason to claim that pound for pound there is hardly a region of this country that has done more for poetry and prose than Long Island.

George Wallace
Suffolk County's 1st Poet Laureate
2003 – 2005

Contents

Hassanal Abdullah

A GLIMPSE OF TIME

Standing at the center of the universe, I would hope to have a glimpse of time.
I would hope to see some teary eyes that hold the desire of such a dream
That was once thought to be impossible.
I would hope to draw an ocean of people
Waving for each other's happiness
And dancing like water that eventually brings the spring.

Standing at the center of the universe
I would like to flow as the Mississippi River
I would like to flow as the Hudson
I would like to flow as the Ganges
I would like to flow as the Congo
I would like to flow as the Thames
I would like to flow as the Nile
And then make my dream as true as the morning sun.

I will bring a founding father like George Washington
I will bring a leader like Abraham Lincoln
I will bring a voice like Martin Luther King, Jr.
I will bring a worker like Rosa Parks
I will bring a liberator like Mahatma Gandhi
I will bring an orator like Nelson Mandela
I will bring a dream-maker like Sheikh Mujibur Rahman.

No cry will be left unattended
No issue will be left unsolved
No hunger will be left for starvation
No food will be left uncovered from the rough ground
No mystery will be untouched
No mother will be betrayed
No soldier will be deserted
No prisoner will be tortured.
At the center of the universe, I will bring the light
That will change into a huge power to bring the sunshine.

2009

Now he is nine.
His bird-size eyes
Got bigger; hands and toes
Started to look manly.
He now stays up
Alone to finish his homework.
That little boy, who could not
Even sit in the bathroom
For number two, now
Locks the door from inside.
He is becoming aware of
His growing up--
He no longer cries for whatever
Happened in school,
He no longer sits in front of
The bathroom door
For his mom to come out
After finishing her bath,
He no longer hunts for
The ant that goes
Around the room keeping
A safe distance with humans.
He is nine now;
He looks at the world
In a little different way.

ANOTHER TOUR OF DUTY

See me, with your eyes closed.
Put your hands out
touch my shoulders
can you even move the weight?

Am I still in your dreams? I see you, no matter what's in my sight,
please see me, with your eyes closed.

Trust the smoothness of my voice,
I know you haven't heard it in months.
You've heard others
they've told you what you want to hear.
How you can't hold on.

The dust that covers every inch of me,
the blanket that keeps you warm.
Wrap it around you as I let the dust cover me.

See me, with your eyes closed.

SHE PLAYED

I wanted a boy,
I'd never tell her that
never have treated her like that.

The game isn't the same

I told her once,
Girls lacrosse takes more skill.

Over the years –
Watching her
running into womanhood
I think it
may have taken more skill being a father
to a daughter.

Michael Ambrose

ASHES FROM MY HEART

Crepuscular light creeps from my silent heart
Beating ever harder the farther we grow apart
When you return to me no longer far but near
The darkness in my clouded mind becomes so clear
I've walked the hallowed grounds beneath the shattered holly tree
And none but one truth remains you were always there for me
Cursed I've been like lesser men to plague's sorrowed hold
Left in the innocent, pure and deadly snows
Until you found me here lost, windswept and cold
And warmed me with love's auriferous glow
When I sit in gold-trimmed church
By countless deities I am searched
Even if I'm condemned for my life of sin
I know to rely on you even then connection close as birth
And my new start may begin

THE TRUEST LOVE

As you face me now in gown white and aglow
Cherry blossoms blowing in the wind a pink whirl of snow
They settle down beside the crowns that are the golden binding bands
So let me now lend a hand beneath your chin, raise your face to the sun
        and kiss your tender lips
Then allow my arms to fold and rest above your slender hips
As I stare into your oceanic eyes the truth now reveals itself
Heaven cannot be a lie I've only been lying to myself
I take you now this day once and forever to share in my world, my life,
My love every sunset, dawn and so much more

I~
can~~~
see~~~~
letters~~~~~
and shapes~~~~~~~~~
swirling~~~~~~~~~
~up
~~~~into
~~~~~the
~~~~~~~~cool
~~~~~~~air
~~~~~and
~~I swear
~they
spell~~~
out~~~
your~~~~~
name~~
in~
hot
vapors of kaleidoscope colors, then disappear as they
float high up to the ceiling like that of a pale misty
morning moon that disappears into the brightness
of the day. I imagine you sitting in your easy
chair, stirring the moon into your coffee
while writing poetry to me, as your
silver spoon tinks off the side
of your blue coffee cup,
creating thoughts of
cinnamon and
spice and I think how nice you are to join me in a daily verse of
coffee and poetry beneath the shade of this tree and silent stars.

WHITE KNUCKLES

Reflection of a wicked sun
burns the retinas of my eyes
as shadows elongate
themselves before us.
A pale moon watches,
whispering softly to me
the secret of patience.

White knuckles grasp
the door handle.
Complete control is yours...
Over-steering, pot holes, puddles,
'round the snake-like turns
of black-top, paved years ago
by intoxicated men rewarded
for each mile with a smile
and whiskey.

A road you viewed not long ago
from a little seat that promised
you safe travel...
your life was in my hands.

Now *my* life
            in your hands.

Philip Asaph

A RED LEAF

Fallen on the step at my front door, this leaf,
as I lift it gently by the stem,
brings me to prayer and becomes a gift
I will bring tomorrow to my lover.
All red leaves remind me of her,
and will every autumn until my death.
My mind was changed a month ago,
becoming a new kind of wilderness, when,
coming home from Zen, I saw on someone's lawn
the sudden flame of a small red tree
and felt windswept within, or like a plucked string–
a man swept clean, a man struck sane--
in this world of pains and pleasures, each
as brief as this leaf in the leaf of my hand.
The word love and her name–
one is the leaf, the other, its veins.

WHAT MY HANDS WANT TO SAY

When, as now in bed, I reach to touch her face,
I wish my hands were lighter, softer,
something other than what they are, the hard hands of a laborer,
and of one who has lived too near the street,
where what is gentle becomes suspended,
like the seeds at the heart of an apple--
this tart green apple I hold before her mouth.
Even when I wipe the juice from her chin,
as she stares through my eyes, seeing everything within,
I doubt my outer hand is capable of expressing
what the inner one intends.
And so I hope her cheek, her temple and her hair
will hear what my stunned touch
is stumbling to say, that her nose and right eyebrow will know
that when I am touching her like this,
she reaches the place in me where I am finally free
of selfishness, a creature surrounded by the field of her.
And though the sound that comes
from my throat is a growl, I want her to somehow sense
that beside her with a tending love
in this body that would defend her to its death,
a being is seeing her being
and hearing the silence in each of her eyes
as clearly as the sounds of *Om*
and *Amen.*

Susan Astor

LOSING ANN

At first a hint of distance in your eyes
a vague expression of perplexity
as if you have just heard conflicting rumors
and do not know which is truth.

Then quietness sets in, not suddenly
but seeping, slightly somber
tingeing conversation with a bit of gray.
Your syllables get snagged in nets of doubt.

Before too long, your poems grow thin
begin to place themselves peculiarly across the page
until the space between is louder than the print
until your punctuation makes the only music.

One day when I put out a plate of cookies
you wrap two carefully and put them in your purse
then move your lipstick to the pocket of your skirt.

My simple questions baffle you:
Where did you go on your vacation?
Confused, you twist the tissue in your hand.
Ask Bill, you say.

Now when I visit you at Maple Pointe
your pants are halfway up or halfway down –
you can't remember.

When you stand up at lunch
and start to walk away, I ask
Where are you going, Ann?
but neither of us knows.

UNDER THE MAGGIE MOON

Delicately, the way you walked, the moon rises
nestles against a soft grey cloud.
It is the night after your death.
The crickets are not loud.
The earth's breathing is no longer labored.
Reluctantly, we have let you go:
your smooth brown coat, the fine flaps of your ears
your perfect paws, your high elegant haunches.
Yesterday, pain swayed you up the stairs
but tonight, your energy back,
you glide where you go.
The moon, still a globe of hope, floats over us
as you, with your old eagerness,
nose open a door we cannot see,
nuzzling your ancestors and ours.

David B. Axelrod

IN THE SAME ROOM WITH YOU

After such slander you'd think
a tongue would swell, but there
you are, smiling and speaking
happily to others you lean
toward. Your white hair
in a perfect bob; a black silk
blouse and single strand
of pearls. And that slightly
British accent though you
never lived there. That
should have been a clue
for me, who told you things
in confidence. "You're a good
man," you comforted, and I
believed you. Any allegations
against me were found to be
false, of course, but who knew
that you were capable of
spreading the lies long
after I trusted you.

OLD MAN FISHING

The old man fishing for pike
in the Barrow River, had walked
a mile out of town to where
the weeds along the bank were
cool and buggy enough for a fish
to take a holiday. He cast a fly
only ten feet out and drew it
slowly in, but fifty times at least
in half an hour. "They can be
this big," he said with hands
spread much too wide to
believe him, but why correct?
The conservation sign nearby
says "All fish must be returned
live back to the river."

RUSTING

Rust populates
those parts of things
that are not touched.

Others are oiled by
fingertips, or polished
by the brush of cloth.

Deeper crevices decay.
Even the thickest
iron will grow porous.

For ships there is
comfort in dry-dock,
welders' arcs of light.

For me, waiting
and wasting. Unlike
love, entropy is slow.

NEW GENERATION

Hot summer party
torpid day
earth smells like pennies

wind teases tablecloths
sheets of rain
montage of sound

jumbles of sneakers
cooling tiles
bare feet dry, slide, dance

hip hop rocks, arms fling
damp hair curls
kids romp, babies squeal

samba, rumba, shake
fusion, bop
splashed images

on a global canvas

TURNING POINT

Day lilies
like yellow butter
surrender to
languid afternoon
their short premiere
a sun-struck boast

three flowers
on one stem
each in its own time
drifts on a mazy river of breeze

on a storm-driven day
my friend fades
ready to float away
no more treatment

the lilies harbor their seeds
their flowers will come again
bringing a burst of creamy yellow
memories as immediate as a blizzard

Bob Barci

A LOVE POEM

Well,
  I'm sittin' on the F train
  writin' you a love poem.
Yea, a love poem.
The guy across the way
  has the music to his headphones
  way too loud.
But, I don't care
  cause I'm thinkin' of you.
I don't care about
  that girl's lousy cell phone reception
  or that I'll soon transfer to the E train,
  cause I'm sittin' here with you in my head.
Well,
  I'm sittin' on the E train
  writin' you a love poem.
Yea, a love poem.
At the other end of the car
  there's a group of young guys.
They look like hoodlums
  but they speak in sign.
And I'm just amused
  with you in my mind.
Well,
  I'm sittin' on the 6 train,
  heading downtown,
  somebody's radio is on,
  and I'm writin' you a love poem.
Yea,
  a love poem.

Stanley H. Barkan

THE MUSICIANS OF XI'AN

So young these musicians,
strumming their wide-circled
banjo-like instruments,
blowing their bamboo flutes,
plucking zithers & lutes,
bowing the one-string "ehr-wun,"
striking some nameless percussives . . .
These sonorous streams make me dream
of an ancient time I've never known
except in movies & books,
reading the poems of Li Po & Tu Fu,
the *Shih Ching,* the *Te-Tao Ching* of Lao-tzu,
and the *Analects* of K'ung Fu-tzu.

THE SHOESHINE BEGGAR OF CHONGQING

He wet my left shoe,
I didn't agree but let him continue.

He rubbed it with a cloth,
brushed it once.

Then he pushed the left away
and pointed to the right.

I moved my right shoe
onto the box.

He wet and rubbed, clothed,
and brushed it.

Then held out his hand.
I gave him 5 Yuan.

He shook his head.
I shrugged my shoulders.

He pleaded with his eyes.
Again shook his grizzled head.

Finally, I gave him another Yuan.
But he rubbed his belly.

I patted his right shoulder
and shook my head.

He went on to another
who refused his footwork.

Now, I think of his thin, gray
stubbled face, eyes full of mirth.

But, most of all, his rubbing his belly—
regretting I didn't give him at least a dollar.

YANGTZE HAIKU

I

Gliding through two banks
  of soon-to-be Yangtze past
    into the future.

II

Gliding past old town
  on both banks of the Yangtze,
Great Gorges rising.

III

Black awning *wupengs*
  poling cascading waters
    of the old Yangtze.

IV

Calligraphs cascade
  terraced hills of ancient towns . . .
Cruise ships cutting through.

V

Between cloud layers,
  sky ship and red sun streaking
    through Middle Kingdom.

VI

Above, the old stone
urges the faltering youth:
  "To strive is enough."

Diane Barker

KARMIC CINEMA

Coworkers obey the gods
but I ignore their warnings
to stay the daily grind
Midday cinema beckons
to revisit a childhood of double features
white hat heroes
extra large chocolate almond bars

Aroma of buttered popcorn
draws me down dimmed aisles
to a ocean of soft chairs
that invite like a mother's lap

Center aisle center seat
enveloped in the cushioned embrace
delirious as each popped kernel
saturated with butter passes through my lips

Small joys ward off guilt
Lights fade
the excitement of playing hooky
heightens as previews begin
but truant officers of retribution intervene
as the vision-blocking head
takes the seat in front of me

WAR WITHIN

Confirmation received
Enemy has infiltrated
First shot fired

Generals convene
Defense required
Battle plans drawn

Resources requisitioned
Ready to deploy
Faith, prayer, courage

Chemical weapon loaded
This soldier alone
Ready…aim…
Drip
   Drip
        Drip

MORNING REMONSTRANCE

Yesterday's dishes I won't put away
though they're thoroughly dry in the rack
For I know they'll demolish the mood of the day
if I should start putting them back.

No matter how gently I place them in piles
the plates will not quietly go;
They are being imprisoned without a fair trial
and they want the whole household to know.

The cups and the saucers demanding their rights
in protest will shout loud and clear.
"Though melmac and Styrofoam keep out of sight,
we're china, we're proud and we're here."

The glasses, for their part, are sneaky today;
these girlish sopranos conspire,
If I take two or three to the cabinet, then they
will become a boisterous bell choir.

I take hold of a knife or a fork or a spoon
and regardless how much I implore,
It insists on clanging objection as soon
as I lower it into the drawer.

The casserole covers, when put on the shelves,
continue complaining. I'm sure
That the pots and the pans consider themselves
percussion for some overture.

If I can preserve for this little while
some peace, then I'm going to try.
So instead of getting the dishes all riled,
I elect to let sleeping bowls lie.

WINTER

Birdsong is quiet.
Winter silences nature.
Now poets must sing.

Leslie Brooke Bell

BLESSINGS

Hear the exquisite sound
of an unborn child's name,
dulcet syllables
strung like precious pearls
into a mother's lullaby.

Witness the radiance
of that child's name,
bathed in the glow of halos
and angels' wings
at the baptismal font.

Marvel at that talisman name
scrawled in schoolhouse print,
perfected in Palmer script,
matured from teenaged doodles
into a flourished signature on the page.

Believe the promise
of two young lovers' names
engraved on golden rings,
exchanged in everlasting vows
to bring forth children

who, in their turn,
will wear cradle clothes
embroidered with melodic,
shimmering, magical names

that shall bless them in this life,
and beyond the eternity
of the chiseled stone.

OCTOGENARIAN ATTITUDE

I will go to my grave
with my collar standing up
like Marilyn and Ava,
and someday,
Lauren and Liz,
starlets of the silver screen,
heroines of my younger years

with necks provocatively bared
above top buttons undone,
pointy bras straining at the bodices
of their shirtwaists,
cinched belts accentuating hips
voluptuously curving under their skirts.

Every old woman I know
from Brooklyn to Nassau
still flips her collar up,
a reminder of her sensuality
before it waned
and the stars lost their shimmer.

I will never abandon my style.
I have passed it on to my daughters,
and I will go to my grave
with my collar standing up.

Linda Benninghoff

SNOWY WINTER

The silence of the snow
this winter
was like two hands praying.

After your death
I sat in the dark room
and watched the single fluorescent light
glint on my teacup.

What is the meaning of the encounter?
Is it the world coming close
to ending--
is it two hands
clasped, meeting, intersecting?
After the whiteness--
the new green shoots rising?

NIGHT

The night comes
With a flashlight
And the sound of glasses clicking.

What is the meaning
Of the ice cream we shared today—
If only that it brings me a day closer to your death?

Each day the night
Shuts its lips and is speechless.
The torn woods answer
Cries of geese.
The rain sends itself down
As if forever.

Byron Beynon

PERFECT PITCH

I'm reading the club manager's letter
inside an intimate room
overlooking a bay
where colours change at a secret pace;
he once shared a space
with Dizzy Gillespie,
a story of perfect pitch and smoke-
filled notes, informing me of how
the jazz trumpeter
once listened to him shave,
the almost-contact of his face
in the cold mirror of light
as he told him something real,
shelled a musician's ear his way,
towards the sound he'd never forget,
that the electric razor
held calmly in his right hand
was in E flat.

TINPLATE

This is the rain my father knew.
My mother would see him to the door

as he left for work
at the tinplate plant.

A worker for all seasons,
his continental shift

sounded like a dance,
a geological movement

over a quarter of a century;
mornings, afternoons, nights,

two of each as he'd wait
for the one weekend holiday per month,

the stop-fortnight of summer
as July closed and August began.

His coil of days,
the overtime for extra pay

inside a fork-lift truck.
I still see and hear him leave,

his uncomplaining silence
I search as the tinplate shifts.

Janice Bishop

A PLACE THAT WAS

Around the corner of BAM
Brooklyn, USA
at Ft. Green and Lafayette
It was on the north side.
Left or right?
Dare I remember?

Dare I go back
to that one room
bath and tiny kitchen
where he taught me
to slice off the heads of fish
to curry rice
and make Jamaican delicacies
to please his palate

Roaches ran along the bath
Feet scurried across linoleum
Amid thick summer air
or cold clanging pipes
we bed and wake
young hands entwined

Dare I go back
alongside that steel and fragile man
whose dreams we shared
in a blaze of noon
racing down the continent
to Kingston town
back again and

      Death
    I dare not speak

On this street of yesterday
I turn outward to Alvin Ailey
and know the dance
Celebrate *Revelations*
the flow fold hold
        release

WINDOWS OF BONE

Under cover of night
woven among strands of stars
I trace the course
of your silver hair
the spill of the same brown eyes
as Father who cradled me
newborn

You easing into me
awakes that child in me
safe at Father's side
with you at home
inside myself

You found me first
through Mother wound
a swirl in hot dark fluid
shaping me into body

Again the wound sheathes
the blade
as we yield to a heave of living

Dawn breaking within ourselves
wrapped in the flesh of time
wrung from our bodies

We will hang skeletons
in the wind
and through windows of bone
arrive Home adrift
on patches of light

Cliff Bleidner

PHASES OF THE MOON
(A Haiku Sequence)

new moon in summer
    only fireflies
light the way

hard to believe
    it's the earth's shadow
first quarter moon

my love has died
    tonight just me
and the half moon

the last quarter moon
    so low in the sky
it could bump the buildings

making a saint
    out of the scarecrow
full moon

Andrew Boerum

THE UNMEASURED MOTHER OF BROTHER HAND'S GLOVE

we may not always be this; and i say that
without vowels i say this
"w my nt lwys b ths"
a caution its suren't - a promise i couldn't
thus currents will guide me to stray

thus wasn't to be might certainly can
emotions are weightless - i belong to the seas
and the buoyancy of consonants will sink you like bait
and thus such i say
"e a o aas e is"

TO JUDGE A SILENT DISTANCE

there was a distance that you weren't hearing
but heard it i did certain   like a fury of silence
[back that up - there was a summons, you missed it]
it was a clearing in the heads   collectively
           an instance of clarity   [the judge was furious]
a severed end to a cluttered catastrophe
…..but you weren't listening   [the jury looked violent]
instead you sat like books in a dream
instead you read from lines yet wrote
lest to hear the long distant scream   of dreams shot dead
[case dismissed the evidence has left]

Sharon Bourke

CHARLES OF THE STEPS

Charles, swaddled against the world,
All burlap
Save for a slit through which he saw,
Nestled himself in a shadowy corner
On underground steps,
Watching, leg by leg and shoe by shoe,
Fifth Avenue go by.

He looked up, not for alms.
He never begged, never put out his hand.
He was too bound up for that,
Arms close to his body,
Body itself immobile.
He was inward and armored,
Reflective, away.

He looked up, pulled his burlap down
And wanly, brownly smiled.
Tired but warm from his past self,
"I'm Charles," he said, bemused,
And I too smiled, I said my name,
That's all there was to it.
He must have seen the back of my heels
As I climbed up to the street.

Charles got around, and so did I.
We met in improbable places,
Uptown, downtown, over the years,
Always on a flight of stairs.
He would find a perch
For the bundle of his being,
A porch on which to rest and rock,
His space beyond philanthropy,
And he would cradle his special
Knowledge of the dark.

THE CAT

The cat rests on the shelf,
Ever smiling while ever sleeping,
Every act prolonging
In a clay eternity.

LA KATO
(Esperanto version)

La kato kusxas sur la breto,
Redetadanta dum dormadanta,
Cxiu ago plilongxiganta
En argila eterneco.

Mel Brake

SPECK OF BROWN

We have lived
In the richest of
Specks   Neighborhoods
Of brown   But are counted
In a sea   Among the poorest
Of white
Cotton   We are
                        Specks of
                        Brown
Since   In a sea of
The early   White cotton
20th century
My people   Since the
Have serviced   Election of
Your people   Obama

As indenture   We have
Servants   Been spotted
                        For a change
We have cleaned
Your homes   Words of
                        Victory
We have cared
For little Johnnie   Headlines
                        In our local
We have fought   Newspapers
Off your husbands
                        But what
But we   Has changed
Have gone   For specks of
Unnoticed   Brown
Like the borrowers
We don't ask for much

And need
Much less to make
Our way
In your convoluted world

TWO SISTERS

Like
Levers on
A kitchen
Faucet

I have two
Sisters

One cold
And the other
Hot

My sister
Who was born
In August

Is as warm
As sunflowers

Baking in
The afternoon
Sun

The December
Sister

Is icy
Like the kind
You slip on
And break your
Neck

I love both

They each
Have their
Own way

One with letters and
Cards of appreciation

And the other
With a cold shoulder

Thomas Brinson

ALONE IN DUSKLIGHT
Long Beach, NY

Three mating pairs of pelicans
glide and soar in unison
They ride gracefully the thermals
webbed feet dangling beneath them
searching for dinner far below
amongst placid waves of Florida Bay

I sit in silence, watch shimmering sunset
wait for my dinner of grouper with Caesar salad
in Sundowner restaurant on Key Largo
a couple of doors away from the Caribbean Club
Today it's a dingy local fishermen and tourist-trap bar
where once Bogey and Bacall seemed to have it all

The orange-purple-pink glow of lowered sun
stretches behind clouds along the horizon
It casts a widening spotlight of color
across the darkening, gentle sea

A lone cry of long-legged-and-beaked stork
skimming the sea surface towards some home
pierces the cooling night air
It rouses in me deep sadness for ex-wife Sara
still so sorry for how badly we blew it all

The sliver of a new moon rising in dark sky
winks in calming compassion at me
Despite aloneness my heart is filled with such gratitude
in wonder for the mere magnificent mystery of simple being

DUSKRISE

Islip, NY

running alone
valiantly fighting
a losing battle of the bulge
during this post-Turkey-day season
i feel the chilled air
enliven my pumping lungs
brush my close-bearded face
with sensations of crispness

the reed-full swamp
on either side of
this ribbon of searoad
aimed straight
into the Great South Bay
emits a jittering cacophony
of waterbirds nestling safe
into the deep shadows of night
as fading swiftly into the darkening West
the Sun pales from grey-orange to grey-pink
while entrails of jet-streams swirl
in wild calligraphy strokes
imitating mysterious messages
which signify nothing to me

across the black shimmering of waves
the lights of Robert Moses Causeway
reflect themselves in shards of broken parallel stripes
as I gaze heavenwards
to see in one sweeping line
the alignment of Mercury with Mars with bright Venus
signaling me to stay the course
through this silent evening's certain prime

Richard Bronson

DOC BLADES

he's called -
wears his speed skates barefoot.
He's an orthopedic surgeon, so I've heard
but wouldn't know;
and they say beware, his blades
will cut you
if you're slow. Ask him
why he skates,
and he'll tell you 'bout
the long glide, strong stride,
steel on ice -
prowl of the pack
full moon howl
flying through the night
mantra of the blade
heat of the meet
rhythm of the motion.
And I thought I heard him
say as he raced away -
high on ice, the stars sing me
their ecstasies!

THE DINNER PARTY

An evening breeze —
candle light shuddering,
reflected in dark mahogany —
a bronze candelabrum, red carnations.
I hold a Bordeaux in my hand,
ready to pour, its dark hue
theme for the evening,
to match the china, the candles;
giving you the 440 glass,
judged A on my keyboard —
a tone to which violins are tuned —
the C goblet for myself,
and E for our absent guest;
a minor chord, this triad,
sounding a *grave* note,
only I could know,
having assessed each glass.
A Chateau Du Bois '98, and you,
knowledgeable of wine,
nod approval as I pour,
deep red filling our glasses,
the third in our party
yet to arrive.
The china, *Rougemont,*
red to match the wine,
was my mother's gift.
She would understand
the absent guest,
the light of red candles
reflected in crystal bowls,
the need for the minor chord.
I raise my glass,
toast the empty chair.

Michael J. Bugeja

PLATH ON PRIMROSE HILL

Upon renting a London flat occupied once by Yeats,
Plath reportedly opened to a line from one of his plays,
which read, in part: "I will get the house ready."

You wander home to William, Fitzroy Road,
As if to hush the filibuster muses
One, Two, Three. Your days are numbered like an ode

Anointing laureates in each abode.
When letters stop, the poems come in deuces.
You wander home to William, Fitzroy Road,

But soon become the swan that Leda rode.
Your hero mesmerizes, then seduces:
One, two, three. ... You like to number "day" and "ode"

Recorded in a diary whose code
The coroner deciphers as he chooses.
You wander home to William, Fitzroy Road,

Escaping yet another episode
With husband back in Devon. He recluses.
"I. II. III." Your numbered days are like an ode

With strophe, antistrophe, and epode.
How easily a tragedy reduces!
You wander home to William, Fitzroy Road
123. Your days are numbered like an ode.

JOYCEAN LINK

A clear blue sky lent a lift
to Tuesday in Dublin,
a fine day for a stroll through
St. Stephen's Green.
Sprawled on the grass
lunchtime regulars
listened to a brass band
blaring brisk American tunes.
Then to my right I spied him
drifting on the edge of the scene,
tilting slightly
as he made his way to
Leeson Street.
His unruly hair
set out on its own route,
while his disheveled shirt
exposed white belly skin.
No bother.
He was determined
to make it up the street
to the nearest pub.
Not a pretty sight.
But oddly fascinating,
this renowned scholar so learned and
so utterly defenseless.

SUNFLOWERS

In foreign lands
armies of golden giants
in waving yellow fields
salute me from trains.
Staring with their jaunty black eyes,
heads tossed to the sun,
massed in thousands,
making a statement.

Provence smells of them.
In the shops
their smiley faces stare from blue and yellow fabrics,
plates, tablecloths.
Papier mâché copies beckon to tourists:
"Let the sunshine in."

Yet, they are awkward.
Alone, in an earthen jar, a sunflower looks forlorn.
Like humans, they need companions.
At flower markets
they are always too tall, unwieldy,
towering over the pretty, dainty flowers.

Sunflowers, are, after all,
the workhorse of the flower world.
Pushing out cooking oil
and tasty seeds.
Not prima donnas
like showy roses and orchids.
This homely family member
must smile to curry favor.
It must wave to strangers.

Fred Byrnes

FOR TJ, WITH THANKS

In Snyder's Pub
during the decade of the '70s
Barry Fitzgerald tall
TJ the bartender
wearing a white apron
would sometimes
in his soft sad tender tenor
break into Irish song

All would stop
All beer drinking
All conversation
All argument

While the world outside
bustled about its business
every ear in the pub
would listen
as TJ gently let loose
those ancient tear rolling lyrics

And even if not
a drunken mother's son
of us in that pub
ever possessed the slightest notion
of where we were going
we'd always remember
where we'd once been

NOT A BIT

On an August night
when heat hangs in the air
real as orange-blue flames
from a never-ending furnace
unpaid bills
on top of a barren refrigerator
a crying baby
thirsty, as the gasless car
abandoned in the driveway.

She picks up the needle
again, her heroin cooked
according to recipe,
offering freedom from
bills, hunger,
high stereo sounds
of a fatherless baby
and rusting car.

Wearing a long-sleeved
flannel shirt
to cover fresh tracks,
she claims to be visiting friends,
the heat isn't
bothering her a bit.

Louisa Calio

BODY OF GRIEF

The mind/body puzzle
calls us to search more deeply,
dive beneath the outer exhortations
or *shoulds*
to know the Core Self as Good!

Too many
shouldering more of the world's weight
than Atlas
demanding perfection
perfection demanded of
live on too few good words.

Hungering for good feelings
they find instead
a lump here, a tumor there
a heart blocked
and leave within the year.

THE CURRENT

Wet and luscious as the snake I come
to lick your body whole
The million-million thoughts
Dissipate
A calm current flows
At a steady rate
Nature, lush and abounding as
the five scents of Eve
Passes
Traces of leaves, salt seas, deserts sands
Passing
Even we.

Paula Camacho

SOLSTICE

Entering a barn
we leave the stars outside to tell their own stories.

We are here to celebrate the solstice
the sun standing still in the northern hemisphere.

Relative to velocity, one and the same motion
different from different frames

there are no absolutes
all motions to the observer are bound to earth
like blood bound to bone
and in the darkness a candle light of reassurance.

We are here again for one midwinter night
past the equinox, past the funeral of fall.

Relative motion stops and changes direction
without ambiguity, without a solar-based calendar,

only souls in the darkness of a planet
our hope lying in the communion of each other.

TRENCH KNIFE FROM WW I

Where will you hide
blade sharp as a bayonet
handle formed in brass knuckles
effective in tight trenches
close quarter combat?

You go to Vietnam
perhaps by then already heavy
with the blood of the dead.

You cannot speak
tell your war stories
you are silent.

Touching it,
the hands of ghosts
the smell of metal
the opium of visions.

You need to be given away
find your own future
a relic with stories only imagined.

Vincent James Carbone

TIME

Time, is just a thing marked by shadows in the sky.
Now, like before, is just a moment etched in time until it passes by.
Then, once was and held moments still to try.
Gone, is what was had until those moments died.

Edgar Carlson

GREEN KNIGHT TWENTY #2

autumn leaves
test
the homeless

old war vet
squeezed
of money
in a rib
of parkland.

an old pond
raised
on granite
where birders
come
with handouts

IS MIMIC COSMOS TONAL ZONE REMOVE

In poison ivy leaves, the first to change,
a few of many red with orange koi
are pressed against a vinyl superwhite
suburban fence. With gravid sides, they hang
in place, about to lay a thousand eggs,
within this roe, a salamander; frog
and toad; terrific lizard; gobi egg,
for sixty million years unhatched; peacock
and penguin; enigmatic fur of shrew

and white opossum's grizzled hair.
As white opossum parklane pocketbook
is walking circles in a garden room,
a man, in separation, from lawn with tree,
is tall is lean is watching possum smooth
a nest in grass with leather naked tail.
Again this man is working in vermont,
where cousins own their farm, and thumbs his way
to alabama, where driver hits a cow;

again ships out to california and
aleutian isle campaign in bering fog,
where rain is mist, is condensation stream,
is soggy tent is soggy boot and sock;
again is mired in south pacific war
beyond the range of guns and waits for dawn.
The sky is tracer white is bullet black.
He takes this time to write his sisters back.
This man is not alive. He knows the dead

are busy in our head. He knows this tree
is oak, the buds are bunched and velveteen.
He taught his kids to color out of line,
to play at cards, to box, to swim, to work,
decide today to let the possum live
or die. His eyes are wheat. His sleep is sand.
From distant rail, he comes and goes, as dead
should be allowed. He rides between the doors.
He wears no hat. He smokes saloon cigars.

UPON THE DEATH OF PAUSUTAGUS

upon the death of britain's eastern lord
iceni knight hip pocket client king
of rome, his wife, boudica, walks a wire
is walking rope among iceni earls.
has even fewer friends on the roman road
where army alpha dog, paulinus, rules
as sword as noose as nero's napalm stooge
too deep in war in wales to keep the peace.
the procurator, catus, left in charge
is tax collector roman butter ass:
repots the status quo with eastern celts
to sate the roots of nero's money tree.
the queen denied defaced deforced misharmed
rethought refused refaced reformed rearmed.

B J Cassidy

AUTUMN

Yesterday we worked
on the stone wall
mortaring rocks
arguing as usual

this morning the wind
blows hard from the north
what is unfinished
must wait for spring

NOEL

The moment they started
to scatter her ashes
the wind came up
from the woods
through the fields
blowing her essence
into to the sky
down to the grasses
in late afternoon
a whirl wind
a gusting
a swirling about
a dance - a dance

SHIPWRECK AT MONTAUK POINT

I lost the well constructed poem
about the retired New York City Fireman
with Irish eyes of infinite light blue sadness
      and how right off
I knew he was interested
while my sort of boyfriend
sat three barstools away
watching everything
out of the corners of his eyes
      and how the lightning crisscrossed the sky
      in sheets of blinding whiteness
and the rain fell
like Noah's ark was outside
someplace up island
      and the rain
the rain over our heads
as we sat inside
this dark and dreary bar
everyone drunk but me
      refusing his offer
to let me buy you a drink
which everyone else took him up on
with little or no hesitation
and him telling me about
his dead wife
      and me trying not to
look like I was interested
in spending this night with him
because he had that look
like he had never been really happy
in his whole life
      and I lost it
I lost the poem

3:00 A.M.

Can you see moonlight
Chase itself in water
As it cobbles a path to me,
Enters my unshuttered window,
Casts the shadow of a wide-mesh screen
Like black net stockings on my bare legs,
While I dance and dance
Through the hours that close at dawn?

I want to follow light
Back to the moon,
The way I used to follow you,
Learning to dance with quick, silvered steps,
Tap-tapping my way, up that cinematic stair,
Chiffoned and rippling.

GONDOLA

Like a beautiful woman who knows
How light paints lips,
How shadow improves a cheek,
And turns her superior profile
To those who admire her,

The gondola enters Bacino Orseolo,
Pauses before the crowd
As a gray-haired singer,
His hands in prayer,
Concludes his aria,

Its final note aimed and glancing
From one white wall of stone
To another behind him,
Crossing the canal, ringing
Like a bell, a cymbal, the skin

Of a drum, until his heart,
Opening the moist pleats
Of his larynx, speaks,
Until the sound of all he feels
This moment enters us and continues,

As time in Venice continues
Circling, like the canals,
Like the cochlea of our ears,
Like the words and melody he sings,
Given to him by his ancestors,

VIVALDI CONCERTI

There are so many birds in Vivaldi.
Once he heard them, he had to have them.
He seized what the earth offered
And gave everything back. Tonight,

A snow bunting calls from the woodwinds –
Soloist in camouflage –
White dress shirt, black tailcoat,
A piccolo for a beak.

Like the first to blow song through a wing bone,
He longs to soar and Vivaldi
Lifts him, lifts him so lightly,
Each bird sings again.

The peak, the dive, the aerial glide.
Our shouldered wings unfold and we all fly.

Sultan Catto

LOST IN PRONOUNS

Searching for those departed songs
that rolled off your lips centuries ago
I am lost again in your whirlwind.

Fearful of falling into the shadow of time
on ever turning wheels of change,
head tilted,
arms imitating a half infinity sign,
a whirling dervish,
I am lost again in your soul's high flames.

In a hazel delirium within a sea of pronouns,
hands upon the revolving wheels of time,
I want to slip back into your spell,
lie in and wait for you, my impossible dream,
to dream me your meaning again.

ON EXILE

Tormented by the absence of your eyes
I live on a faraway island.

Everyone around me is young in here,
except the wind.

Palm trees, iguanas,
cormorants and laughing gulls,
nights performing tricks to old stars,
flame moths burning their wings
over unending camp fires.

And you, my forbidden word,
you're always at a distance
spread out on some space-time sheet
sunbathing over its golden sands.

The wind of my glass blower's soul
doesn't have the strength
to reach your arms, climb your hills.

Exiled, I lie here on white sands
converse with the waves, write poems,
scribble them to paper boats with imaginary sails,
release them to the waves in the wind, hoping
they will reach your shores like ancient sailors,
carry pronouns to your eyes in lines of salt.

QUESTION

Tonight the full moon is in your house.
Tonight you drop your handkerchief,
close your eyes.
Tonight you're afraid of the bull,
of the matador too.

You know all sorrows last long,
joys always come to an end,
river never sleeps,
memory of the sun fades,
heart grows numb and time grows old.

We endlessly scribble mislaid words,
talk with speeches never uttered,
take everything in,
lie to ourselves it will all come to an end.

Will it ever end this infinite pain?

Will you, one day place your naked self
into these arms that long for you
and surrender to love without words?

ESCAPING IT

Ho Hum with daggers,
here it comes again, more memory,
pouring on smooth, I'm thick
with it:

Bent double almost,
with all the hot times turning
cool; my parents stiffening,
bent into my back—their zest is airless,
painted in, they are a wax tableau—
I carry them
And it, a mohair relic—
their chair, fabulous with bumps;
and the man who sat in it, I clutch
his sneer

I carry unshocked secrets:
weighed down with mold; grimly buttoned
things. And bobbed,
the quiet flapper, I carry
her

I carry excruciating cuteness, old
babies, who coo in wax. But when a
dapper derby hooks itself, and
underneath, where
uncle and his moustache
perch— I cry, go back this is
too much!

Still, rosewood comes:
inlaid with melancholy, it's just
a desk—but bulging
with photographs—a drawer
of impossible youth, of blinkless
eyes—all wax! I am encased
in it, the past

O turn it blank! I'll live happily
there, amnesia's floodlit room—no dark-eyed
loss, no words,
that for any pale reason, resonate

No linkage, just
a crystal man; lightlight inside,
with nothing held—no trace of moonlight—
or a quarrel—not even the
cobwebbed burden
of a glance

MADMAN SPEAKING

New storms up there—thunder
in the head—bravado-brained, it *bursts!*
and with
such force, that I, with terrifying hands, now coddle
meteors! Will myself
cruciferous. And briny dazzled, turn sudden
clam! owning, as if born into it, its

Morbid juice. I will—I *must!* toward
foreign ecstasy, creep newly born—or
eel-like, twist; work heavy human
into it, find glass and there somehow, re-silver

Youth
and touch in mirrored memory
the acned boy; slim blush and fumbled
sexuality—to be ingenious! To throw off cells,
leap *leaping* from oneself, pop-eyed
and singing madrigals!—to be another's
bloodline, flowing

Smooth. But pity—all these flame-lit
possibilities, seem repugnant
now, they bring me, tugging madness,
to the
sharpest edge I feel

Unhinged. This brain has rust corroded
lobes, they make me thrash; or glued
to stodgy platforms, make me sit; watch
fireflies; the deep bending
of a continent, the twilit haze—but not,
full-flood organic, to partake
of them, to simply

Sit; grow thin, dry husked, and papery—to lose
the wing; the latitude; the infinity
of lines. And who
denied their liquid fingers, touches
light? This sanity is

Too sad for me. I'd rather say—come here
magnificence! *you* be
gardenia; and I, turning leather—oxford
or anklestrap, I'm someone's

61

BICYCLE DAY

and they said; "perhaps"
but I was aware of at least hundreds that I could speak of
perhaps more with my tongue removed

and these days pierce like morning after the doldrums

but its numb,
and a dull sensation remains.

The nature of everything is natural
and when we circumvent the cycle
the deliberate becomes ambiguous
and the caustic, abundant.

Yet the flesh remains
and the days bleed into the dwelling

and I contemplate the complement
of crimson, fresh rain, and Lysergic Acid Diethylamide

after a bike ride with Albert Hoffman
I soon realized that every high ranch
should have a built in portal for viewing rain storms

ROMANCING ETERNITY

Upon an axis she dances, romancing eternity
Enchanting, unfurling, unfolding it all to me
The bastion of passion spoken through poetry
The actualized anthem – ohm is me!

Qualify the music by the quantified musing
The compromised viewing is a cosmological misusing
In other words it's other worlds that are looming
While we canonize the categorized characters of our choosing

In tune to the universe tune into the verse
The movement of luna, sea - the moon and the earth
The un-compromised cycle, The eternal promise
The piety in prose, the poise of the forest

The sound of the harvest, the reaping is piercing
I put my ear the ground and hear the earth weeping
I found myself sleeping upon a moist fertile clearing
And most of this dream has been the mist of my nearing

Kneeling, endearing myself to the sky
For she is open to me, as to her – am I
I do believe indubitably I've been duped as a youth
The truth is nothing new to me, now I have proof

Do not be fooled when I'm silent for days,
I'm merely sifting the truth for the right things to say
And when I pull away, know it's for the best
I'm honing the glowing for whatever comes next

Lift me upon an earthly display
Release me in rivers where the energy sways
And I stay unwavering - the undulating yawn
The open aired odist with unorthodox form

Who's to say who's more insane?
The cynical madman or the laughing deranged
The pivotal moment when you figure it all out
Grants you the license to critical fall out

With unkempt hair you tear at the field
Alas - you've gone mad! At last, you can feel!

At last, it's all real! BLAST! – it's the numbing
And this is the way we enter the strumming

The humming of struggling through this
The something of sun things summed in the riff
The misplaced grace, this listing technique
Will they find me brilliant, obtuse, or delete?

If it's left unsaid it's left unremembered
The unspoken oath over your head
When promises are meant and kept to yourself
The sentiment is seldom more than pelt

Wrapped in my warm trophy of self-loathing
The selfish, self sensitive song of the longing
Seducing the soul at the dawn of the morning
Soothing to know I have caused all this

Upon an axis she dances, romancing eternity
Enchanting, unfurling, unfolding it all to me
The bastion of passion spoken through poetry
The actualized anthem of enlightenment – ohm is me!

Vince Clemente

DREAMING LITTLE AFRICA

> *Little Africa, just above Porpoise Channel here in Stony Brook was once*
> *solemn burial ground for the Algonquin tribes that first inhabited this*
> *part of Long Island, the Paumanok of our Native-American forebearers.*
> *Guidebook: About Old Stony Brook*

The doe
straining for the saltlick
bathed in foxfire
an arrowhead lodged in her flank,
I am so close
I see her eyes washed in blood
the scarlet sheen of her lashes.
Dazed, she leans
against a white birch:
the only sound
in the still forest

Always the same doe
the same dream,
how many times
must I return?
Canoe beached,
I raise the bow
to a clump of woodfern
pad through the forest's nave,
where she waits for me,
scraping her wounded flank.

I cannot remove the arrow.
I must cradle her in my arms,
ask her, *forgive me*
  forgive me
    forgive me.

65

KEROUAC IN NORTHPORT

He slept with a brakeman's lantern by his bed
 for the Muse on foot, up from the harbor
  to the cottage in Northport &

woke to *St. Matthew's Passion* & black coffee &
 where to set the ampersand
  to piece together the graph

which was the poem
 for the lightning
  in his head.

MARGARET FULLER TO HER MOTHER

Mother, can you see
the bud about to open,

periwinkle blossom
of a delicate hue,

and the brash geranium, stipple-pink
like the blush on a young girl's face,

or the laurustine, butter-colored,
that spiral their way to heaven?

Why, I hear such flowers blossom in winter,
Mother; I've been told such a thing.

Mine in the garden, the footpath
below the shed, I fear are barren,

with not a leaf on them, nor a single blossom
to hold against my breast,

place under my pillow, summon the angels
there, chittering beyond the meadowfence.

SO SWEET THE LINDEN

So sweet the linden
 why, enough to lift it
  from the sky, caress
   its yellow blossom and leaf.

It clings
 like the arm
  of a lover
   waking

from a fretful sleep,
 and delicate as the pulse
  beneath a quivering
   philtrum, or

sacred
 hollow
  along the valley
   of a woman's thigh.

I must ask then: why
 does love come
  to us, from such
   chaste, fortuitous things?

TRILLIUM FROM THE WOODS

Thoreau left Monadnock
 with tundra petals, crustaceous
  along his breastplate.

it is said, their fragrance
 followed him
  all the way

This must be true,
 for only yesterday
  long before dawn

I rambled through the woods
  beyond Otter Pond
   and found a single

star-veined blossom
 to carry in my breast pocket,
  and as light as air: a trillium.

Now, at night
 unable to sleep
  moon laving my room

I find a star
 seared into my heart:
  three white petals

and an opal flame.
 It smells of the woods,
  the musk of long sleep

(the kind animals take)
and the Lord's aspen fingers
  viscous with pinepitch.

Jonathan Cohen

HORSESHOE CRAB

O *Limulus polyphemus*! O long-enduring creature of the sea!
Sword-tail, king crab not really a crab, arachnid, sea spider
unchanged over time, since 500 million years, living fossil
modern trilobite, wanderer of sea floor, plowing for food
onward, digging for worms, feeding on life, surviving
covered in armor, domed shell, the shape of a horseshoe
like hard leather, dark brown, darkening with age, in time;
sea creature with multi-lens eyes on the sides of the head
like those of a dragonfly, light sensors, and with other eyes
in the middle, close together, as if the one-eyed Cyclops
son of Poseidon, the sea god, seeing at night, finding mates;
ancient mariner with blood as blue as the ocean itself
translating oxygen from water to blood, breathing with gills
like books whose thin pages turn constantly in the water,
like the leaves of a living book about the secret of life;
marine scorpion that crawls and swims from the depths
in late spring to swarm in shoals under the full moon,
countless waves of them ascending toward the shore
to spawn in evening flood tides of Atlantic bay and cove,
males clinging to the back of females, swimming together
mating, the females laying their eggs in the sand, onward;
each laying many thousands of eggs in successive tides
the males fertilizing them, completing the spawn
enough surviving predators, shorebird, fish, sea turtle,
enough surviving wave and storm destroying their nests,
crab larvae emerge and swim and find the sea floor
growing, molting, maturing, as always, onward!

NIAGARA FALLS

Tremendous torrent! for an instant hush
The terrors of thy voice . . .
—José María Heredia, "Niagara"
Trans. T. T. Payne & W. C. Bryant

"WHEN YOU DISCOVER no extravagant Falls here,
you must excuse me. I can't make Nature into
something different from what I find. Let people
in the future say that I depicted the Falls
truthfully, and everything agrees with my
account."

     Peter Kalm writes to Benjamin Franklin in 1750:
"At Niagara Falls—you can look up the river
and see all the water flowing from lakes
that appear more like great seas
with many large rivers, the most blue magnificent part
of which throws itself over the Falls"
     The largest group of freshwater lakes on Earth
"And all the water comes dramatically to the brink—
you can't look at it without being stunned
watching so vast an amount of desperate waters
plunge to the bottom rock of the Falls
and fly up to a great height in the air
all in motion like a boiling cauldron"
     3 thousand tons of water per second
"And the water cascading down from that Olympic height
foams in the ugliest way, as if lather or suds
and makes an ominous thundering sound
that's louder at times and believed by the Indians
to surely warn of approaching bad weather"
     15 million cubic feet of water per minute
"And every day when the sun shines
a rainbow appears below the Falls
and under you, when you stand at the side of the Falls,
a fine rainbow, and sometimes two rainbows,
one on the outside of the other:
the more vapors, the brighter and clearer it is;
and when the wind blows the vapors away,
the rainbow disappears, then reappears
as soon as new vapors come . . ."

5½ billion gallons of water per hour
And now multicolored neon signs everywhere
are greeting the tourists as they arrive:
"The nearby village," a New Yorker writes in 1822,
"abounds with mills, shops and foundries, iron works
and a dramatically growing number of other factories
        Eternal clang and bawling hammers"
BETHLEHEM STEEL
            UNION CARBIDE
                    CARBORUNDUM CORP.
            HOOKER CHEMICALS & PLASTICS
                    OCCIDENTAL CHEMICAL
And now, at night, a thick fog rises from the Falls
and creeps into the sleeping town, and out over the land.

Lynn E. Cohen

DREAMS AND DREAMERS

Summer's end again:
an almond tree,
sweet, hard nuts,
the tart taste of tongue-laced kisses --
soft like a southwestern rain shower.

My hair traces our lips
tangles with your mustache
your fingers caress
my breasts
tan; tentative
after too many years
too many changes
too many mixed messages.

Tall, taut; tired;
gaunt; grayer; with
teeth stained by coffee and cigarettes;
your face inflamed in a perpetual flame.
Time has not been kind
to dreams and dreamers.

"ON THE DEATH OF W. D. SNODGRASS"

You loved blondes with blue eyes
replaced them when they turned wives
forty-five to my 19
I was Larissa
in that near-Russian winter
defying your misogyny
I navigated ice tunnels and became my future:
Moved away and continue to write
questing for an inspirational chalice
addicted muse
holier than thou grail
and found you on every rail
on the trail of summer
the tail end of late autumn
in each turning of the equinox
in Indiana late one February
on Long Island in his alcohol-laced lips
in His November kisses
cold by sleet time.
But now that you are gone
I will know when you try to reappear in another form.
I will sacrifice the poems
for sleep
And self-induced suffering is no longer a treat –
for I am older than you when we met.
Yet I am very much saddened by your death.

YOU EXIST ONLY IN MEMORY

My memory hears
a mesmerizing Venetian melody:
"Al Di La; Al Di La; Al Di La"
strains played at a Seville bullfight
against a Franco red sky
Guernica still at MOMA
Picasso's painting doing time:
an upside down minotaur falling out of line
characters screeching off the canvas
and causing grim thoughts
to invade my berth
through the Basque Country
toward Tuscany
summer 1970
the Bolshoi dancing in Madrid
mandolins and balalaikas
babushkas and blankets
dotting the backdrop of gypsy camps
twentieth-century pointillism
seen through time's prism
when I wander
in search of lost days
that were stolen away.

Lorraine Conlin

RADIO DAYS

Dad went junking
found radios tossed on dumps
repaired some, dismantled
and reinvented others
He'd rewrap wave transmitters,
thin coated wire, 'round bits of twigs
said "save it for a rainy day"

Mom used his so called *junk*
to keep busy nights he was away
She'd accordion-fold sheets of crepe-paper
draw free-hand, cut out perfect petals
shape them between her thumbs
use an old butter-knife to curl the tips
with homemade spools she'd wire them
to stems devised from discards
create beautiful bouquets
in colors of the season

She taught me how
to make her favorite, paper roses
bend wire back and forth
feel the cold metal get hot
just before it breaks
I'd cut my fingers on razor thin radio wire
wrapping petals on scraps of metal
learned how to stop the bleeding
cover bare stems
use common sense
never waste
and finish whatever I begin

WAR WOUNDS

Dad, an Army vet
told war stories
showed me scars
slivers of shrapnel
expelled from his body
the half inch lift
nailed onto his left shoe
his Purple Heart
how he earned it
why he hated damp weather
took so many pills
visited the VA Hospital
shock treatments   cold water

He'd whistle a tune
add lots of da rah rahs
sing *"Never trust a sailor an inch above your knee"*
invent lyrics of his own,
"Boys never buy the cow if they get the milk for free"
always a lesson

I'd blush, promise him
there would be no free milk
kept my word till the day I said "I do"
when I married a Vietnam vet
whose scars I could never see
whose stories I will never hear

Victoria Cooper

OVER AND OVER

This is her.
This is the woman you love.
She doesn't have a name yet.
But one day you will ask her and she will whisper it to you in a soft, ginger pitch.
You will remember the very instant she leaned in and talked close to your ear
and the s-curve of your neck.
You will replay this moment over and over in your mind;
Sharp, static heat will race down the backs of your arms and your breath will go
shallow in the very purple center of your shaky chest.

You will feel her breath over and over on the lobe of your ear,
her words slipping out like white hydrangeas; subtle and stately.
Between tongue and tooth you will believe the time means something so much
    more
but she will not remember the exchange.
Her pupils will shrink and disappear like slushy, highway-snowflakes on your
    windshield.

There is a tape in your mind and it will roll over and over
those dusty, dull moments of doubt that
stick like honey-grease to your fingers.
And when you take a sip from the glass on your nightstand
your fingerprints will shine
brighter than any word her tongue has ever twisted to say.

The thought of her still bobs like an off-shore buoy
and her face is burned on the backs of your eyelids like a weathered muscle.
For a moment you believe that chivalry might be dead (you were right.)
But it was the photograph that made you think over and over
Of the minutes passed since you turned your back to the fog
Resisting the spitfire, blood-boiling madness of her voice.

You will notice that her smile is wrinkled.
You will hate that this is her.
She will not recognize your mouth when you try to talk back to her
and she will forget to look when you point out at the field
to the rain coming down on a sunny morning.

You remember her name and when you finally switch off the light and go to bed
you will stare up at the ceiling and say it low and hushed,
over and over again. Penny. Penny. Penny.
Between skin and skin there is only light.

JUST A GLANCE

that was all,
maybe
a slight of
hand,
maybe an essay
written in longhand.
There was no
stuttering,
no pale moon
light,
no love poems
to verse.
But there
was a revolution,
and a picture
to keep
in my purse
where all the
rest of my
wrapped breath mints
are
living.

Yolanda Coulaz

FEEDING THE FAMILY

At ten years old
I walk home from school
in my parochial greens
and sensible shoes
wondering what vegetable
goes best with the steak
that's defrosting in the fridge.
My fifth grade friends ride the bus
planning afternoon activities.

I have my own key
let myself in
to an almost empty house
where the dog greets me
wanting a walk
and something to eat.

My brother nags
my friends play tag
outside the kitchen window
as I prepare dinner.

Mom cooks at the convent
for the nuns
for less than minimum wage
to help feed the family
and I am at home

cooking for a brother
who complains
about my food
and always has seconds
sometimes thirds.

THE SIDE STREETS OF LONG ISLAND CITY

just south of Steinway off Ditmars.
The cobblestones of Astoria Boulevard.
This was my world—

The haunted house just three doors down
where my brother and his friends
illuminated by candles and flashlights
told ghost stories
that smuggled their way into my dreams.

The boy who ate worms and pissed
through the bushes that lined our back alley
aiming for whatever unwitting cars came by
who sent me Valentines and Christmas cards
and wrote me letters like we were oceans apart.

The girls who made fun of the crooked cut
of my hair, stole my toys
and locked me in the neighbor's tool shed.

The older boys who waited for me
to pedal by on my bike
so they could knock me on my ass
right where the boy who ate worms would piss.

The spinster woman, or perhaps she was a widow;
I don't recall. (Yes, that's it! A widow! A widow
who fed her husband a daily diet of arsenic
and ground glass until he was gone.)
who always found a reason to scold
or punish me for something I didn't do.

"Always listen to grown-ups; they know
what's best!" my parents would say; and I did.

They are all one way now, those side streets of Astoria.
They linger now in nightmares and memories.

Lisa Cowley

IN UTAH

I was reminded of the age of the earth
how it was all once under water.
These canyons I've seen
once held massive rivers.

The horseshoe crabs I see, here, in Orient
really masters of the sea
really ancient knowledge in their sea souls.

And I complain that
the large red jellies
lining the shore
are blocking my entrance to that

blessed salty water
that's been modernized
and polluted over the years
yet still remains my holy place
for a swim
for cool thankfulness.

Their dark maroon bodies won't let me enter.
Maybe they're taking back the sea.

NIGHT DRIVING

You'll notice them:
deer munching the sweetest grass,
which grows by the roadside.

Young does carefully lick that barrier
on the darkest roads—
seen by headlights, but safe from the dayglo
hunter's watchful eye.

I wonder whether their elders remember
acres of woods, outstretched farmland.

STARGAZING

At Yosemite at night
I searched for shooting stars
to start my wishing.

The stars taught me not to want
and refused to fall.

Walt Dawydiak

GOODBYE POP

I Miss You Too

Your house, once shingled white,
is vinyl-sided yellow.
I don't recognize it.
No, that's not you in that box.

> *It's full of shells, like empty whelks*
> *that litter beaches after hurricanes.*
> *With driftwood oak bones.*
> *Burned from salt of age.*

Your living hard has finally paid off.
All systems failed at once.
No purgatory nursing home.
No waste of useful organ life.

> *Those years of steak and hard potatoes melted,*
> *like the butter-lotion*
> *from my scarlet body*
> *on that gritty Belmar beach.*

You're here, though, I can see your spirit
through the pall of Newark air.
You're golden. Azure.
Wild. Unleashed.

> *In lilacs and tomatoes that I planted.*
> *Roses, flowing like my hair*
> *in wheatfields, sixty years ago,*
> *more handsome than I'd ever be again.*

Our final Father's Day,
your eyes burned blue as ever.
Bunsen-burners glowing
on your mouth, imploded.

> *Every moment of my life lit up,*
> *like flaking Christmas bulbs*
> *we labored over each December,*
> *perched atop the soft gray stoop.*

You'll run now,
to those verdant fields of childhood.
To your white-socked boyhood dog
that howls from the woods.

> *Our final conversation:*
> *fishing at Cape May,*
> *the day the storm tide*
> *swallowed marsh.*

83

Now evening falls. Your boys have saved a spot for you.
They're dressed in suits and playing rummy-bridge
and drinking Seagram's
in a cloud of smoke.

> *I carried you crying,*
> *safely through a minefield filled with horseshoe*
> *crabs,*
> *those cancers old as dinosaurs,*
> *as hard as wind.*

I'll play with you, in time.

> *In tides, of just enough.*

STRIPER

Cancer is the spiny crab
That crawls within your ebbing flesh.
They haven't told you yet you're dying.
But like geese sense south,
You know.

I've seen you once before,
In the brow of my grandmother,
screaming at the ghost of her mother
who had laid herself on the train tracks
one hundred years before

I watched you in that bed, too many weeks.
I watched the morphine dribbling
from the teaspoon, through your mouth,
as the quart lay invitingly
just beyond your reach.

The thin and icy blue of your eyes
and the low moan that rumbled and floated
far longer than any cloud could.

The faint cringe
as you dangled, exposed,
as people chattered regrets
while she changed your diaper.

In my dreams, you emerge,
a Poseidon from the depths.
I am in your beloved boat,
landing a striper you might have tagged.
It pulls so hard that I pitch and
the water rips over the transom.
And I can barely see the bony fingers of your hand
in the foam of the churn
as I'm pulled under
and everything is salty-sweet
and sinking, and still.

And stunningly painless.

Cassandra DeMario

MADNESS

on a shaking Prozac high
I hear the mad laughter of a dead woman
and think the house is gonna explode
wait outside in frozen night
nothing happens -

stuck in visions of bloody catheters
bones bulging out of thin bodies
    that craved fast food and chemo
faces that stared from their wooden boxes
    now beneath my feet without eyes
and green moldy beds
    soaked in disease

There's little hope
for someone who sees the world and vomits
but, if I survive
then I'm a beautiful damned angel
Worthy of salvation

THAT PRETTY FACE

I saw a murdered woman's picture on t.v.
What a pretty face,
now beneath a weeping mother's feet
bloodless
being eaten away
by worms and time
eyes, tongue, and brain gone
nothing but bones and teeth
not a face -
lonely without flesh
and lips
that kissed the killer,
tasted his poison,
and suffocated.

Joan Digby

AGAINST THE GRAIN

The thoughtless builder
stacked his concrete forms
against a dormant pink azalea
that I could only hope
was sleeping soundly
and didn't feel the pain.
Still it angered me—
heavy metal dumped
on fragile leaves
without concern
about how easily
a life may be spilled—
emptied like the gray cement
wash he flung appallingly
over the helpless bush.

BUBBLE

Inside the tennis bubble
there is no blinding sun–
or gusting wind–
summer scapegoats
for the double fault
that happens anyway.

In the white cocoon
the game establishes
a winter rhythm
to the sound
of droning heaters
that circulate stale air
salted with the acrid
smell of sweat.

Outside
the winter rain
chills to sleet,
and the high pitched
hollow patter
of the taut shell
plays counterpoint
against the slow
percussive beat
of he the long rally.

On the hour
courts change players,
silently, like workers
changing shifts
without ever knowing
the next team
that replaces them.

Cold simulation
of summer games,
winter tennis
casts no shadows
on the gray surface
overhung by
floodlight.

WAKING THE STUDENTS

Grandmothers are dying;
it's final exam week,
papers are due
and grandmothers
always take the hit.

Sorry I missed the test–
my grandmother died
and I had to go to the funeral.

I thought she passed
in the flu epidemic
at the end of the fall term.

That was my other grandmother.

The ruffled student had played
her last grandmother hand.

Now there were only cousins
aunts and uncles from Massapequa
to carry her through
three more years of college.

John Digby

I NEVER ENTIRELY LOST MY RECOLLECTION

Early in 1816
I stopped to rest
Took a drink of water
And finished my bread

Next morning
I was awakened from my dreams

I never entirely lost my recollection
It was about o'clock on the morning
The sea had a beautiful bright green colour

On going upon deck I found
Four of the seamen were dead
But had so far recovered
As to be able to walk away
In clouds like volumes of steam

The following morning
I came to a bend of the river
And here I must interrupt
The course of my narrative for a moment

The black forms of a steed and its rider were seen
Suspended amid clouds of snow

It seemed as if I was alone with nature

Night came on
I hastened to it
After bathing my feet
And was soon asleep

Immediately I arose
Applied snow to my head
The next instant
I took a snap-shot
As a means of meeting several ducks
That walked round the camp

How well I can realize
The feeling of a shipwrecked mariner
When he first catches a glimpse
Of a cotton-tail crouched behind a sage-bush
It was a moment of achievement
I comprehended all

MY WORLD WITHIN THESE WALLS

It was an awful sight
My trembling feet could scarce support me
As they helped me from the chair

My hand shook with fear

The bed of evil spirits
Passing in the night could not
Take the souls of the sleepers away

Down the corridors nothing could be heard
But the most brutal howlings

Dinner consisted of a wooden bowl
Laurel-leaves a water jug
With a broken lip
There were no napkins

Perhaps the Doctor in his dim room
With dried bats hanging from the ceiling
And a dragon's egg close by his hand
Fled the country and wandered abroad

An insufferable stench filled the whole place

I can say this terrible sight nearly killed me
I felt a suffocation come over me
I fell to my knees

But father loved the place
And taught me it is the silence
On the house-tops that
One can hear the spirit's call

He often said
We are a caravan of beings
Wandering through pathways

The house on the mountain top has lost its soul
It is nothing but a palace with empty windows

Camillo DiMaria

COUNTING PENNIES

The jar—
(big and heavy
in both hands)

amassed to the rim
with old and new
pennies—gets tilted:

spills, crashes, slams
in mounds
around the table.

Slide coin
                    after coin
off the edge

filling your palm. Once full
fling them back
into the jar.

DE-POEM: SONNET 18 BY WILLIAM SHAKESPEARE

all I comp   thee to a sum   ?
   art more   and ore temp   :
      winds   shake   ling   May,
And   me   ease ha   all to s ort a date:
 me I too   t   ye   eave sh   ,
   oft is   old- plexi dim ;
    e ery air   om air   time de lines,
        , or nat e hang   c urse, trim ;
But t   tern   me   hall   fad ,
 r ose   session   hat fair   west;
or sh   eath rag o wand   his s   ,
hen n et   lines   me th   grow s ;
      g as men   eat ,   yes   ,
        g ives his,   hi ves lif t hee.

93

HIS LOVE

Tonight he walks home
from the station
by way of 85th Street
which becomes Avenue T.

He walks at his usual
unrushed pace
under the trees
by the closed down café.

On the other side
of the block
where 86th Street is
there's a huge empty building

next to a fenced-in empty lot
that he would've had
to walk around
had he taken that way.

He doesn't see those tonight,
cool in the shadows
of the leaves
on his walk, the couple

of blocks it takes
to get home,
one of the many things
he thinks about

are the girls
he stopped calling...
then wishes
he could play piano well.

Slowly,
atonally
he plays a piece
for them tonight.

Arthur Dobrin

DREAMS ARE NOT AS BEAUTIFUL

How many times?
Who can remember?

Callow first from college
Until your belly swelled.

Nine years later a stone
House on a green hill.

The silence of safaris,
Lavender sky and savannah.

Yours the elephants,
Mine the giraffe.

The buzz of mosquitoes,
The flight of butterflies.

Our names: Moraa, Osoro,
Nyakundi, Kwamboka.

Theirs: Ongesa, Maranga,
Pereira, Singh.

The places: Africa, Kenya,
Kisii, Tabaka.

Dreams are not
As beautiful.

To return and return:
This our hearts.

WAITING FOR A BUS IN KENYA

Small boxes and those large enough to accommodate big men
Are stacked along the main Kisii road. The hewn
Homes for the soon to be dead wait beside plastic
Jerry cans, bananas and petrol pumps.
Walkers tend to the balance on their mobile phone cards
And wonder when the next bus from Kisumu will arrive.

Attention must be paid to the dead, it is said.
Tell that to those who go on despite losses counted
By mosquitoes working overtime after the rains—
Only so much attention can be paid before the bus
From the lake city arrives and the minutes are used up.
The dead take up too many rooms to be allowed to roam.

Kufa—dead—the day before yesterday, last year,
Kufa until the last who know them are themselves laid out.
Then the dead are no longer *kufa* but *kwisha kufa,*
Completely and finally dead, as though never having waited for a bus,
Never having called to say, "I have only a few minutes more.
I'm on my way. Let's talk."

Kathaleen Donnelly

ASLEEP AT THE WHEEL

A gas-guzzling truck
pierces through prairie land
heading cross-country,
its driver half asleep,
unaware
of the Native American
who dismounts his horse
in front of the last station
for miles to come,
fills his watering can,
fuels his transportation.

DEAD OF WINTER

On a December night
all is still; no wind rustles
through frozen shadows.
Snow covered tree trunks
sigh quietly, wait for
the warm sun to come
to their rescue. They'll wait.

Brown leaves dead and gone,
buried under frozen snow,
numb, having severed all ties,
protect their mother's roots;
purpose in their demise.

This is a night for reflection.
A walk through these woods
is a solitary tryst, no one
ventures out to meet you.
Stand still among the old trees,
try to be one of them…until you breathe,
give yourself away.

MUSIC

The low notes of a cello
settle in my solar plexus,
fill the air between beats,
cushion all other sounds;
make me want to lie
supine on the earth's floor,
in the grass, on the sand,
look up
from the line along the bottom.

Walter Donway

SPRING POND: FIVE HAIKU

Through the pond's clear water
The sun finds water lilies
Asleep in the mud.

Green spears of Iris
All thrusting at the spring sun,
Like chanting tribesmen.

The pond is so low
That the big carp's wet green back
Pokes out of his world.

The white egret stalks
From step to menacing step,
A snake with a spear.

In the sun a turtle
Is a motionless black stone.
But its pulse quickens.

ON READING DESMOND EGAN

The poet proffers his considered words,
Close trimmed and set atop an honest scale,
And I must heed, must hear that our spare world
Will ever lay within the Humean pale,
The ghetto of our senses, beyond which lies
But dreaming precincts of reason, where once
Our smug, high-minded kind presumed to go.
I seem to hear his midlands brogue pronounce
That no fine heart can sing the measured song,
Pretending meaning in our farce of pain
Incomprehensible, so long dumbly borne;
The true voice breaks to sing of it again.
But what if reason's brief, appealed at last
Before an honest bar, should be sustained:
A verdict deemed but chattering abstraction
By minds in which mere reason is disdained?
How, too, if all that pain, that rote debit
Duly weighed in weary calculation
Of man's undoing, prove but the price
Exacted for our reason's liquidation?
Poet again could lift the human voice
To sing the human order, a human song
Of man-the-maker, with his sufficient joy,
And man-the-knower: well sing him, and long.

NOT A POEM

We'd walk beneath the twin-boled birch
Where oddly soft and floppy grass
Caressed bare feet that hot stone steps
Had stung. And then perhaps we'd pass
An itchy August hour outsprawled
Beside the patch of four-leaf clover;
Or pitch the lumpish, worm-pocked apples
So high, high and twirling, over
The peeling white, roof-sagging barn.
The scent of sweetest, rotting brown
Delighted bees in buzzing orbits
Round apples, pears. We might race down
The hay-laced, furrowed orchard path,
Where stickling stubs would poke small feet
And crackly grasshoppers would scatter.
Among cool tents of vines we'd eat
Our squishy fill of purple grapes.
No poem in this, nor so much more,
That did not happen in this world
and is too real for metaphor.

John Dotson

BEYOND REASON

> my spine just sprung loose
with a good snake-jolt
> on the path

> my heart fluttering like
a pale blue eggshell
> weightless in the breeze

> i can sense the whole
planetary energy
> growing within me

> beyond any reason

SOLITUDE

The lowering sun slits the clouds and light
gushes through the wound onto the far Pacific.
I know my work is with others, but I need this time
alone to remember our origin, to hear the hymns
of human destiny tolling with the sea waves.

Mammoth clouds move stealthily southward toward
the Big Sur ridges. Lobos lays low—natural haven
for the secret forces of night. The sea is roughened
by storm after storm, the beach eaten away
by January's voracity.

The pen is cold in my fingers and the crescent moon
won't leave me alone, touching me softly, intimately,
in the mirror-wet sand's reflection. Can I walk away
with that cool burning ember over my shoulder, dropped
in the deep blue cove of the heavens?

Like moon and tide and the freshness in the sky
of the evening star's light is the miracle among us—
all who hear and remember.

WHERE THE RIVER MEETS THE SEA

thrust by gravity rippling forward
verdant fresh-water surging
is overflown by exploding waves
infusing their collapse
converging superimposing
subverting now emerging
rising again translucent
aquamarine tunnels rounding out
then thunderously plunging purified
and released and forever seduced
by whirlwind and by moon

* * *

across sculpted granite the wet salt
of time dissolved seasons our cheeks
and tongues as flame-tips penetrate
the ruby-slit sky above the bay

billowing driftwood-smoke
and evening star and all
the blazing points of heaven
affirm the incorruptible

joy passing through
our bodies

as light sees self

DIVINE MADNESS

I am caught between mirrors
        while clowns with painted faces
reflections of the infinite
        ignite the cobwebs in my head
surrounded by a heavy veil of darkness
        with a continuous oratorical ramble
where lost souls roam the streets
        citing some lame excuse
like rabid dogs in heat
        for the ineptitude and incompetence
no bounds, no borders
        perpetrated upon us
where wealth is accrued
        a melodrama of words
and then wagered
        beheaded and disemboweled
with delusions of deliverance
        woven, spun, bound together
in the light of new ideas
        a choreography of language
fused by logic and reason
        inciting and inspiring
with natural instincts
        these word and images
opposing outdated moralities
        twisting and turning in my brain
and decaying values
        curled like a coital knot of snakes
a torrid entrapment
        drowning in the stream
beneath the shadow
        of conscieniousness
of the street corner gurus
        a stagnant water, without any depth
singing the suburban blues
        I know it is time to turn off the TV
these young lions roar
        and write a poem

FRESH

What can you tell me?
What can you say to me?
New, used, borrowed or blue
        It doesn't matter
Just make it plain and simple
Communicate and connect

Don't dabble in form or specified style
It can go clinkity, clankity,
                      Clunk
As far as I'm concerned
You don't need rhyme or reason
Or speech measured by meter

Just put one foot in front of the other
And you can vary the pace
A walk, a jog, a run, a dance
                   Or a shuffle
Long lines and short bursts
      Surprise me

Take me on a journey on the road
        Past a farm
And a red wheel
Barrow or down a dark city street
To hear the howl of blues
       Emanating from Mexico City

I'm getting old and tired of waiting
I want something fresh
       Pure and innocent
Or am I just talking to myself
      In the mirror
I want words that flow from within

Let me hear words that incite
      And inspire
Spoken in a language
      Not spiced
With adjectives or adverbs

Give me words fresh,

Red meat
Sliced right off the bone
Raw and unseasoned
Give them to me in
                    American

STICKS AND STONES

was it the spicy cuisine
or was it too much caffeine
that shattered the serene, poetry scene
at the Sunshine Coffee House

detectives say the verbal carnage began
with an argument that spilled out of the café
into the parking lot where it escalated
from threats, insults and innuendos
to four letter words and abusive language

potent adjectives and adverbs were added
to nouns and verbs to increase fire power
causing word to ricochet off the pavement
and leave graffiti marks on the walls
bruising egos and shattering self-esteem

what began as a placid poetry reading
turned into a boisterous slam
police were called and a swat team
stormed the coffee house where
they found some poets in possession
of toxic verse and explosive prose

the bomb squad along with a hazmat team
were dispatched to the site to clean up
the spent casings of commas, colons
and other punctuations that littered the area
three ticking exclamation points wired
to haiku hand grenades were disarmed in the parking lot

defendants were charged with poor oratory
skills and copyright infringement
all pleaded not guilty and no bail was set
the judge knew no one makes any money doing this

Robert Dunn

PANTOUM: THE BIG CRABAPPLE CIRCUS

Watching lions and tigers and boars
Run the concession stand,
The Ringmaster's getting awfully sore ...
While the Lion Tamer whips the band.

Run! The concession stand—
Condemned by the Board of Health,
While the Lion Tamer whips the band,
Hoping they'll all play something else.

Condemned by the Board of Health,
Trapeze Artists swoop down on the Clowns,
Hoping they'll all play something else,
Like *Hamlet* (in a see-through gown).

Trapeze Artists swoop down on the Clowns?
The Ringmaster's getting awfully sore ...
Like Hamlet (in a see-through gown)
Watching lions and tigers and boars.

VILLANELLE: STAMP ACT

We stamp your hand to prove you paid
Your admission. Go in. enjoy the show.
The impression usually takes weeks to fade.

It looks like a tattoo of dusky jade—
A status symbol for those "in the know."
We stamp your hand to prove you paid.

No, it doesn't come in any other shade.
But water it and sun it and it just might grow.
The impression usually takes weeks to fade.

You'd be amazed how many jokers try to evade
Our modest cover charge. Don't try it, Bro.
We stamp your hand to prove you paid.

It gave you a rash? Then take a razor blade
And scrape yourself back to your status quo.
The impression usually takes weeks to fade.

We started with paper tickets, but they just made
Us trouble: they got lost, stolen, counterfeited, smeared,
        stained, folded, stapled, mutilated, etc. So …
We stamp your hand to prove you paid.
The impression usually takes weeks to fade.

MY FIRST MRI

MRI, I was given to understand,
Stands for Magnetic Rosicrucian Imagining,
Or something to that effect.
It's what you get when PBS modalizes
Your GNP through LSD-laced LNG in an ICU CPU (PDQ).
Yoo-hoo! Are we straight about this?
At the time, the technology was so new
I thought I was making a CD.
They were looking for soft tissue injuries,
But I didn't find that out until later.

So they shoved me into some tube,
The diameter of which was ¼ inch shorter
That the width of my shoulders (not unlike
Shoving Play-Doh® through a Fun Factory®,
And let 'er rip. Oh, but before they did,
They offered me music during the process—
It prevented fidgeting, or so they said.
I asked for Led Zeppo Lynne, a punk rock
Band specializing in updated 1930s movie
Musical music, but they said the vibrations
Would skew the readings, so they foisted off
Mozart on me instead—they insisted
It would make me look smarter.

Insults.
Always insults.

After it was over, they gave me
A refrigerator magnet.
I figure that if I get enough of them,
I could go into business for myself.

Desmond Egan

BRONZE HORSEMAN BY McKENNA
...what I do is me: for this I came *

down the shaft of the Notting Hill
terminal below London
deep in this fluorescent underworld
his hammer and chisel
began to squirm again

and where commuters would crowd
he started to re-invent
air and daylight
the imaginary fields
the lost summers
as horse and rider
began to emerge to
gallop into the bronze idea

now that cave
the buttressed corridor
its *tunnel tigers*
the might have been
the dead creator too
all toss together within this
fierce jockey this resisting mount
half mass half urgent bodies
bursting towards outdoors

a blink and half a century later
they gallop motionless on my desk
in that very moment as
his horse twists its strong neck
out of the earth its rider

so where's *the gaffer* now
the minister who joked
no barbed wire round the mailboat
where are those who proclaimed Irishmen
let us make a profit
the insiders outsided

while it
sooner than later will stand
lighted on a pedestal
in time's wide open spaces

nourishing passersby
who won't know why

*... *what I do:* Hopkins, As Kingfishers Catch Fire

FRESHLY GROUND PEPPER ANYONE?

early bird and she is part of the hush
leading us to a window table

when we take our places
she begins the ritual
smiling from another country
the tabloid menu
their specials by rote
and of course the wine list

she comes from where

a basket of covered bread
while we scan and choose
concentrating on the text
our host adding
a bottle of house red

discreetly in the background
Charlie Parker dies through *Lover Man*

before our waitress returns
checks sets down
plate by warmed plate
carefully onto the white tablecloth

Iraq

Carolyn Emerson

"WEST MEADOW BEACH TETRADYCT"
BY CHRISTIAN WHITE

If I am the sand,
then you are the Sound
and together we
love the sky and how
it moves faster than
my changing shoreline,
the ripples as you
retreat from me and
your many currents.

The sky's colors change
affecting you and the
clouds whisper our love;
sometimes they darken
and rush off
to other places.

If we are the beach
and the Sound
and the spit of land
then we are all
loving how the clouds
come and brush us
and the blue above is something
that reflects on us,
that we reach for.

WINTER CONCERTO

Pale blue sky, light streams
through white clouds,
bright, allegretto.
I sail through days
on these wind currents
until free-floating like a
balloon high above,
feeling suddenly lost,
I glimpse the tether that
binds me earthward,
feel the resilience while the wind buffets
hear the resonance in the low-pitched string.
As the tempo descends to largo,
I listen in that white passage
where time stretches out
and every note has weight,
nestled in blue space.

Duane Esposito

HERE ARE THE DAYS

Here's this memory:
the age of eight.

I nearly died from an explosion in my brain.
When does a lifetime begin to speak?

Here's this memory:
the age of fifteen.

I walked across the L.I.E. stoned on Quaaludes:
there goes September & the sky.

Here's this memory:
the age of seventeen.

My parents are divorced, my childhood dog is dead.
My mother's boyfriend buys the family a new dog.

& this one: I give that miniature poodle
a hit of white, blotter acid.

You see, I've refused to let anyone take
what I'm unwilling to give.

These days, regardless of memory,
the voice of God is a stillness in me.

I haven't died.
Faith is a still voice.

I'm forty-two, & I fear death.
This is not a memory.

Dear God, Here are the days
that will carry me toward dying.

SEPTEMBER

Those nights when the cold's slow to settle,
the planet barely holds itself inside its own space.

The soul's roots grow stringy, & there is
the certain moon we chew in September.

It echoes like a childhood fever, & we wake terrified.
September, the mind tries to freeze the sky.

I mean, there are no carnival rides for the families left behind.
The odor of charred bodies still lingers under ground.

May we ever have a month-long memorial to grief?
September is the reason for the sickness in our lives.

It's the reason for our dying-- this dream without a narrative--
as the faces of our loved ones blur & disappear.

Oh to equal radiance must we pray to God?
Are we certain we even live on earth any more?

We try to find an answer for how light travels.
We sit beside a field of purple flowers.

Love says hello again
to something we believe.

Faith insists there might be recovery:
but there isn't-- there never is.

You see, we can't think back before collapse,
before limbs were torn from bodies

on the bluest day--
now pure abstraction.

God is surely miniscule,
so It must be in the dust & blood.

When the hell is October, & where the hell
is any other month but this one?

September is the weapon
we use against the people we love.

I think: there is no cure for us--
if we want to go on living.

Sasha Ettinger

NIGHT WATCH

You try to shake sleep from your eyes
    months go by in a blur
hands
   still warm to the touch
      I hold them in mine

The slim space in your mind
tugs
   at lone thoughts
     drifting
back and forth
   with few faces left to draw from

At the blunt edge of the lake
    dusk
pulls down light
     night's swell
     props up stars
Wind
like a ghost
    roams the sky

Soon
you will breathe
    the last hint of life
Soon
I will weep
    the tears of a child

THIS MORNING PORT WASHINGTON ROLLED OUT OF ITS SLEEP

But I've been waiting for you
all winter
       in the upper room
         of my mind
Our two faces
        in the lost clean landscape
          the sound of voices
fused
       in my flesh
Let me be silent
     as your voice warms
       like honey
falling
      from a stranger's lips
Your shadow
       bent toward mine
hung
  to ripen
    in a gesture of love
With no light
       or pilot to guide us
stained
      by invisible birthmarks
      we set off
        a bonfire
          of the heart

Apologia

Walking on the moon
light shed in pools on the rug
at the top of the stairs
I turn toward sleep again
where dreams of what others
do wake me filled with prayers
for each and all of us, then
I get up, let the dog out, then in
I feed the dog & make the coffee

though nights later
I think there's not much
we need besides what we have
even if that is not all we want
It's time to ease up on the complaints

A map of the world in full detail
unveils : small spots   fixed focus
holds then fades, updated, shifting
a couple of inches north, northeast

Then it's time for dinner
though nights later
I'm not hungry

Another month and the moon's full
in a couple of days, hard days
back and forth with the masses days
What is not my fate is still my fault
What is not my fault is still my fate

WINTER'S BONZAI

Colder before the sun fully sets
Though it does nothing of the sort
flying around so far off that
as we orbit and revolve
the sun from our point
      of view goes around us
seeming to rise in the East, setting
      in the West – like other ideas
standing beside this small, bare tree

WORKING CLASSES

One:
Been working all weekend looking for some fun
Before the work-week begins again
                I'd like to find me some

Low on energy – missing basic curiosities
I stay at home, roll up those spare quarters
         & think about the bills I owe
& the thrills I let go a long time ago

Two:
Saturday Night. I'm listening to the hit songs
of the latest diva everything goes smooth,
the weirdest pieces fit the gift of a peaceful moment

Three:
Things poke out of the winter mulch – persistent
green things…prongs of plants opening
as if that *green fuse* really were a force!
Then back in the house to the work at hand
patching & sanding walls, prepping for a new
paint color – two coats!

The reaching & up & down on ladders & stools
Stretching & bending – maintaining balance!
The satisfaction of a job done & done well

Four:
The story of my self-employment starts early

First job at nine, I loafed the summer past puberty
& dropped out of the market in my mid-twenties
Slipping back into shades of respectability
I got a paying job in my late thirties
Running low on the government radar

Barely enough in the IRA to get us through
three or four years of retirement unless
we cut back on everything: groceries

Too bad tattoos can't be resold, too bad
love doesn't come with rebates or refunds
Too bad, bad isn't as bad as bad used to be
Elsewise we might waste a lot of time

better spent on spiritual growth no matter
what you think about the result, it's the same
you might be who you think you are
yet you're also more or less than that

Five:
& when I'm riding true to my view
I'm thinking of you – the things that
                              we still can do

Six:
I work because I like to do things
& a lot of those things take work
else I won't be doing them right
or wrong. But, hey don't listen to me

I ain't got anything new to say
just a little spit & sway in how
I say those things I say

Seven:
The back is shot, the knees hurt & pop
The lungs are laboring, wanting a beer
& some chips as I watch TV to stay awake
so tomorrow I can sleep late

                    Then comes Monday
& I get up & do it again
                    as long as I can –
                    No hallelujahs here or there, buddy.

Gil Fagiani

LISTENING TO "PEANUTS" BY LITTLE JOE
AND THE THRILLERS

I see the emerald sheen
of a ring-necked pheasant.

Gargle with sunshine.

Do handsprings
in a field of apple blossoms.

Chase cloud-shadows
along a path of pine needles.

Backstroke in a sea
of beach ball marshmallows
bobbing in chocolate sauce.

UNA PAROLA
Finale, Sicily

-- one word – the old Italian ladies say,
holding up a single finger,
as they step in front of you at the bank, post office,
ignoring the half hour, forty-five minutes, hour,
you've jockeyed behind the ragged excuse
for a line, always about to hemorrhage
into three or four smaller lines,
inching towards a single window teller.
Una parola becomes a paragraph, page,
and while you slowly burn, the old ladies
are opening their purses, transacting business.
"I have diabetes, gout, heart disease," they say
if your eyes betray your anger.

VESTA

A woman bringing fire from her mother's hearth
to light her own in her own new home.
I like this story, an ancient Roman ritual, and tell
it to my daughter though I get it wrong on the first try.
I say the mother *gives* the flame, hands it
to her daughter like a bag of apples
or cash against emergency.
But a daughter needs to choose before she takes,
use her hands as she sees fit—for culling grain
or spreading seed, replacing broken d-strings
on an old guitar. And what about a knife or a gun?
Within arm's reach. Scale fish, sculpt form,
ward off anyone who comes into the house unasked.
Let me not be one of those unasked.

2.

News from afar of war; nearer too, political unease.
Signs and omens read me, compel me to the story's end:
women bringing fire from hearth to hearth
to the center of the city. I tell this to my daughter,
pacing like a lynx in the room I gave her
long ago. "We must," I tell her, "separate, as completely
as the morning you were born, your raging flesh
rent fast from mine. I'll find you when the war is over,
by the wounded bridge or in the last abandoned building.
Let me hold you, briefly, just for a moment, just
for all eternity. My spirit's blazing, burning in and out
my own wild life: feel it, hold it, keep it in your own
mind's eye, heart's core, deepest dream cupped and
closed and open then move on: go with it, go with it, go."

VIRGO

I look into the mirror, where the future looms
in present tense, then walk out of the house
into the stark day.

I want to prod the moment open like a soft jewel,
whisper intimations, unmask the mask of *now*
and put it on to forget.

Trees know how to do this—the massive Oak
with her thick black branches. Gnarled and thick
and hard: so sexual. so open. legs and oval crevice.

And standing on an island in the middle of the road,
a sapling Maple. No new leaves though the old
dry dead ones have finally fallen off.

Walk up close to. examine. round swollen buds.
Just last Tuesday they were tight and brown,
now they burn with blistering green.

(still the opalescent essence,
safely hidden)
come up close to. walking to take with.

Johanne Farmer (Veroflame)

ANCHORAGE

Inherent figures
come from multiples faces
a slow procession of bands
with their simple echo
flirt on the slopes of old adage
and I listen in stereo
haunted by their upheaval
I know
that this line descends
I admit
searching in the imperfect
my twin ego
I strike up on life
and awake lover
for too long a solo,
a shooting star, a loner
I bind in discreet bodies
and linger
along my eternal bends
until I discover new anchorage

ANCRAGE

Figures sous-jacentes
la venue de multiples visages
une lente procession de bandes
avec leur simple écho
flirt un peu mon adage
et j'écoute en stéréo
hantée par le remue-ménage
Je sais
que la file forme une descente
J'admets
chercher l'imparfait,
le double de mon ego
J'entonne le célibat sillage
d'amante,
d'étoile filante
Censures discrètes
me tiennent au chaud
dans mes courbes imparfaites
car l'éternel solo
se rapproche de son arrimage

125

DEEP BARRICADE

As if a split Berlin
carried in my heart
this moment when collapsed
every plot of land in my being
digs on this barricade
Set up by a wall of fear,
I try to know
where my soul hides its facade
so badly loved
as it only knew hours
of intouchable solitude

As if this morning, I awoke
fractured in my heart
a starving place
where I felt being reborn
Eager for feeling an embrace
whatever your mood
I don't care about appearances
I open the way for remembrance
Wanting to love you
without any apprehension
and hear my desire to be lived in

BARRICADE PROFONDE

Comme si Berlin, scindé
portait dans mon cœur
ce moment où effondrée
chaque parcelle de mon être
pioche sur cette barricade
Érigée d'un mur de peur,
je cherche à connaître
où mon âme cache cette façade
si mal aimée
qu'elle n'a connu que des heures
de solitude intouchée

Comme si ce matin, réveillée
se fissurait dans mon cœur
un espace affamé
où je me sens renaître
Avide du sentiment d'accolade
quelque soit ton humeur
je me fou du paraître
J'ouvre la voie du mémorable
Je veux t'aimer
sans aucune frayeur
à l'écoute de mon envie d'être
habitée

Kathryn M. Fazio

A BRAND NEW GOD

A brand new God
exploded
in a (near
by)
toy factory
yesterday,

where physicians
gathered for the 2000,
2001, 2002, 2003, 2004,
2005, 2006, 2007, 2008, 2009,
health care conferences.

Bystanders
wedged between
Pokemon and Minnie Mouse
stumped attendees,
who discussed the grave state
of a handkerchief,

and the sole remains

of leaves
of grass.

TWENTIETH CENTURY

Oh God, what choice do we have in life.
And what is a victim?
And who is a computer,
That has a box and the nerve to answer a phone?

And who has a short. No, a dress for me.
Wearing like thoughts,
Like the clot of thought that lives between the mind,
And acid etched in the lining of a metal frame that looks like mind.

Pure ignorance is genius cut
Bad like an order...
A what powdered drug, that doubles one over
A banner

A banner in the highest.
A flag that warns Stop. Don't go on.
A flag that warns Stop. Something is wrong.
A banner in the highest.

But, where do liver-tinted dishes belong
What box? I cannot tell by smell.
The switch from civilization to specialization teases me when God
isn't looking, and leaves my senses numb and unsettled, like an
African's foot sole.
What form is this, I wonder
That spins a turntable with a record on it
Or makes the sound a gold.

I wonder about forms in a fog of forms.
The face of the boss, the screen from a machine with questions written on it
calls me.
Nervously, I puff on smoke
And reach to answer the phone that rings unsympathetically, like a street
light annoyed,
blinking in complaint of the state of street these days.

I think
I'll extend an arm to do the dishes,
And go to bed alone.

Harvey Feinstein

WINTER SOLSTICE

The pale moon
Washed of all color
Yet with still a hint
Of China yellow
Shines through poplars
Twisted like charcoal
Sketches in the snow

Night has barely set
And the sun is rising
While the moon
Westward in its flight
Lingers in the garden.
A mourning dove sighs

You sense me stirring
Call me away from the window
Pull me back
To the patterns
Of the bed
Your body in my arms
Ignites a fire.

HAY(NA)KU EXFOLIATION 9

Spine
grunt donating
a minimal animal—
figures to
sacrifice. But never
cruelly dead to doubt.

We smell bimbo
savvy. Ordinary darkness taught
insanity (a pinch) to light
up quietly. Underneath, perhaps,
the collected lemons, his secret

exercises. (To be dissected after cremation.)
Thunderous banality was reason enough
for secrecy, his glossy education and
its flowering fed to an inertial tunnel.

HAY(NA)KU EXFOLIATION 11

Sometimes
I'd appreciate
a day's gift
(perhaps not
in me?) of
extreme sustained emotionalism. Her

closet brags. Many
things betray the unnamed
to which we could strain
to lend figures. The
"Great" Depression, her sole professor,

has been radically more infectious than
your common catachresis. If another's
decision menu keeps standing at odds
with the odds, one's pragmatic persuasion dodders.

BEE 10

Oh yes, over a million.
He won a long time ago.
IBM has been lousy since your father died.
I come from a rich house.
And boy, did your friends try to take it away from me.
I should have done a lot of lot of staying home.
Nothing in that room must be sold.
Ask her; she's the seamstress.
She's way in, in, in.
Maybe I would pay her to stay with me, if it felt safe.
We would hire a policeman.

FROM ROWING, TO AN OLD MAN

1.
Summer trees and I
trade oxygen, CO_2
like two people working
the same oars: one pulling,
the other pushing.

2.
In early fall—leaves.
I stand under them with my
rake, waiting.

3.
Sugar-maple leaves
bright yellow in the eastern sun,
a million golden butterflies.

4.
The leaves are red-
orange tipped
as if a child mixed up
her brushes putting
the orange
in red paint
then colored
a thousand
leaves.

5.
Leaves, still wet from last
night's rain, polished brown chestnuts,
sleek coats of stallions.

6.
Leaves after last night's
freeze are dry, shriveled tan
like the face of an old man.

WALKER IN THE CITY

On a carnival-closed-off-street
kids bounce on a blow up castle.
A guy takes your photo, sells it back in a button.
A girl spins cotton-candy from a swirling machine.

A hefty woman in tight
clothes eats at the Euro Café
while Latinas from nearby offices
flirt with the handsome,
barista at Starbucks.

On the subway a well-dressed man
like a model for Barneys,
but probably a banker or broker
goes home to a pretty wife.
A Mexican hard-hat with heavy
boots, torn jeans leans
against the door, exhausted,
then slumps in the seat
with the bottle-blond
who's swaying asleep.

A woman in her fifties,
displays her boob job,
like Trump Tower
with its garish excess.

The street cleaning machine rumbles
by the curb, sweeping candy wrappers,
dirt, issuing a faint spray of water,
like a snail leaving its track of slime.

Two men, unshaven, scuffed shoes,
soiled jackets, play chess
next to the pansies in Bryant Park.

DAWN AFTER THE ART WALK

Line of a train on the north side of town
an hour before sunrise.
I open the early morning window
to snow under the street lamp.
In my bedroom, a chill in the walls,
a loneliness deeper than my bones.

Changing my shoes after the waltz,
I walk into the cold air alone.
By the door to the Landmark Hotel
at exactly the wrong moment,
I witness a marriage unraveling.
In one evening, in front of me
all of the reasons I left this place.

Dreams tumble like the paintings I saw –
tree frogs splotching a red barn
inside an arch of cottonwood branches,
a dancer climbing blue star stairs
to the Pleiades after midnight.

Five years ago, I packed up
what was most important to me
in my Toyota and drove
west across the mountains,
in the back seat,
my cello, my dance shoes, my favorite books
including the one I was writing.

Somewhere inside, beyond the snow
I knew about you
and knew you were not here.

RING OF FIRE

At the edge of the continent,
fires are everywhere.
Lightning strike at Point Arena.
Then a wide band of fire
traveling northeast on a summer wind.
Hundreds of lightning strikes
inside a ring of fire
torching the solstice night.

In the Mendocino Woodlands,
echoes of stellar jays,
a family of pheasants,
a mountain lion stalking in the meadow.
In the distance, burning mountains.
Images of the enigma
weaving themselves together
inside a larger vision.

For some reason I don't understand,
my mother decided to walk
back from the edge –
unable to leap at this time
through the ring of fire.

This is for my mother,
the older version of the three-year-old
who stood on the piano bench
and belted out radio tunes
and folk songs from the old country
when her relatives said in Yiddish,
Sing Mamale, Sing Little Mama.

Somewhere
in the middle of the continent
peonies in full bloom
now filling the still warm nights
with their sticky fragrance.

Somewhere
while the rest of us are
are still dreaming,
a meeting with her Guardian Angels,

planning how long she will stay
and the next adventure on her soul's journey.

Mamale,
you'll probably burn a path of fire through the sky
wherever the meteorites and snow angels
take you.

In the middle of the redwood forest,
I feel you singing
inside the spirit of the trees.

WHAT IS THE SOUND OF AN ISLAND?

A millennium of coral
angel skin pink
resting upon the eardrums

full of ocean,
with a cello singing in the distance,
somewhere between memory and the soul.

Billions of blue barnacles
in galaxy of voices.

MOOM

Your small boots crunch
down into crisp white
you roll a ball small
as your small hand
and throw it laughing
you point up to gulls circling,
saying 'brr, brr'.

Your eyelids have
small white flakes
on their fine hairs.

*

I carry you outside the house
to look up at the moon in full
you point up and say
'moom, moom'.

I forget speech
and say with you
'moom, moom'.

*

How you like to see
the yellow school bus

the big trucks and tractors
and the train, a great saurian

rumbling through the station,
how you like these noisy things

how you like to read
your bookies also.

*

The rains all day rain down
into this night
and the house becomes large
without you. It is to say
tear down these walls,

the small boy is not here
and in the morning the sun
will say five days now I
am not where you are.
Bueno. I am busy, stringing
the guitar with new strings,
feeding the fish, the cats
and dogs. What is the night
out there like, what
is it like on the desert?

*

This house becomes a vast building
a circus tent where
the stands are empty
the ring bare
all the dancing animals
gone out to the desert,
where you are.

*

Out tonight under the moon
almost full, looking up
it is you carrying me

you buss my cheek and say
'look dada up there is
what you will grow into,
the universe of stars'.
But I am small, and like
to watch the ants crawl
on the kitchen floor, and
cannot understand your experience.

*

In this winter I face my fortieth year
and you gain your eighteenth month.
The raspberry bush is dormant now
where you pulled from its branches
ripe fruit in the summer.

First thing out the back door
you steer your small boots
toward that barren bush,

you don't care winter
denies you fruit
your hands are my hands
our ears hear
winter winds whipping,
the Atlantic surf pounding
on clear sands.

We visit your great grandmother
whose furrowed face is older
than any flowerings,
more ancient than snow,
and give her
fresh berries
she can't understand.

                    *

Behind the house past
the raspberry bush soon to bloom,
out to where trucks and tractors rest
heavy on the ground and pheasants nest
I hoist you into the cab of a rusted
deuce and a half dump. You stand on
it workingman's sofa steering us
right and left, making truck sounds
hrmm, hrmm, we travel forward
and backward in our truck.
I'm not sure what brings us here
to this forked peninsula this Sunday.

Later when stars and trees have
reached communion we go out again
among steel monsters dead and dying.
It's too dark for play so we stand
looking up. Your eyes
are equal to mine
in them I see
moon and stars reflected.

                    *

Wind whips through
the almost budding branches
a cold April snap.
I care for you

as the shell
cares for the turtle.

Much later, when moon
has traveled and the winds
become unbearable
and Time has had
his small dinner of us,
trucks back up to unload the house.

                    *

You sleep now
your innocent sleep
beneath the starry arch
oblivious to any tomorrows.

If I should go before you wake
to some far place
beyond understanding
the Dakotas, let's say

or far Australia,
or up into the heavens
and you, should you go
before me to these places,

now I lay me down to sleep.

James Friel

FLIGHT MEANT ALSO PASSAGE

between the last whisper and the first gasp we overreach eternity
till nibbled away by time
perspective is restored in dissolution

man is a vagrant dreamer
never becoming what he holds in his hands
half-led half-pursuing
ever returning to caked footprints threatened by unbounded sea
salt licks its way to the heart
we are unearthed at tide turn

till shells toss, we burrow for love to be more like gods
but in the mirror we find human traces
clay marks tell us we are prey to errant hunter
yet a bond seals us forever in one another
and all the sea minding cannot remove from our lips second breath
we are double image in a one vision world

we promise through eternity in this feeble grasp of nows
to be with one another
we who never fully become
and as our garments unravel we are never quite exposed
nor in warmest union ever quite contained

it is the lisping that would defy the angels
yet this tale must be told
and we who hover know at least that flight means also passage
though we do not bundle in divinity.

OCEAN SONG
To Umeiko

The fisherman casts his line in the stream.
Salmon swim north to spawn.
Against the current they jump
and leap wildly,
splattering ashore in their effort,
in the frenzy of seasons
that tick savagely to be seen.
Behind your eyes wildly you watch the world go by,
white caps whipping up the ocean song
as it beats against the shore.

Celeste Gainey

(OVERHEARD!) A SECRET THAT COULD
CHANGE THE WORLD . . .

someone
could
make
a lot of   *hush!*
$ $ $
if

they
invented
a   *silent!*
leaf
blower

ssshhh!
pass it on
hear what happens!

GERARD DRIVE

It's hard to beat the bicycle's
perspective. Today is always fresh
as I peddle down Old Fireplace Road
out onto the spit.

The bay is sun-tipped and winking,
the harbor's edge green and marshy,
and always, the egret
alone and white against it all.

A few folks plugged to iPods
pant and power walk;
an SUV muscles through
to the beach down the stretch.

I bike by the modern house
shaped like a dog bone, its nose
at the bay's edge; it's one the real
estate agent showed us years back

when we'd finally decided to change
it up, go for quiet and simple close to the sea.
The house was tidy and exact on the inside,
everything built in like a ship.

Too small we thought, so we bought
another, tore it down, built our own:
a mid-century shrine; all long
and lean, clear cedar siding and cork, but

the dream house held us captive
then cast us out;
it's really not important anymore.
Still I wonder

if we had bought the dog bone house,
how many glances out the window
would it have taken for me
to see what I see now?

Christine Gelineau

ENDOW

What's it like there, Mother?
Have you been there long enough
to be happy? Have your bones
cleaned off to silver now, holy and exact?
You did so love to dress
in pure lines and simple elegance.

That insistent black elegance
was your signature here, Mother,
but it was Dad and I who chose the dress
that you wore last and we had had enough
of black. We put you in the teal, an exact
gesture; by now, soil-black and moist, your bones

wear only what becomes the bones.
Even the outerwear of mahogany elegance
we gave has softened into exactly
the embrace we had intended. Mother,
that last evening we talked, I remember well enough
the look of you in white: the white dress

the hospital issues; the room dressed
white, white ceiling, white walls, bone-
white bedclothes, your face floating in whiteness enough
to release you; your hand in white air, elegantly
waving goodbye, goodbye; so like you, Mother,
to be, even at that moment, exact.

But it was more than I could imagine you would exact
of me the black sophistication of a funeral dress
while you wore blue and wouldn't leave your box, Mother.
Sucked down with grief to a model's high cheek-boned
look, I came into a sudden, adolescent elegance
but paid for it. Can we ever pay enough?

Even decades have not been time enough
to compensate the cost. The exacting
interweave of you and me, that elegant
embroidery of dreams, demands, losses and redress,
continues to work its intricate details, the bone
needles pulling bright venous threads, Mother.

I wear our crewelwork close to the skin and dress
to camouflage the truth: we each are silver at the bone,
and what you must endow, I must inherit, Mother.

HORSESHOE CRAB

In truth, your shape is less
like a shoe than like the hollow
a horse's hoof describes:

ancient as absence, you glide
the ocean floor, sword tail
susurring in your wake,
a stylus tracing the small
poem of your passage.

Waves roll in glass-clear and
loquacious: exhale

and then the long
gurgling back of the sands.

Beneath that bright film
the black exclamation
of your body persists,
persists.

MY FATHER FISHES FOR STRIPERS

In darkness it begins :

He stands in the surge
and retreat of the sea :
the unremitting inspire /
expire of the surf's
swallowing : he casts out
the glint, the live bait
of his own hunger to hook
that silver muscle of what we know
to lurk there, nearly out of reach :
slowly dawn smudges the horizon

stripped : striped : strike:

the line keens out of the reel
like a shriek, the jerk and rush
of that filament all he sees
of the struggle : knowledge now
a province of the body not the
intellect : he holds clear
of the frantic line and grips
the shuddering rod two-handed
as it pulls him deeper : he plays
the live line :   deeper
but diagonal, holding
as best he can to the shallows,
the shore, the electricity
of that strand steady now :
thrusting with an energy pure
as any desire

stripped : struck : strung

Desire is tireless but the flesh
is not :   the glitter of menhaden
with a hook for a heart : the bite
and drag of it : the exhausting
tease of the man's grip and release :

closer to shore : closer
to shore : hauled towards
          the light : the fire
of oxygen : air

  : beached :

whose element the amnion?
fish the length of the man's
toddler daughter : the mylar
glitter of the scales : the eye :
fading even as the glistering
water drips from the body
back into the sea

PICKING PEACHES

Even before we're close enough
to reach to them we smell
the sweet offertory of their ripening.

Birds lift with loud reluctance
leaving behind opened suns
of soft-fleshed fruit.

He steadies the ladder
while I rise among the leaves
handing down the warm-skinned globes.

Peach by peach they drop
from my fingers to the cradle
of his outstretched hands

and for that moment we
too are as filled to the skin
as fruit.

Gail Goldstein

FLUCTUATIONS

Like the stock market,
My life goes up and down,
Hoping to avoid steep crashes.

It's those steep crashes that will do me in—
But economics of experience teaches
I will bounce back.

Zeniths of joy, good times, new connections
Follow declining lines of depression.
Again, the bull charges upward,
And again, is followed by
flashes of downward dipping.

How do I insulate myself in bare times?
Allow myself pleasures of peak moments?

It is difficult to grasp
the fluctuations of a free market.
My life, like the market,
is not defined by any wink of time,
But rather by the sum
of all the surpluses and deficits,
The balance between bear and bull.

Remember, the flat line spells death.

WRINKLES

Like hands of the clock
ticking away, moving
slowly around the face
passing each number,
lines on your face appear
small and shallow at first,
then cutting deeper into smooth skin
indicating seasons that have passed.

Each line holds another experience,
moments marked, visible for all to see
their meaning invisible to all but you.
I notice them all—
tiny markings above your lips
like small blades of grass,
longer lines down the sides of your face
            that do disappearing acts,
only to return with each smile.

Distance keeps them hidden.

I feel the urge to
smooth them away,
push them into nonexistence,
they are a reminder of how long
            you've already lived.

The gesture is a temporary solution,
gravity drops us back to reality.
They are beautiful;
they show strength and
determination,
wisdom and
endurance,
a powerful reminder of
your indeterminable worth.

AT DUSK ON THE TOP OF THE WORLD

Stone upon stone in mortarless order, stones like words worn
smooth singing the mystery of tides, stones the size of stars chiseled in the
mouth of gods, each mountain peak a fist flung up to the star-carved heavens.
The ancient city of Machu Picchu sits above a river which carves deeper a valley
whose rock Inca once lifted up this mountainside to align the heart of the sun
with the stone of the moon.

Over a freeze-dried dinner a thousand million stars unfold their
light, unfold the mortarless order with which the rock he rests on moves within
the moving night, spatial harmony like this never before: kidney, liver, thyroid &
spleen, moon rising over the altar-to-the-moon's ruins, river roaring against
boulders beneath him.

Though campsite rulebook restrictions will have him out of
temples tomorrow, though the memory is recent of resisting to hike one more
step up the four-day Inca Trail ascent, only this lost city at the pinnacle end of the
world remains---incomprehensibly here,
like whatever level of mind takes over when beauty we have no breath
for appears, floating in the air.

THE ANCIENTS

Find us waving a field's barley wheat invisible under sheets of cerulean
sky and melted sun streaks. Find us in dough's leavened rise, in crusts of barley
bread broken, eaten & baked by hearth's augured heat. Find our unheard word in
a wind flittering red magnolia blooms on spring limbs that unfurl ruby-throated
hummingbirds. With the light just right you'll see in a wing span we're no more
than remnants of stardust & phosphorescence while the ocean-spun memory of
its dinosaur limbs opens to you as your limbs open to your children. Later, when
the breeze announces a season's change, find a golden leaf falling in a red-hued
wood where jays carry under southern soil such tiny seeds that make a forest
complete: not for granted would we remain in small things. Find us on the gusts
for wherever you open in understanding we already are: the sun in the sky, the
rain on the rise, the bread on the stove, the curve of a bird's wing meeting the
bend in the road, the shape night takes against the ebb & flow of the ocean
shining within you.

Roberta Gould

FARIDA A. WILEY LEADS A BIRD WALK
TO OYSTER BAY IN HER EIGHTY-NINTH YEAR

"An osprey," she said
looking out over the bay
where she'd taken us to see
the fledglings

Their parents in classic
plumage feeding on spring
foliage we pierced
craning our necks back

Field glasses fixed on one spot
steady as the season
returned for another round
of song and procreation

Always creation's
first bird
April present again
fish in the hawk's beak
over Long Island sound

Her face a presage of skull
10th year before death came
took her and made us
the leading generation

Her suit indelibly green
under the strawberry blond hair
and her twanging voice ever naming
each bird with wonder

THE CHICK PEAS

Spilled through the funnel
they fall
into the destined bottle
each one revealing
a verse
joined to the next one
lying over and under it
rounds of birth death birth
they tell where they are going
and their dark original home
Listen!
Each common bean of the epic
constellated sings
its secret

Leonard Greco

GLORIOUS

before winter's enduring bleak
autumn's glorious death
walks

awash in golden hues
umber offerings
amber blaze
third leg necessity

limping as it were

into winter's aging bleak

latter years
at times sweet
often hollow

blistering chilled
to
the bone

crusting
blood droplets
spell
in fresh-fallen snow

a beginning

winter's frosting bleak –

RIFF ON LEONARD COHEN

I see her in black
dark as night
a survivor of horrendous nightmares
beckoning me to join her in her
nightly dance with death

And I sing to her of my
youthful horrors
how they plague me like black death
in the alleys of medieval London
so far removed from the light
so close to those
deepest moments of my psyche

And I am awash in self pity
even though I have more
fame and fortune
than god himself
because I am a poet
and
as such
must suffer or
my art becomes empty

As empty as a bottomless bucket

Oh woe is me
covered am I
in a shroud of gray flannel

Oh woe is me
woe is me
woe is
woe –

THE CHRISTMAS PARADE
December 9, 2008

Here,
in the heart of
the Great Smoky Mountains,
Hayward County,
where loyalty takes decades
to die   if ever;

Cold Mountain Fever
runs deep,
marches proudly
along Main Street
in old Waynesville

I smile at the visage
this wintry night
of eight chilled men
in frail Rebel garb
just behind a Baptist float,
carrying a banner
celebrating
their heritage as

Sons of Confederate Veterans

Yes here,
deep in the heart of
the Bible Belt:

Old loyalties die hard –

Geraldine Green

A HANDFUL OF STONES

she stands wide, legs
apart, arms raised

fists shaking. she
makes faces

at the sun, bends
down

collects pebbles from
the shore

tucks each one inside
her blouse

she has five nestled
there - maybe more -

she imagines they'll
hatch into baby birds

she imagines they'll
grow wings she imagines

the stones will fly
across an ocean

meanwhile the tide
comes slowly in on the moon

the wind blows a
ballad across the sea it enters her

like a lover the wind
enters her as she stands there

a dreaming tree. it
enters her the wind like a dreaming lover

so she stands wide,
hands raised makes fists

pulls faces at the moon.

inside her blouse
warm as figs --

nestles a handful of
stones.

EVERYTHING WAS MURDER

everything was ardent back then
she said, everything was turning
everyone was enamoured with crystals
the men on the dock preaching christ's
anger showed a film of murder called
'murder.' everyone was angry back then --
she paused in the telling, sliced open a croissant
sliced an apricot, placed each piece of
red-juiced flesh on the skin of god's anger, flicked
crumbs from her dress opened her mouth and
sang hymns for the crazy. everything was ardent
she said, and murder back then. the man preaching
god's cinematic death closed his lips folded his
director's chair and headed for the beach.

YOUR EYES

were seagulls to me once
your heart the moon
the razorbill edge of your
mad arm the sun
reindeer ran with your gladness
then inside the deep indigo of your skin
inside the deep red heart of your winter
in your skin, red diameter
in your skin, coal eye of Andromeda
your smile, the susurrus of wind

you were a seagull to me then
cool as beelzebub
cool you were,
with your seagull eyes wide open
cool, you were
with your yellow razorbill mouth
opening and closing
a blue letter day you
held sky in your wings
held moon in your smile
held jupiter in the dead red
muscle of your thigh

you, with your wings of madness
your red hot soul of
indescribable longing
your trade headed winds
wrapped isobars round my limbs
my skin became incandescent with
your myelomas

you, with your yellow
sing song seagull eyes blazing
your beelzebub acid
eating into matchstick ends
your licorice eyes
stick stock stacking
your hairy arm pits

riding storms
your eyes
snail shells in the dark

tell me, you
with your
pin-a-penny smile
with your
skull abandoned mouth

you, my yellow seagull lover
with your arms outstretched
ready to devour.

Russ Green

BAD KARMA IN PARADISE

The Flies! The Flies!
They are ravaging me
Little black demons
invade my meditative
vista They buzz by
my ears rest on my
skin They hover so
close as if they are
next of kin but oh
just the same they
are out to kill and
craze drive me to
sin Maybe they *are*
family come back
to haunt me again!

BOWERY RELOCATION BLUES

Car got moved
Wanted to slap Mike Bloomberg
slap his billionaire mayor forever monarch face

He wants to pave the way to economic recovery in
New York City
instead he paved me out of my parking space

We weren't there
We were tasting food from exotic lands
India Nepal and the old Siam
We were just there to see George
and the brilliant poets he had in store
The problem was *we* were not George
We could not be everywhere at once

Like Dorothy's house in the Wizard of Oz
my Ford Explorer was picked up, whisked
away, mysteriously moved, like a restless toad
it hopped across the road

Just as I thought my car was on the lam
I found out it had become part of the
Vehicle Relocation Program

CHAOS THEORY

Chaotic tendencies sliding through
sometimes it feels as if it's more than I can chew
someone's opened the door,
let the universe fly in

The cosmos is wrecking my kitchen,
what happened to my lonely planet?

It must've gone on vacation,
found a quiet little black hole
in some secluded galaxy
where all thought, any sense of organization,
is shredded, crushed
All sounds have been rounded up—hushed

As lamplight fades, against the distant sunset
As darkness pervades

Swirling winds, cosmic debris
it ain't The Wizard of Oz
No wicked bitch here, no Emerald City
no Emeril Lagasse
no control, no <u>BAM</u>!!!
No kickin' up, no kickin' it down,
no lost, no found

Where is that confounded bridge?
Where is my kundalini karma?
Does kundalini bother you?
If he does, call me. I'll send Federico Fellini.
They'll be weeping at his funeral
playing Henry Mancini
or maybe its just the word
kundalini, kundalini

Hey man, this is New York City,
things get a little crazy here
You survive black holes, rogue universes
disappearing planets, flying debris
falling cranes, exploding planes

Who's to say what kind of innocence remains
So excuse *me* if my eyes look lazy,
it's just that my head's a little bit hazy

George Guida

CABIN IN THE SKY
for Don Leo

He was swinging the boom, and
Ninety-First Street is closed to
traffic: twelve feet of rubble,
balconies sheared off, a cloud
of dust, one presumed dead
in a city of faces without end.

You woke to this and your seed
in a small vessel labeled
with mate's name, on its way
to doctors' hands. You watched
the morning news, thought of rising
from the bed for a day
with your would-be mother-bride.

The last day of the week,
the work week, three weeks
before his wedding day, a week
removed from his bachelor party
getaway, cigar ashes on pink beach
and sunset the shade of
daylilies ready to bloom.

Where he sat this morning
they call the cabin, home
of the working man taking stock
of the site and his reasons
like the peregrine falcon's eye,
the impulse of freedom tripping
the instinct for nest and mate.

You are almost asleep again,
tempted to postpone the day,
forget your lovely cousin doesn't know,
as she glides to work believing
him husband and father, counting
tables of wedding guests
who'll come in spirit.

165

In the cabin he heard music,
a Seventies story song from
the window where the dark-haired woman
always waved, relieving
the mild tilt he might have felt
had the day been overcast or cold,
the kind that doesn't make you feel
you could step from the cab,
measure with bar, circle and heart
all points along the azimuth's promised arc.

SONG OF THE ROCK DOVE

The nuthatch chips insect niblets
from bark strips. He is bright blue
as poisoned rain.

UNTITLED

In life what's spent
is spent. In lassitude
I died at 38
in languor, yet
I stand here, yet
I stand as if
nyet were *da* and *da*
were *nyet*. In flight

I have no net, no
parachute, no peer
to judge my past
performance in mid-
air. I died at 38
of a wingless heart.
I sing old melodies
monotone, passion
silent in my
frontal lobe. My

bones are foreign
spies on my flesh.
My flesh is set
to melt around
my bones. My unborn
children fidget in
their nest. I spend
the days in flight,
where *nyet* is *da*
and *da* is *nyet.*

Chao Guo-Hui

THE PACE OF LIFE HAS SLOWED

Each time I decide to walk
a life a quicker way,
it turns out to be the opposite,
and I have to lie down and wait.
Day by day I have realized that
it is not my say.

I look up towards the endless
white heaven. It is silent
and conquering. I've felt it,
and bowed down to examine
my heart, and know
what can be known is here known--

As the sky is higher than the earth,
so is His way than mine,
His thought than mine.
If only I could breathe in His breath...

Russ Hampel

SHADOW ME

While there is luster
in the evening light,
it does not reflect on me.
A calamity of geese
trumpets overhead,
yet I do not hear them.
A rolling boil of fish
entices me to swim,
but I cannot.
Sorry, I can't play today.
I'm wearing my shadow face.

From the woods,
a soft-eyed deer watches.
Her warm breath
billows into the cold air.
I see… but do not notice.
Even when I am beckoned
by the long track of the moon
on the pond,
I do not follow.
Sorry, I can't dream today.
I'm wearing my shadow face.

THE INFINITE HORIZON

She travels east
on her Kawasaki
down Interstate 8
toward Pine Valley.
With the sun at her back
and an open road ahead
she gently accelerates.
It feels so good,
so familiar…

She remembers
being a proud Cherokee
racing across a dry meadow
on a paint horse
at a time when
America was free,
the streams unchallenged,
and the skyline unblemished.

She remembers
breathing the cold clean air
and how invigorating
it felt on her skin.
She remembers
how the colt responded
to her subtle urging
and ran faster… and faster.

In this life,
her horse is a machine
with fire in its belly
responding only
to the twist of a throttle.
But once again
she is racing the wind
to a common destination,
transcending time,
and forever approaching
the infinite horizon.

CARRIAGE DRIVERS

There comes a time when
you can't write about
what you know about-
because it's far too close to your nose.

Simple is how I would
like to find myself.
Maybe left alone with the phragmites
at the end of the road.

Better yet, cunning.
Until ignorance turns
everything I have
into droplets of suspicion.

I know nothing from carriage drivers
on a Central Park West evening.
Cotton fingers projecting through
gnawed-off brown jersey gloves.

Night wind cuts a path
and suddenly I'm somewhere else.
Flickering lanterns have turned into
much more than citronella dreams.

FLASHLIGHT

You poor miserable beam,
jailed behind a once transparent
scratch resistant
piece of faded plastic.

Darker days are done,
snuggled by cold zirconium.
Gently set into place
above a corkscrew spring.

Fifteen years now,
fifteen years.
Banging my head
against the wall,
waiting for the
cauliflower to freeze.

Chase your shadows
and start to realize,
you're living your life's
own consequences.

But if I roll these "D" cells
between my fingers,
I can almost catch
the slightest glimmer
of light vibrating from
your beveled silver sides.

THIS COULD HAVE BEEN A LOVE POEM

I always wondered if you'd make it to the funeral,
pierced lip and a Holden Caulfield t-shirt.
You'd slip behind the minister and realize
open-toed shoes in the mud just don't work.

Then you'd think back to the secrets
that you whispered in my ear,
showed me your journal pages
when you didn't think I'd care.

And softly said, "tell me your secrets
and I'll be one of them."
You gave me all your pages
and I handed them back again.

When sometimes, but not often,
we'd hear the saxophone's solo sounds,
and lose each other in the sad light
humming a melancholy song.

You would cry for all the good reasons
and for absolutely no reason at all.
Makes it easier to touch the earth.
You said it was good for your soul.

The smell of yesterday's air
lost some taste in the barroom smoke.
Still we ran down the driveway giggling,
not giving it a second thought.

This could have been a love poem
if the words and feelings went hand in hand.
This could have been a love poem
if you ever paused to think that I gave a damn.

Barbara Hantman

WORSHIPPING WOMEN *

The priestess holds large key to temple gate;
The patriarchal polis cannot pose
A threat to woman's ken in sphere of rose,
Libation, love nest, lair for heroes' grace.
Though demos denied suffrage through the land
Retreats on sylvan isles bore mater's curves
With sister's fawn-like charm, friskier nerves
For chant and dance of Dionysos's band.
Withheld: a chance to stamp discourse's tone
When Caesar, king, or emperor opined
The sorry state of Carthage, Tyre or Rome.
Bequeathed: marble bond of marriage chiseled
On stele showing hand-in-hand drizzled
About with tender deference in stone.
In life, in death, hearth's heroine sublime!

* Insights and details were gleaned from the Onassis Cultural Center exhibit
entitled "Worshiping Women: Ritual and Reality in Classical Athens" (and
accompanying pamphlet); December 10, 2008 – May 9, 2009 in the Olympic
Tower, 645 Fifth Ave. & 51st St., NYC.

Patrice Hasbrook

CHECKERBOARD PAVILION

Fugitive and hesitant, papery birds
seize a hypnotic patina from

       tarry
       velvet
       streets

Streets worn by scowling destiny
feather etched in humidity-fattened air

Streets divided into a mosaic mewl,
symphonic, in equal parts

Spring-green birds that have lain
with bloom, in 2's, 3's, 4's

now lie with strewn flowers
their folded paper bird's breath,

       aloft

"GO FOR A WALK?"

I'm a great prow walking into the carnivorous wind

    blood sang
          into the musical wind

          lunar leaps, rise
          jubilant foxy trot,

          leaps tease upright
          planes in space

  Prow from the slip, Orion, (only lately clairvoyant)
    at the helm

        so on

           and on

  Pauses only to batter land   prowl   describe sand
    beside sea

Inky night silencers
       Sinewy   bleats weepy   gulpy chokes

Now Goya's astral air
   seats huge figure
      crisscross giant legs
         hug blurs lusty kiss

Who stares into skies blue-black crevices

    vanquish earth's extra amber flow
    beside the milk-like transparencies
    of a milky way

  "Go for a walk?"

Meredith Hasemann-Cortes

POEM FOR MY FRIEND TOM KOPKA

Three years ago we stood
outside the theatre just before midnight,
awaiting the premiere of Revenge of the Sith.
I wore jeans. You wore Jedi robes.

Three months ago, I sat on a rattling plane
piloted by a captain with a quavering voice
clutching my children's hands,
vowing to hold them until our fiery end

so they wouldn't be scared.
At the same time you lay in a hospital,
your five young children gathered around
trying not to be scared.

As my family finally landed at JFK,
fellow passengers crying, clutching rosary beads,
the airport abandoned by incoming and outgoing flights
due to extreme weather,

the storm of your mind
quietly slipped from your body,
away from that hospital bed,
your children gathered around.

By the time I landed you were gone.
Four days later I visited your body
in the casket, arms folded
across your last Star Wars convention ticket.

Why is it that my plane landed and yours did not?
I suppose yours landed, too, but far far away.
I'm still standing here
with no Jedi robes, no light saber to guide me.

But I do hear distant whispers from the force
like the one that guided my plane home.

OCTOBER 14, 2006: FOR ROBERT LONG

Just a week or two after my car accident,
chopping carrots for chicken pot pie,
planning weeknight dinners to pull out of the freezer,
I sink to a wooden chair and cry.

The kitchen fan is on, but there's nothing cooking.
I haven't even gotten a pot out of the cupboard yet.
Strangely, I am home alone, and you are dead.
You weren't yesterday.

My car is totaled; there are skid marks on the road near my house.
Outside, the windshield of my rental car
reflects the trees, staccato notes in the wind.
If there's any hovering going on, you'd see me here:

hand to my head, eyes wet, windowpane patterned
in sunlight relief across the floor and over my jeans,
wondering what song is playing. I recognize it,
but can't put my finger on the name or where I heard it first.

Somehow, it seems important. It reminds me of this:
the same death that hangs burning leaves off trees in fall
is not sad or awkward like death among humans,
but pregnant, beautiful, and deep.

In every crunch of leaves under sneakers or tires,
a chord is played, a poem is born,
silence is crushed.
It's a fitting season for death, October,

the month itself hovering with contradictions:
clear, crisp, perfect days too cold to spend time in;
sunlit, aromatic kitchens too cloistered to cook in;
nature reflected in man-made objects.

I romanticize beginnings and ends,
elusive waves pulling back
into the ocean after crashing hard
on the shore all summer long.

It's fitting that you died in October,
when poetry stands in the window
of the Hertz-rent-a-car, life contradicting itself
in a world of chopping carrots for meat pies.

SILLY RIGHT BRAIN WILD TURKEY POEM

Every day they crowd the curves: I nudge my car
through rhythmic feathers on the way to and from work;
hordes of them strutting. My son says they are dancing
and sings his third grade anthem: "Who let the dogs out?"

So many of them, so suddenly: Where did they come from?
They don't really belong here, not these days at least,
like the thoughts crowding my mind, elbowing
into corners, strangely welcome and unwelcome.

Confluence, quotidian: I am learning so much –
but at the same time I know so little
of what I am supposed to be doing
about all of these wild turkeys crossing the street.

I weave my way to work and back
thinking things I shouldn't, singing songs
that send me into wanton flashbacks, triggers:
a symphony of memories playing to me,

myself, the audience in my own drama, feeling around
for the music, the answers, like the turkeys, pecking about blindly,
unsure how to dance to this new song, in this new place.
We sally forth, bit players in the dramas we create.

Deborah Hauser

PARISIAN LOVESCAPE

I want you to prime me like you're Chagall
and I'm a smooth, blank canvas
splayed taut across all four corners of the frame

propped on a rough-hewn easel
in a cramped studio on Boulevard Saint Germaine

the light streams down on me from the one casement window
set high in the paint-splattered wall,
shutters flung open to the late afternoon sunlight

not the interrogating high yellow sun
but deeper, lower on the spectrum
a thick forgiving honey tone

that warms and flatters my bare ass
under your broad, swirling brush strokes

BLAMELESS

She lay
In their bed
A scent of diluted flowers
Permeates
As they grope in the dark
Time drowns
He rolls away
A vacant expression
Passes across his face
All the love felt

Brushed off
Like morning toast crumbs

PARASITE

You
Are an overdressed memory
Bloated
Bathing around my heart
Intoxicated
Basking in a vein glow
Used, numb
Harvest complete
You detach
Fangs still moist with my blood
You troll for your next host

CESCA AND THE SWING
for Francesca Gioeli

You've been such a strong swinger,
Pulling yourself so high you took away our breath
Lest you'd turn upside down
And land on your crown.

You've been such a swift runner,
Flying downfield to score in sudden death.

But when the swing broke at your apex
And you fell on your ankle back on earth,
You learned that life's not just flight
But free falls and bad breaks.

Healed, you'll soon swing and fly again,
But wiser with memory of pain.

FEEDING CHICKADEES

(Morton Wildlife Preserve)

Black-capped mendicant,
why do you put your life in my hand—
just to snatch an easy snack,
beaking seed from my palm as you straddle
my thumb and forefinger?
Not one extra instant do you linger:
the black cap dips, the sharp beak plucks
a sunflower seed, and you skedaddle
to the nearest branch that's out of reach
to hull your catch,
then gull it down
and cast the husk aside.

Chickadee-dee-dee you call,
and the flittering wings of your kin
announce that they've forsaken
sedulous forage for seedy feeding
at this strange pink perch
that wavers slightly
as your feathery ounces weigh upon it,
claws clenching skin,
while I sit on my urge
to snap my fingers
shut like a trap
and have my way with you.

Frane L. Helner

THE SUNDAE GOWN

The color of hot fudge,
its silken fabric
languidly oozes

across body's length
to pool, a luscious syrup,
at the feet.

Neckline's deep conic vee
plunges between generous vanilla scoops
and scattered caramel-chip freckles.

Kimono-shaped sleeves
extend like spoons,
ready, waiting to serve. And note,

unlike the wanton scatter of walnuts, these
decorative buttons, like firm, round hazelnuts,
stand aligned along zipper's spine, alert

against enticements
of frivolous maraschino cherries.
After all, this gown's formal!

WAITING FOR POETRY

As if it were a *Shule* and we,
congregants gathered for morning *Minyan*,
our stanzas of liturgy held before us.

We wait, watch the door,
give name to each entrance: "...here's Sandy,
anyone know about Dan...?" And count

eight, nine, then the anticipated tenth,
the one who, by fortuitous number,
may make our prayers acceptably

unselfish, yet still cleverly designed
to fulfill,
or purge,

each self's own needs
within an agreeable
stanzaic arrangement.

Gladys L. Henderson

ON THE EIGHTH DAY

Once the word is out,
the garden is filled:
crackle,
    blackbird,
        red-wing
and sparrow.
All flapping
    with acrobatic
poise to eat the seeds offered.

Later they splash
    in the birdbath,
       spinning jewels
of water onto the waiting flowers.

For all of us, a gusto of joy,
those who wait,
    those who splash,
and we who sit on our porches
overlooking all—

Understand now,
    how a god feels,
three minutes after creation's hand.

WALKING STEGE'S POND

1.

Along the way we name the flowers.

Mom in her straw hat
and Dad in his red woolen shirt,
fishing rod in hand.

My brother's pale skin
is protected by a baseball cap,
the hospital and war behind him—

he doesn't have much to say anymore.

I walk with ease,
run ahead of them.
At the turn, they are out of my sight.

2.

The path is unchanged.

Along the way I name the flowers.

A small blossom,
with a pink center
grows between the granite rocks.

It is unnamed, an orphan.

I have lost them all.

William Heyen

A POETICS OF HIROSHIMA

Imperial Air Force pilot Sachio Ashida, unable
to fly over the burning city to report
to his superiors what had happened to it,
landed his plane, borrowed a bicycle,
& pedaled into it. He'd remember
a woman in front of her smoldering home,
a bucket on her arm. Inside the bucket
was a baby's head. The woman's daughter
had been killed when the bomb fell.

This is atrocity. You've just now descended
from a stanza wherein a baby's head—
were its eyes open or closed?—was carried
in a bucket by her mother.
An Imperial Air Force pilot stopped his bike
in front of what had been her home.
I've wanted us to breathe ashes & smoke,
but we cannot. This, too, is atrocity.

What's true for me is probably true for you:
I'm tired of trying to remember this.
Somewhere in Hiroshima the baby's head
is dreaming, wordlessly. No, it is not—this, too,
is atrocity. Ashida went on
to live a long life. He felt the swing & weight
of that bucket on his arm. No,
he did not. He did. He sometimes dreamed himself
pedaling backwards away
from that mother. I don't know whether
he did or not. Meanwhile,

we rave about the necessity of a jewel-center in every poem.
I've used a baby's head
in a bucket on her mother's arm. Whether
this is art, or in the hands of a master could be, or whether
art is atrocity, or not, I'm sick of being,
or trying to be, part of it, me
with my weak auxiliary verbs which vitiate
the jewel-center, me
with my passives, my compromised stanzaic integrity,
my use of the ambiguous "this"

188

which is atrocity. No, it is not. It is.

For years my old high school coach visited my home
with dahlias in a bucket,
big red-purple & blue-purple heads
my wife & I floated in bowls on our tables.
Have I no shame? This, too, this story
that evokes another, this narrative rhyme, this sweet
concatenation of metaphor,
is atrocity. Coach fought on Iwo Jima
for ten days before & ten days after
the flag-raising on Mount Suribachi.
He returned there fifty years later, brought me
a babyfood jar half-filled
with black sand from one volcanic blood-
soaked beach. He did. But at Marine reunions,
he couldn't locate any of his buddies
from his first outfit. No, he could not.
He once laid out on my desk aerial photos of runways
the Japanese used to "wreak havoc"—his words—
& said that hundreds of thousands of GIs would have died
if HST had not given the order.
As a participant in necessary atrocity, I agreed.
I still agree. But it doesn't matter if I agree—
what matters is whether poetry itself agrees. Incidentally,
Ashida was in training to become
a divine wind, a kamikaze.

    1945. I was almost five. Col. Tibbets named
    our *Enola Gay* for his mother.
    The 6th of August. Our bomb, "Little Boy," mushroomed
    with the force of 15 kilotons of TNT.
    "A harnessing of the basic power of the universe," said HST,
    as though the universe were our plowhorse.
    In the woman's home, her daughter was beheaded.
    I don't know if Ashida learned exactly how,
    though we & the art of atrocity would like to know.
    In any case, what could this mother do?
She lifted her daughter's head. She laid it
in the aforementioned jewel-center.
She was not thinking of the basic power of the universe.
Did she place oleander blossoms on her baby's face?
Did she enfold her daughter's head in silk, which rhymes with *bucket*,
 & *sick*, & *volcanic*, & *wreak havoc*? ...

(Buckets appear often, as a matter of fact,
in the literature of exile, for example
in Irina Ratushinskaya's prison memoir *Gray is the Color*
of Hope—coal buckets & slop buckets,
ersatz food placed in what were toilet buckets.
"Time to get up, woman. Empty your slop bucket."
Irina drags her bucket daily to the cess pit.
She doesn't know if she can ever become a mother.)

Ashida attained the highest black belt, went on
to coach the American Olympic judo team.
He did. I spoke with his daughter
at an event where I received a poetry prize,
a check for a thousand George Washingtons
& an etched glass compote
for a book on the Shoah. I said I once heard her father
lecture on Zen—the moon in the river,
River flowing by that is the world with its agonies
while Moon remains in one place,
 steadfast despite atrocity.
I remember that she seemed at ease,
she who had known her father
as I could never.

While teaching at the University of Hawaii,
I visited Pearl Harbor three times, launched out to the memorial
above the *Arizona*. Below us, the tomb
rusted away—a thousand sailors,
average age nineteen—for nature, too, is atrocity,
atoms transformed within it, even memory.
We tourists, some Japanese, watched minnows
nibble at our leis.
No, we did not. This was my dream:
I knelt at a rail under a Japanese officer with a sword,
but now there are too many stories for poetic safety,
for stanzaic integrity—woman & daughter,
Ashida at his lecture, my high school coach carrying heads
of dahlias grown from bulbs
he'd kept in burlap to overwinter in his cellar,
even persona Heyen at Pearl Harbor
above the rusting & decalcifying battleship that still breathed
bubbles of oil that still
iridesced the Pacific swells as jewel-centers iridesce

our most anthologized villanelles….
A bombing survivor said, "It's like when you burn a fish on the grill."

I end my sixth line above with the word "home."
My first draft called it the woman's "house," but *home*
evokes satisfaction, *mmm,* a baby's
contentment at the breast, the atrocity
of irony, & *home* hears itself in *arm, & bomb, & blossom,*
& looks forward to *shame & tomb.*
I cannot not tell a lie.
Apparently, I am not so disgusted with atrocity
as I'd claimed to be—my atoms
do not cohere against detonation, but now time has come—listen
to the *mmm* in *time & come*—for closure,
as, out of the azure,

into the syntax of Hiroshima, "Little Boy" plunges—
I've centered this poem both to mushroom
& crumble its edges—
& "Fat Man," 21 kilotons of TNT,
will devastate Nagasaki. What is your history? Please don't leave
without telling me. Believe me,
I'm grateful for your enabling complicity.
I know by now you've heard my elegiac ē.
I hope your exiled mind has bucketed its breath.
I seek to compose intellectual melody.
I fuse my fear with the idea of the holy.
This is St. John's *cloud of unknowing* in me.
This is the Tao of affliction in me.
Don't try telling me my poetry is not both
beguiling & ugly.

"There was no escape except to the river," a survivor said.
but the river thronged with bodies.
Black rain started falling, covering everything the survivors said.

I have no faith except in the half-life of poetry.
I seek radiation's rhythmic sublime.
I have no faith except in beauty.
I seek the nebulous ends of time.
This is the aria those cities have made of me.
I hope my centered lines retain their integrity.
I have no faith except in atrocity.

OH, EVE

If you hadn't nibbled that fruit
you and Adam could have spent eternity
naming things repeatedly
trying to find something useful to do.

Every day - no dishes, laundry, shopping
just pluck a pear or tangerine
from any other tree.

For all we know, you only wanted
to test a new ingredient
for your most recent recipe

or perhaps there was another reason
you couldn't resist trying just one bite.
It's easy to sympathize with cravings

we women know how hard it must have been
to get a bagel at midnight - in Eden.

RHAPSODY
in honor of George Enescu

Let's play again that rhapsody
that starts with tingling trill

the one that lures me to find
a place where Gypsies camp
where I shall fling myself
in frenzied dance
to the throbbing of violins

skirts flashing flame-colored
ruffles above my bare legs

tousled hair, radiant
in the fire's glow

my wanton glance
inviting you to dare to try
to kiss my naked toes.

Barbara Hoffman

BAD CONNECTIONS

in the dream
the sales clerk throws
my long black coat
out on the street

it lies on the pavement
like the chalk outline
of a police drawing
at a murder scene

I run out   pick it up
the clerk says
they told me to do it
I gather the coat in my arms

bring it inside
continue shopping
he throws it out again
then I remember

in your house
I opened a closet
to hang up my coat
but you took it

laid it across the table
where it stayed
for the 24 hours
you allotted me

BOTANY/BIOLOGY

he brings me
seashells
as sheer
as the membrane
of an egg

as thin
as my skin
awake
to every nuance
of touch

stroke
opening
to him
I am the vulva
of an O'Keeffe flower

petal folding
upon petal

DINNERTIME

mother calls us for dinner
a burning rises   acid
in my throat

I sit at my place   break off
a piece of Italian bread
butter it

father tells my brother
eat your bread
damn it   eat

father's words fly across the table
followed by a smack
to the side of my brother's head
the sounds thud
heavy as the bread and butter
in my stomach

mother stands at the stove
stirring soup

something boils over
on the back burner

Martha Hollander

AFTER SCIENCE FICTION

From upside down,
the ceiling's acoustical tiles
blur into roiling grays.
My head is hanging off the bed,
and I see the first pin of light,
the second, the third.
A firefly is caught in the room,
I say. *Should we let it out*
to be with its firefly friends?
You see it too, turn over and sleep.
No, no need to step outside now,
for a blessing of sweet night air.
It was just the smoke alarm
winking and dying.

So life is a loop,
our small son had said
at dinner, having been told
that death returns us to
the nothing we came from.

Reading a whole sf anthology
in a single evening,
I see why his discovery
propelled him to the fishtank
to stare at the fluttering tetras.
Those imagined worlds
are all based on loneliness,
on the absolute despair
of being imprisoned
in that time, that place,
stuck in a horrible world
of another's making.

FLOATING ISLANDS

Coming at the end of a gorgeous
French lunch, the floating islands
appear at the girlfriends' table.
Under the crust, three desserts
Are awash in amniotic warmth;
offwhite, with a touch of sea and liquor,
hot as the earnest, fierce
mantle of earth.

Float far enough and you reach
the harbor where each of us began;
a shrieking solitary little person
running to the tip of the continent,

out of the restaurant and down the boulevard,
gliding, lined in egg yolk,
back into the summertime crowds
which murmur like fat flies drunk on blood.

Tony Iovino

ECHOES

Kermit's laughter lingers,
Where Thing One and Thing Two once scurried,
While the Owl and the Pussycat sailed away
And we whispered hushed goodnights to the Moon.
Now the child enters
Asking Daddy not for a bedtime story,
But for the car keys.

SUMMER, 1968

There is no great river here,
No raft to sail with a runaway slave,
No flying laboratory to share with Tom Swift.
Native spirits don't rise under a full moon
From ancient graveyards
To haunt this suburban row.
Just Chevys and Fords in every driveway
Dads pushing mowers, Moms cooking dinners.

There's marches and riots on TV
But they don't come to this neighborhood.
No protestors trail the Good Humor truck,
No chants ring out, just Pavlovian bells.

Jesse James and his gang don't gallop down this block,
No pirates pillage Tackapausha pond.
The only thief hereabouts is
The high school bully who cheats at flipping cards,
Taking the third grader's cardboard heroes,
Three-card monte meets Topps.

August sun baking in the summer boredom,
He imagines the Russians invading,
How he'll hide behind Mr. Tom's bushes,
And hurl rocks at their tanks,
Or ride his Schwinn ahead of them,
Paul Revere with a banana seat,

To warn, to save.

Holding his thumb tight over the end of the hose,
Beneath the water line in the blowup pool,
Counting down from 10,
He starts the liftoff, hose water splaying
Like the exhaust from the Saturn rockets,
And he dreams of being first to the moon.

Lazing, backs against the picket fence,
Shaded by the old sidewalk elm,
The older boys talk of jungle war and muscle cars
And girls, always girls.
He looks down the block as they banter,
Watches an Impala turning left at the corner,
Disappearing behind Mrs. Fisher's hedges
Heading to the main drag.

He wants to sail away, become a privateer,
Storm exotic shores.
He longs to ride a train
One that doesn't have a dashing commuter as a logo,
Maybe a freight train, rumbling long through the night
To the square states on the map.

He yearns to explore new worlds,
Be the new Lewis and Clark, or John Glenn.
He wants to pitch for the Mets.
He wants to be President.

He wants to bike down the block,
Turn left at the corner,
And follow the road 'til it ends,
Until there is no more pavement,
No more Levitt houses,
No more picket fences.
Just go, ride until there is something else,
Ride hard until there is anything else.

WHERE & WHEN?

Dripping from the shower.
I can't tell where the ice cream begins,
And the pecan pie ends.

Where exactly in this paunch
Are the chocolates?
The cookies? The Doritos?
The salted peanuts, the buttery popcorn?

Where have I stored the donuts?

I can't recall the ordinary days.
I can't recall the ordinary snacks.
But they've left gray in my beard
And bulk on my belly
To let me know they were here.

FEATHERS

Lisa James

Primaries, secondaries
A season's molt scatters.
You've got new wings to fly,
If flight was your goal.

But you won't go.

Oh, now and again
The half-remembered myth stirs
The flights of forgotten ancestors
The weariness of migration
The beating, beating
      of leaden wings
The relentless press
The urge for new sky to steer by.

But life's soft in the suburbs.
Endless grass and easy beggings
Your once-gaunt sinews are larded
     and loosened with ease.

Then you spy your wilder, earlier self
Winging high and straight, a perfect vee
Aimed at tundra and endless, glassy blue lakes.

So you try.
But the formation's all wrong
Beats all out of time
And a low, slow altitude.

You flutter back to familiar puddles
Garlanded with plastic bags.

MOTHER LOVE

Your swallowed anger could strip paint.
The endless acrid cigarettes
(which would eventually end your days)
etched lines into your lips that no amount of
blood-red lipstick could erase, yellowed
both fingertips and the hair roots peering
from beneath bottled color.

Yet despite the tomboy who ran
beyond your forties-fashion ideal,
despite the adolescent who argued politics
from the opposite end of the spectrum,
you loved your enigmatic eldest with a fierceness
that hid the empty space where a childhood should have been.

RAVENOUS

It's almost
obscene, the way
the juice of a good poem
drips
thick and
glistening
down your chin as you
eagerly
tear into its perfectly
ripe body
bite
after
lusty
bite.

A WILD DANCE

The back fence has returned to hedge again,
arching rose above a wild dance,
binding and winding of root and stem,
bramble arms form a linking branch.
A reach for light in the dense green,
flowers of pinky-white, raised hands
to the music of sun and rain,
steps of the soil know no commands.
For long, wires and poles were divides
and planted privet struggled to grow,
but now the moorland strides
towards us and forms a row.
In the ceilidh whirl the birds emerge,
a reel with seeding air its urge.

BIRDS ON HIGH WIRES

Up on the high wires
                              I heard them first -
                    a charm of finches

          persistent
                    'Chick, chick, chick!'

     telephone lines
               the staves -
                         green notes from a distance
a trick of the sun
               through binoculars
                         white-capped
                              a flash of white
                                   across wings

          as though
                    premonitions
                         of ice and snow
     I'd seen the weather-map
          systems from the north
           not south Atlantic warm wet
           but winds with icy breath -

                    did they know too
                              even if
                                   today was highest
blue?
     when they flew
          in feeding fits and starts
               their butterfly motions
                    were fragile as the season

     before owltime
               they had gone
                         it was a resting-place
                         on a long migration
                         in search of the sun

          the telephone wires silent and bare -
          a manuscript without a song.

Evelyn Kandel

THERE IS A GAME CALLED SOLITAIRE

it could be called *forgetting*
it should be called *burglar*
its ending begets a beginning
like a long listing in Genesis
no one says it is required
to sit long hours
no one says there is a reason
to play alone
to avoid some things
and this is the answer.

WHERE WAS I?

Where was I when they burned bras
menstrual blood ran in the streets
women gathered in living rooms
to take back selves
        they never had

Where was I when they stormed the halls
of hallowed universities with raised fists
flinging fingers in victory signs
tearing the flag
        shouting *pigs*

Who was I in blue silk suit
holding children for an Easter photo
a flowered silk hat worn like Jackie's
        smiling into the camera

What was I thinking when they murdered Jack
Martin and Bobby bled on cement floors
tears ran in the gutters for demented minds
my son asked
        Why are you crying?

The answer   my friend   is blowing in the wind
still *blowing in the wind*
that is what I was thinking
when I was there

Rita Katz

DREAM CATCHER

ashen sky suspends a stone gray roof
geese barks cross the night of Christmas lights
it has started to snow
and I am wrapped in my blanket cocoon
holding my dream catcher

images brush lightly as a butterfly wing
I see my childhood home
fireplace still warm
father in his green velvet chair
puffing on his pipe
mother brushing and braiding her hair

their togetherness invades me
together yet apart
we are each other

NERUDA

surrounded by winter's drab presence
I read poetry and for a short time
live inside a stranger's world

what day is today?
today is my birthday
I blow out candles
if I am lucky
my wish will be granted

should we mourn
suddenness of time
listen to past pleasures
ask for more?

aware of destiny
I feel the need to touch
hold onto integrity
of each new day

SHRADDAH

her life in photos & e-mails

at one month
almond-shaped eyes
newborn down hair

> top on the list
> Shraddah assigned to an American woman

nine months
thick brown hair just above her ears
heart-shaped lips slightly downturned

> Nepal closes adoptions
> all regulations revoked

12 months
sad eyed
in the arms of a child care worker

> the government collapses
> re-stabilizes

14 months
standing together
with 2 other children in a single crib

> new regulations drafted & approved
> annual adoption limit: 10 children per agency

21 months
wearing a pink sweater & barefoot
outside the orphanage

> adoption reopens
> children over 10 given priority

TONIGHT

the ticking of grandfather's clock has stopped
and the dog slipped into sleep
in the back room an hour ago
the windows are closed against the cold
outside sounds wisp away
soon the noise of children
and grandchildren
will enter our home
then I might well long for quiet
but now the echo of stillness
startles this dark night

PERSPECTIVE

"You only really need
five brushes," he said,
"fat down to thin.
But you have to clean
the paint off every time."
Dads are the ones
with the rules. The man
worked in insurance but
lived for painting. He never
owned a suit he didn't
ruin. He tried to make me
paint like him, sing like
him, be Irish like him.
He taught me how to
knock myself to others
and hide behind Mozart
and the Met and Monet,
how to look down on
Barbie and the Beatles,
how to be at once
above it all and less-than.
Daddy's little mini-me.
He collected weird
geezer friends, garage-sale
picture frames, tear sheets,
coffee-table books, museum
postcards. At the end
they put him in a wing of his own.

TO NOT ONE BUT SEVERAL EXES

I built a tower of money
tended a garden of sex
banked a fire of security
embroidered bed curtains
in a pattern of children
put up and preserved
figs nuts pickles candied berries
fed my intellect on the arcane
my skin with the oil of second youth
inside and out all I
was did knew had
was calibrated to woo
and I will never get why
none of it was good enough for you

TO PATRICK STEWART, AFTER SEEING *MACBETH*

For you
I would lose 30 pounds
get my veins done
maybe get some other work done
I would understand the rigors of fame
be the most interesting woman
you have ever met, ever
my subtle eyes would speak volumes
only to you when you're offstage
that *Vanity Fair* columnist would
go on and on about what a perfect couple
we are and how the men with the talent
get all the luck and the good sex
I would shield you from the press
and weird fans who try to make you
notice them while you're working
(like my moron ex-husband
that time at *The Tempest*)
I would be the jet-setting
decorator of all our houses
I would buy you stacks of black turtlenecks
put them in all our houses
I would be whatever you desire
just as right now you are
the notepad I am writing on

Kate Kelly

LONG FALL

into the
promise
of snow
we drifted
before
the fire
we sat
too warm
too shy
to mention
that
we peeled
off layers
cooled
our skins
skinned
our hearts beat
too
shallow
breathing
as one
we caressed
each other
blades
of grass
flattened
by
heat
in
summer.

NO ACCIDENT
for Jackson Pollock

Gravity floats grey sky above sea,
an impish eye moons the night
hawking the moan and mad laughter
of man wrestling nature.
Ahab is caught in a maelstrom
while the innards of sole sweep in schools
beneath a brash stroke of blue
crush and curl.

You wrest yin from the grip of tired roles,
pin manhood to the mat
sweat through with the passion drip of
spent strength. You deny accident,
have sense enough of self
to dance cheek to cheek with unbridled danger;
sifting through shards of broken paint jars,
you piece together curious questions.

In a studio somewhere in this world
a bulb dims, the switch fails,
wooden floor planks splinter and the pilot light
is snuffed; arabesque of the mundane world gone mad.
Everyone worth their salt has been there where
sounds at night wiggle-wobble sax flow
through automatic drip drive,
wailing.

You stumble through a blue moon night,
beg a fresh brush, barter for a pair of brown eyes,
the color of Rembrandt.
"Just," you implore, "lend me back the raging groan
of youth, sketch into this picture
the strength of my third wing
and I will pad softly up the stairs and under cover of sleep
dream of war cries over the creek bed."

There is no accident,
the center folds in on itself, and holds,
and will never be wholly gone
as long as you remember walking on snow
under a clothesline strung with gloves,
and pair with this memory, the firm belief that
everything belongs in the frame.

215

THINGS BORN TO BE SACRIFICED

a swallow with one wing
a white alligator
a blind squirrel
a hare-lipped girl
a cat without a tail

the men marched
as an army
not seen
since the days of Caesar,
through cities in ruin and
desolated rows of
abandoned plantations
burning

leaving
bitter
widowed women,
orphaned mothers of
fallen sons.

some men chase history,
re-enact the casualties of battle;
dressed to play the part
they fall in great numbers
beneath a barrage
of forged cannon fire.

some men chase the future.

born to be sacrificed
a soldier cradles his head;
inside
a
howling
boy
swallows hard
an awful
music.

Ann Kenna

THURSDAY AFTERNOON AFTER THE
DEMONS HAVE ESCAPED
Inspired by "Locomotion" by Jacqueline Woodson

The monsters that live in our minds
Don't have blue fur and purple ears
The monsters that live in our minds
Don't wait for the night or stormy days
They come on Sunday afternoons when
Your eyes are fixed on yellow tulips
They come on Tuesday mornings in stalled
traffic on the Long Island Expressway
The demons in our minds do drive
by pickups of ten dollar bags
steal twenty dollars out of your wallet
but leave the ten so maybe
you think you must have spent it
on gas or lotto so the monsters that live
in your minds will lay low, far enough
under the radar so you won't see that
five of your tablespoons have gone missing
and you think they must have been thrown out
and you don't believe he's one of them
when his eyes are glassy
with pinprick pupils and the demons
that live in our minds have fangs
that are needle sharp and breathe liquid fire
through broken veins
and on a Thursday in April you come home
early and the demons that live in your mind
have crept in and stolen
your blue-eyed baby boy

WEIRD

It happened again today
a regular everyday word
just typed on the page stared back
looking strangely odd
some days
words
seem
wrong
squint
look
out a corner of your eye
viewed from every angle
something seems awry
the word appears to smirk
written on every
page you've ever read

someone else should take a look,
then squint and shake their head
as if they've never seen the word
like a virus it has spread
words of warning about words
don't look too close
concentrate too hard
or
words
may
appear
very odd.

Teri Kennedy

I AM NOT A POET, BUT…..

From time to lengthy time,
I bear the pain
To write a poem.

From thought to thought,
From word to word,
From tear to tear.

From thought to word to tear
And back again.

From time to lengthy time,
I bear the pain.
I write a poem.

MOTHER'S DAY

Why didn't you want
To make babies with me?
Why didn't you?
Why didn't you fill me up
To sprout arms and legs
And fingers and toes?
Why? Why didn't you?

Well, that's it.
You did not.
So, there were no babes.
There are no children.
That time is past.

No christenings,
Birthdays,
Graduations.
No first steps,
First days at school,
First dates.
No little voice ever said, "Mommy"
No grown up girl ever said,
"Mother. How could you?"

There were no babes.
There are no children.
Why didn't you want
To make babies with me?

X. J. Kennedy

LAMENT FOR COPS

When index fingers fired like forty-fives,
The louder you hollered the quicker they fell,
Those good guys whom you didn't want to play.
You haggled for the robber's role: to hide
Fighting back giggles, flattened to a fence
While the dull flatfeet plodded on your trail.
Cops were the kind who ran when Mother called
And picked their Lincoln Logs up after them.

Now crime's a matter of technology: sly banks
Hand over cash laced with exploding dye,
Preserving robbers' looks on videotape---
Efficient, though I miss those gentle men
With shields the size of hearts, who kept the cars
From clashing in the street, whose lifted hands
Broke paths for children and the faint-of-heart
To crosswalk home, who strolled past shaded rooms
Where others kissed by night, who as they hummed
Bad sentimental songs scrawled parking tags.

AFTER ALL

There is a give in nature
Something that sets the wounded coming back
Even in the wake of heavy damage

That takes me when I am not looking
With an insight, with a lift,
As in a dream,
Releases me, who mostly can't, to cry
At lights that cascade radiant down the sea,
Surprises, in a wave of change
Washing over pain,
Invites me to discover
The loveliness in someone lovely.

It has to do with grass that keeps on growing
Up, between close cracks,
With butterflies that ply their brief silk wings
All the way to Mexico.

It is the vast prime essence
Staying the earth, the water sky,
That opens without ending like the dawn.

LINGERING
for Louise and Bob

Both boats move out, slow like the swans
Onto the evening
Slicing through blue silver water
Heading for the sun dance that is the open bay.

Ice laps inside the plastic cups of wine
Last week's Stilton cheese still tastes of cream.
We drift the wind-warm channel.
A doe, two fawns, are grazing soft ripe greens onshore. A heron
Rises out of high tide into stark September light.

The sky goes vast goes crimson wild,
The pleasure is so sure no one is laughing.

We navigate the long late afternoon
Of nearly eighty years,
But we can't see beyond
The end of summer in each other's eyes.

WAITING TABLE IN THE CARIBBEAN

Jasmine grew up over there
In the sunlit valley
Of that slow mountain
That lies long at the horizon
On this prowling beast, the sea,
Marsh mallow roses spring up in those jungle island hills.

Her father is long gone. Just up and drowned, poor scrawny guy.
And her mother died last year, stoic, feisty, warm.
Her dapper Jim has cut out, too, on some tramp trawler
Going somewhere. They had planned to make her seaside shack a coffee shop.

She serves the champagne breakfast
At this three-star beach resort, across that old surprise, the ocean,
On this island that reflects her own.
She rarely looks at the innocent, brutal waves.

She isn't letting on that her back pains from these trays
Or that the rent is overdue. Three weeks.

One of the guests, from New York
In his Ralph Lauren shirt, his orange shoes,
Beats a drum on the table with his knife.
He's been waiting for this coffee half an hour yet,
God damn it.

Jasmine heads in to the kitchen once, again.
The cook was late, not she.

She does look over this time to her island
Through the gnarled old grape tree, past the mystic, throbbing water,
Emerald and lilac.
She tries in vain to think Jim home.
If she started that shop herself, the coffee would be on time.

She brings the now brewed coffee to the man. Who claps.
She once more turns a wince
Into a gracious memory of her smile.

Alan King

IN THE KITCHEN

Cut mackerel soaks in a tub
of vinegar and floating
lemon slices before

dad puts it to simmer in
a salted broth of sweet bell
peppers and chopped tomatoes.

He'll tell you mom was his first
student of the stove and before
their diabetes,

she'd make each dish a carnival --
tongues lost in the loud revelry
of crushed garlic and curry.

Several times of cooking once
a year for her, and dad never knew
mom snuck in the missing spices,

the seasonings he overlooked,
fumbling through pots and pans
to prepare mother's day dinner.

PERCEPTIONS

Your body has slammed shut. Forever.
No keys exist.
The window draws full upon
your mind. There, just beyond
the sway of curtains, men walk.
                              --Maya Angelo, "Men"

I watch my sister gape at
boys from the passenger seat.
Her eyes, electrons spiraling
these walking helium atoms.

I've seen guys hijacked
by hormones, their bodies
propelled like kamikazes.

I know a fella whose lies were
whispering serpents in girls' ears,
swaying them from mother's warnings.

I remember the trail of women
my friends neglected, dismembered
mannequins strewn like *Legos*
behind toddlers.

Those images of my sister lured
and gutted makes a guardian,
a spectral hound protecting her
from anglers she will mistakenly see
as angels.

THE URGE

In the checkout line at Safeway,
fighting the urge to blush when
a cashier says, "if I was five years
younger, you'd be in trouble."

Boy, you gotta do more than
just grin at that fine woman,
my father would say before
going on about dental cost and
how I better show his money
well spent when I smile;

he could never let me forget
an overbite and 3 years of braces.

"Have a nice day," the cashier
winks and the urge over-
whelms me, a fortune
pops into my head:

a smile is your personal
welcome mat

A month before, I caught
a woman's eyes in passing;

a circuit board of nerves
lit up inside me when
she grinned, and said hi,

but out of shyness the urge
to speak deflated and like now
a smile was all I could muster.

Brendan Kirk

HAVING LIVED FOR THE PAST WEEK –
BEFORE WINTER I THINK

having moved from the regulatory houses for education
to the sordid houses for education
to the divination apartments for education
to the friendly hazes for education
to only have been found waking up drunk
with headache
and the sun

having searched for endless venues
and shining crescents
in the shivering air
and running
because my flesh is exposed

having woken with limp arm
to mazes of blankets and books
and a dog comes and licks my face
and i go back to sleep
so i can dream

having assembled mass gatherings
near bodies of water
to see what was going to happen
and finding nothing
and going home
to write poems

having shuffled through new york city stop lights
with blow-job girls
over patterns of trance and dry heaves
outside of cozy hookah smokers
and their uniforms
that stand semi-enlightened
in early hour sleep deprivation

having moved with little caution
through the disasters of streets
that are as lost in the vortex as the noisy boys

who stand screeching on their bricks
and developments
as they smoke cigarettes of misdemeanors
in between their relationships

having stumbled through the dreamiest piles
of the life that has yet to come
and wondering
if it will all be worth it

LATER THAT EVENING

I was eating language and you just watched my mouth.
And I asked for help and you gave me flame.
And I asked for reasoning and you gave me two hands.
And you asked for exploration and I gave you a cigarette and a flower.
And I demanded for purpose and you showed me the moon.
And you asked me for desire and I told you nothing.
And you cried out for acceptance and I dug you a hole.
And I cried out for simplicity and you destroyed the forest.
And you begged for opportunity and I disappeared in my clock.
And we both mourned for our foolishness but neither of us was there.

Denise Kolanovic

THE TREE TALKERS

Is there such a thing as instant money?
They say Americans grow it on trees.
In 2005, that thought is quite funny.
The real estate market begins to freeze
no matter if it's cloudy or sunny
with blue skies, constant rain or soft breeze.

Is it about weather then, a changed breeze
that plays through your hair blowing your money
along the streets? You run fast to catch and freeze
those flapping bills which push past you, funny,
how they heckle you by those money trees
you planted on a day, oh, so sunny.

Who, in their right mind would not plant on sunny
days, while the soft wind breathes the sweet breeze
along the lilacs, and the leaves of money
sway hypnotically making you freeze
there, by the roses, looking quite funny
as you stare at the branches of your trees?

Some people know the language of the trees.
They speak in murmuring tree talk, sunny-
faced, vibrant and joyously as the breeze
passes again through the leaves of money,
not yet ripened to fall, for that might freeze
the process. The tree talkers seem funny

to some of us for they have a funny
way of knowing the secrets of their trees.
Touching bark, caressing leaves of money,
they somehow transform the wood while a breeze
blows onto those tree talkers on sunny
days. One or two squirrels scurry then freeze,

for that is also nature's way, to freeze,
even stifled economies. Funny
how seasons come and go, changing the trees,
or, at least, the way they appear sunny
in full bloom, or splintered in icy breeze,
barren of all those green leaves of money.

In the winter of 2005, freeze
or melt, the ways of weather are funny,
but to the tree talkers in the midst of breeze.

BUT

She said, "No.
No, buts about it."

I said, "Oh, but I must."

It went back and forth
and forth and back
that way for the longest while.

Then, she said, "No. There is no way."

I said, "Where there is a will, there is a way."

She said, "Then I will have to break your will."

And I said, "No way."

It was then, she said, "Oh, but I will.
My Dear, I will."

UN-VALENTINE
for Tom and Rose

Valentine's Day was over
before it had even begun
the call
the flowers sent
directly to the wake

The visit
to that place
where Death
takes no notice of this
or any other day
to bid good-bye
to one of two
who together
brought so much joy
to hug the one of two
who is left

How strange to think that
two who were inseparable
two who after fifty years together
          were playful lovers still
two who were together one
are now two separate
          Ones

One on each side
of that greatest of divides
where for awhile
as each one must
they
will go separate ways

She will live with memories
He will bide beneath a stone
Till
Their destiny fulfilled
Two are One again

D-DAY PLUS 60

I am caught
in a web of nostalgia.
How we accepted everything,
the whole ghastly
upside-down world,
drab olive-colored uniforms,
war and death –

goodbye kisses at the RR station,
telegrams at front doors,
U.S.O. dances, rationing.
The music of Benny Goodman
and finding ourselves
in the midst of it –

with no more choice
than the dandelion seed
in a summer breeze.

OCTOBER

The pine wants to sprout
new needles, but the
season is wrong.

The wind would like
to chase a few clouds
but there are none.

My heart
wants to beat faster
but has no good reason.

The holly, surrounded,
droops
with wild weeds.

THIS TRAIN

is heading for the station –
only a few miles to go.

I have crumbled the warm earth
in my fingers; watched seeds sprout;
planted trees; seen a hundred
praying mantises emerge from
a pale nest; watched an inchworm
measure my arm; the sun spill gold
over the horizon; green leaves
born from stiff branches; snow descend
like torn clouds silent and pure;
had someone who loved me.

I cannot imagine that life
is more than this.

Belinda Kremer

JAVA

5am / slanging around / airport morning
    haze

"you" were gone for years / before
    "you" were gone

why? I offered us the door
    so many times.

someone is talking about fedex

I guess someone always is now.
                               control, packages
    —short lines, moving packages

                   —the hiccups
between two anything.

a skinny boy with a calla lily grins at the jet-blue lounge
    his grin a little too wide

a light woman in loud heels runs toward a rollbar
    gate scrolling up scrolling down

the moment she ducks in
       she has coffee brewing for the bleary irate
bellowing in /out of a tetchy line

(tetchy that the gate's back down)

the women working, not yet open
    the open smell of the coffee brewing

I've got a new trade paperback
    without a cut / spine clean
        pga tour shop
           new york new york to my left

— but it is not catalog time

backwards-speaking steps to trace a flight path

nothing to do with airports
                              of course
I am sorry to state what is obvious
          but troubling

pero disolución: there is sometimes still something

PETAL

        the leaves
plastered on the sidewalks

charming, charming. all out of
    order —

what happens when there is
                          conflict

still an open question.

for years I spoke

having divorced word from feeling.
    now our face is hot with the effort

from our throats. it wants

at the same time, to stop and leave.
at the same time

            we are leaning

toward disclosure, a lock runs

                    slips   catches   closes   clicks   snaps

across our thighs.

& in dream I ride
    a bike so tiny the pedals

bang my bare feet on
    rough asphalt

every revolution
& I am an editor
being a bitch to myself
    til I say

            Do you have any new work?
I would love to see it

Mindy Kronenberg

BERNIE'S STORY, 1943

When I was a soldier
in the Pacific Theater
my mother pleaded that
I send her a photo
of my entire naked body—
front and back, side-to-side,
to prove that no part of me
was missing or bloody.
My buddy took the picture,
laughing as I stood there
embraced by the thick heat
of the Philippines.

My fellow soldiers
teased that I was a momma's boy
-- at 23! --
but we all tore open her care packages
wrapped in swollen brown paper. We sunk
our teeth into the glossy red meat
of hard, marbled salamis,
fragrant ovals of seeded rye—
"Jew bread" they called it—
and we ate like starving children.

When we were on the hunt
the jungle devoured our company—
the air blackened as a winding cave's.
My gun slung over my shoulder
as I pushed aside leaves
nearly the size of my body,
my boots sinking in the muddy soil.
In a thread of moonlight
I faced my yellowed twin
as if looking in a clouded mirror.
An eternity passed in the seconds
that froze us into recognition,
until the thunder of my gun blinded
the darkness with a burst of fire,
removed my strange and silent reflection,
his body swallowed whole
with the bullet I fed him.

THE CARETAKER

It's always angels that captivate him—
voluptuous on their pedestals,
wings spread like an accordion mid-song.
Their plaster gowns twist behind them,
sandaled feet arched, their faces
blind to the darkening ground.

He seeks their refined stature
along the city's burning skyline,
the enflamed clouds thinning
to the song of dying stars.
He relishes the word, *Angels,*
as if he could taste their wonder,

his mouth arching and braced
for the sound, the hard *a*, the soft
g, the soothing s that liquefies in prayer.
He places his lips on the names in pitted
stone, ignores the lengthening shadow
in the grass, the angels' and his own.

Herbert Kuhner

EBONY AND HICKORY

Jo's hands were made
to hold sticks.

His long slender fingers
never gripped the sticks,
they merely rested
in his hands.

The sticks just needed
Jo's hands
so they could touch or hit
skins or cymbals.

It was as if
they had a life of their own.

And you know that
the sticks could only do what they did
in the magical hands that held them.

The sticks that Jo held
were live wood
that belonged to him
and would never have served
another drummer
the way they served Jo Jones.

EBENHOLZ UND HICKORY

Die Hände von Jo Jones
waren geschaffen
um Sticks zu halten.

Niemals hielten
seine langen schlanken Finger
die Sticks fest –
eher ruhten sie in seinen Händen.

Die Sticks brauchten
Jo's Hände nur
um das Schlagzeug
und die Becken
berühren zu können.

Es war, als ob sie
ein Eigenleben führten.

Und die Sticks konnten das nur tun,
was sie taten,
in den magischen Händen,
die sie hielten.

Die Sticks, die Jo hielt,
waren lebendiges Holz,
das zu ihm gehörte,
und niemals hätten sie
einem anderen Schlagzeuger so gedient,
wie sie Jo Jones dienten.

Translated by Ilse Zelenka

NIMROD'S REHABILITATION

Nimrod aimed his bow
at the sky,
pulled the string back
to the breaking point
and let go,
sending the arrow
as far up
as humanly possible
to determine the height
of the Tower of Babel.

Nimrod foolishly thought
he'd reach the God's proximity,
and when the work was finished,
he could climb to the top
to shake the Deity's hand.

After all, wasn't Nimrod a great ruler,
greater than his fellow men
and worthy of God's company?

And perhaps his ambition
could have been realized,
if the biblical Deity,
who did not enjoy a reputation
for being congenial,
hadn't struck his subjects
at what amounted to
being dumb.
They weren't mute
but couldn't converse
since they broke out
in multiple tongues.

Thus no one could give
or follow orders
and work had to be abandoned.

Without Nimrod,
what a wonderful world we'd have,
we'd all be speaking one tongue,
everyone could understand everyone;

there'd be no major and minor languages,
less chauvinism and nationalism
and no need for the farrago of Esperanto.

But what about translators?
Nimrod may very well be
a curse for the word,
but he's a great bowman
and a boon to translators.
In fact to them,
he's Saint Nimrod.

NIMRODS REHABILIERUNG

Nimrod richtete seinen Bogen
himmelwärts,
zog die Sehne weit zurück
und schoß den Pfeil so hoch wie möglich
um den Turm zu Babel zu bestimmen.

Irrtümlicher Weise dachte Nimrod,
daß er Gottes Nähe erreichen könne
und nach fertiger Arbeit könnte er
den Turm besteigen, um
des Schöpfers Hand zu schütteln.

Nimrod war ein großer Herrscher,
größer als alle andern,
und sicher Gottes Gesellschaft würdig.

Vielleicht wäre seine Vorhaben
zu verwirklichen gewesen
hätte nicht der Schöpfer,
der nicht gerade zugänglich war,
Nimrods Untertanen
mit einer Art Sprachlosigkeit bestraft.
Sie konnten sprechen, aber
einander nicht verstehen.
Jeder sprach eine andere Sprache.

Es folgte, daß niemand Befehle geben
oder dies folgen konnte
und man mußte die Arbeit aufgeben.

Ohne Nimrod
hätte wir eine herrliche Welt
mit nur einer Sprache.
Jeder könnte jeden verstehen,
große und kleine Sprachen,
würde es nicht geben,
weniger Chauvinismus und Nationalismus.
Esperanto wäre tot statt ein Totgeburt.
Und Übersetzer?

Vielleicht war Nimrod
ein Verfluchter des Wortes,
aber für Übersetzer.
Ist er der größte Patron gewesen,
sicher Sankt Nimrod.

German translation by the author

Phillip Levine

INVITATION TO A NAP

Sleeping, like breathing, is an act
of forgetting and remembering
over and over.

If you forget and sleep
and dream that we kiss
I will remember
the sound of water
pouring over stone.
And forget how simply glass
can slice to bone.

So I say:

Choose to forget and come to me
like feather down and
spill on me with fingers.
Place one hand on my belly
and your other
wherever you wish,
and I will show you
laughter so silent
our mouths drift open.

Ok, I've told you.

Now, let's remember a field
where the sky drips beautiful.
Melts green to yellow.
And forget how easily clouds
swallow this prodigal son.

Maria Lisella

FOG IN VENICE or *LA NEBBIA VENEZIANA*

Robed and twice-twined
with the plush terry cloth robe
that came with my posh room,
I dress for the steaming pool
on this chilly winter night.

The first night of *Carnevale* in Venice
Beyond this mineral bath
children run among the shadows
with red capes, devils' horns,
men wear three-cornered hats
as they do in *Rigoletto*
and women press bulbous breasts
above lace bodices and jeweled skirts.

I can barely see the pool
the fog is so thick
the steam heady-the odor
of boiled eggs rising.

The fog never touches me,
never settles on any surface
swift as a breath,
steam without the fear of heat,
a mist that leaves shadows in the spotlight.

I part the steam with each movement.
It folds over me, behind me,
protects me from the cold night air,
from the light, from the eyes
of the other solitary swimmer.

I hear the water
part in lopsided movements.
Not synchronized,
but in jagged intervals.
He is passing me.
He is invisible.

I would like to ask him to swim in silence,
to make no waves in this temple of steam.

HOW EVER DID YOU KNOW?

What book should I bring on the flight?
How did you know which poems I'd love,
want to read over and over?

My lips form the words,
my ears hear whispers
of phonetic harmony
accents, my favorite vowels
while riding trains past
the Postojna Caves in snow-
lacey edges of the Adriatic.

How ever did you know?
which words would kiss me
with each passing birch, willow.

SUGARED ALMONDS ARE

parceled out one by one
on a subway car in summer
by a small mother with a ponytail.
Two brightly colored children -
she with pigtails, pink-framed glasses
he with defiant waxy hair spikes
and a boy's precision to irk and test.
Magpie chatter, Spanish interrupts
English commands, mother beams
at kids' quicksilver tongues.

Wes Magee

FORTY YEARS ON

> *'What will survive of us is love.'*
> *'At Arundel Tomb' : Phillip Larkin*

i.

Teenagers, they fumbled in the cinema's back row
and, one iced night in the dead of winter long ago
when totally togged-up in duffle-coat, scarf and glove,
they clung and trembled beneath a dripping, humpback bridge.
A passion play rehearsal performed inside a 'fridge!
So, what became of her, his mini-skirted first love?

ii.

Forty years on just one 'phone call had him seeing stars
- Venus must *surely* have been in conjunction with Mars –
and they rendezvoused in that same town: she now long-skirted,
he greying and rotund. They lunched in a pub, rambled
non-stop through four decades of lifestyle news, then ambled
around a ruined castle. Like teens, they flirted.

iii.

And it came to pass, at the far end of middle age,
a five-star hotel's four-poster bed was the soft stage
for a grand performance of their synchronized sex show.
And who cared about stomach bulge, sag, or wrinkly face?
It was like a comet coming back from deepest space
to be greeted with orgasmic cries of *"Wow!"* and *"Oh!"*

iv.

And today? Another decade's almost come and gone
and assignations in chill, distant towns just aren't on.
Passions have cooled to postal gifts: silk scarf or suede glove.
Those fumbling, unrhymed efforts when the weather was hard
have shrunk to trembly one liners of the Christmas card:
'Memories..... and good wishes for the coming year.   Love.....'

249

RODIN ON THE UNDERGROUND

      It's late.
A tube train rattles deep beneath London,
and in the carriage's unforgiving glare
two are entwined across an arm rest.
Weary passengers affect not to see the pair
who remain sealed mouth to mouth between
Kings Cross and Russell Square.

Out on the echoing platform they stand
- still from a Fifties' film *noir* shot in half-light,
as solid and dovetailed as Rodin's 'The Kiss.'
Glazed eyes view this sculptured sight
before grating doors slam shut
and the train jerks off into stygian night.
      It's late.

STARS, SAND-DUNES, MARRAM GRASS, SEA-THISTLES, AND SURF

Three Cliffs Bay, South Wales

  A bar beside the bay
   and after last orders
  two teenage boys and their girls
 streak along the flat sands,
 barefoot and exhilarated,
  shouting beneath a canopy of countless stars
   until they reach the high dunes
    where they scramble up,
    slough their clothes in excitement
   and, naked, leap and roll
  down the steep slope,
 sand between their toes,
 sand in every orifice,
  grains grating between teeth,
   sea-thistles pricking flesh,
    legs rasped by marram grass
    until they flop at the bottom,
   a gasping, laughing heap of bodies
  while all around the star dome spins
 and the moon weaves drunkenly
 down a sea swell path,
  and as surf shushes endlessly on the shore
   they taste the salty tang of freedom
    when all restrictions are discarded
    and there is a certainty
   that this shared moment,
  this glimpse of joyousness
 can last for ever,
 for ever and ever,
  world without end,
   amen,
    amen.

Rita Malhotra

HIV POSITIVE

a sunless universe bent double
under grief-jammed clouds
twigs fall off the broken nest
from the farthest branch of
life's desolate tree.
wicked winds scatter them
like straw in the wind
thoughts take shelter
in the dark cave of solitude
the last drop of a lacerated existence
rolls out,
a stranger to the hostile world
life crosses yet another tedious milestone
across the smouldering debris of love.

LAND-SEA-LAND

baby jasmine nestles warm
in earth's embrace
in the fragrance of its motherhood
nestlings fly to conquer skies
return fatigued to waiting arms
to her lullaby

her divinity follows destiny's path
patient, smiling, through nature's fury
the thirsting sun's plunder
of man's relished evil
disfiguring, devastating

silent, she absorbs convulsions of history
then echoes bloodshed
that decimated peoples
she veils dark memories

beyond the dark memories
night descends in golden splendour
with sounds of the conch shell,
land and sea become one
sins float away
feminine desire flows
in unconcealed affirmation of love

tomorrow the ocean will reach out again
and touch the heart of earth
as devotees carry offerings
of rice, marigold petals, earthen lamps
on banana leaves
and float their prayers
to the Ocean-God.

RHYME-MEMORIES

As Jack and Jill
went up the hill
stark-still she stood
in earnest longing
to discover secrets
of a lost childhood

trudging along
the forest path
hand in hand with
Red Riding Hood
she longs to feast
on granny's love

time summons,
as the clock strikes one
she climbs the mouse-path
up grandfather's clock
in recall of faded memories
when the pendulum chimes
and sings aloud
hickory-dickory dock

but as the clock strikes at the day's end
her fairy-tale thoughts
on fantasy-wings
fall off the edge
of childhood dreams
and plumb the depths
of dark thoughts of yet another
disfigured dawn

in the filtered light
of a melancholic morning
she resumes
the meaningless ritual of survival
beside the straw-basket
of white flowers
weaving funeral wreaths.

Mankh (Walter E. Harris III)

A ROOM COLLECTS THE ESSENCE OF
EVENTS THAT UNFOLD
from a line by A. Molotkov

could not see the forest for suburbia
so i went inside a small room
to collect the essence of events
that unfold inside four walls

one day in winter the idea of sunflowers came to me,
in august they bloomed

one day in summer the thought of hot soup,
in february the stirring

the ongoing pondering of trees
how they gather as forest
how the trees in suburbia remember this
even those in the city

don't let any *thing* own you—
ah, the night air!

LIVE THEATER

a bead of sweat flies from an actor
and hits an audience member in the face

a feather from a magician's pigeon
floats and lands in a little boy's lap
and his life changes forever

[years later,
 at the crossroads]

where the script breaks down
because that's where this could all go
in any unscripted direction

if the wind is right,
if the mood is up,
if fate extends its bony finger and says
"go that way now, yes, it is time
for such adventure, you must"

and there
on the new path
a pigeon appears again

but this time the boy is older, a man
with long wavy hair and
the whole world in his sights and
another whole world inside him

[cue the floating feather,
 put a touch of sweat to the brow]

as he enters his life
and the pulse quickens and
this is where it all starts to come alive!

Maria Manobianco

MOMENTS OF CHOICE, A VILLANELLE

Moments of choice wrong or right
Decisions pave the road ahead
Life can change from darkness to light

With each thought grim or bright
With every word you ever said
Moments of choice wrong or right

Doubt clouds the mind in black or white
You cannot hide or run with dread
Life can change from darkness to light

Try to rely on inner might
Although fear shares your nightly bed
Moments of choice wrong or right

You can take what comes with a fight
Or take a stand with feet of lead
Life can change from darkness to light

Lift your decisions to heaven's sight
Actions you take will grow and spread
Moments of choice wrong or right
Life can change from darkness to light

SEASONED JOURNEY

in the spring
the child plants imagination
visions of fairytales, playtime
first time discovery
each step exciting to touch, taste
heart fills with the warmth of love
under the comforting hugs
of parents, the safety of home

in the summer
the child walks among flowers
tends the garden of aspirations
prepares for the future
study, honing potentials
experiencing independence
heart fills with dreams
husband, a family of her own

in the autumn
the child slows her pace
takes the time to savor
precious moments
laughter, joy, pain, tears
heart fills with compassion
acceptance
covers the broken with scars

in the winter
the child recalls rainbow summers
bursts of warm autumn colors
knows it heralds the cold grays
heart, unconditional
        gratitude for each breath of life
family, friends, and fellow travelers
sharing the path of discovery

Joan Marg

THAT WAS MOST WONDERFUL

at a poetry reading
chairs filled the room
a poet read, something he said

my grandfather was there
speaking to me
I am little again
we are at the kitchen table
it's early before others rise
he offers me forbidden treats
black coffee laced with sugar
slabs of Italian bread with butter
he tells me, "go ahead it's okay"
I dunk my bread
some of the butter swirls to the top of the cup
I sip, it's hot sweet delicious
a most wonderful forbidden treat

back home
memories swarming
I think of other times
walks in the park
Grandpa would buy me a Charlotte Russe
small piece of cake nestled in a paper cup
whipped cream on top with a maraschino cherry
not my favorite
but he loved buying them for me
so I never told him

poets read, generously offering parts of themselves
that night that poet never knew what he had given me
it was a road into a time long gone
a slice of my past
a time for me that was most wonderful

THE LESSON

He was dirty probably homeless
we sat next to him because we wanted a front pew.
Then I noticed he smelled
I moved us over a bit further away
took notice of the people around me
not everyone was dressed for Sunday mass.
I was uncharitably offended by this motley crew
couldn't properly concentrate.

It was almost time for the Holy Communion
as always to wish each other the blessing
I extended my hand,
 "Peace be with you," I said
then leaned over to kiss my mother's cheek.
Out of the corner of my eye
I saw him
the dirty homeless man
reaching out to shake hands
and wish us the blessing.
My mother's hand reached over to clasp his
and with that gesture I saw him through her eyes
a gentleman who had fallen on hard times
but who had not forgotten the Lord
he had come to worship
and wish us God's peace.

Maria Matthiessen

DISGUISES

When I was six more than anything
I wanted to be a boy.
It was easy in Africa because I wore
my brother's shorts, a khaki shirt,
white socks and brown lace-ups.

The boys seemed so free,
shotguns, mud brick walls,
allowed to go off on their own
leaving us out and anyway
my sister was a bit of a whiner.

I must have persuaded my mother
to cut my hair, because there it is
in photographs, straight, short,
parted neatly on the side.

I was startled once
at the club when I approached
The Ladies and a man said:
In here sonny boy, I ran away
red in the face.

I cut off my hair again at thirteen
and slicked it back
when my mother died untowardly.
It seemed easier to be a boy again.
No sissy tears, boys are allowed
to be silent; they don't like to be hugged.

LOSING

The teddy bear passed down
four times from my oldest brother,
worn, sharp-nosed.
A perfidious friend
saw me pack it in my tin trunk
to leave at school.
"Poor Teddy" she mourned
"*I'll* take it home and
bring it back next term."
"You promise, you promise?"

She never did.
I needed to pass it down
to my little girls.

More recently I lost my
mother's signet ring.
A loss that symbolized
so many losses: a country, ejection,
loss of face, loss of innocence,
loss of a mother too young.

Brooding over other kinds of losses
from the Latin – adulterium, to make impure,
to dilute – has erased whole regions -
Wyoming, The Selous, New Mexico,
Bronxville and the railroad track.

Now I'm losing friends
that change my landscape.
Not to mention the loss of land,
the pure Bridgehampton loam,
defiled with spec houses,
driving out the hunkering, pheasants.

The loss of youth, of cells,
of mien, of bone mass,
of mobility,
of memory sliding by -
well, none of that is anything
to be ashamed of.

JB McGeever

THE TOURIST

I hate being a Tourist
But at the Chateau Marmont
I wanted to see where Belushi died

I hate to be a Sightseer
But at The White Horse Tavern
I needed to stand where Thomas fell

And whenever I approach The Chelsea
I always pause out of respect to Ghosts

I have very little tolerance for the Rubberneck
But back home on The Island
I often stare at the House
Where Kerouac lived with his mother

And as the New Owner
Eyes me with suspicion
I always turn to him and say

You're not gonna let me
Enjoy this
Are you

CHARLEY AND JANE

Charley and Jane were fooling around, and one day Jane told him she was pregnant. "You'll marry me, of course."

He thought about it. "On one condition: You have to lose thirty pounds. Then I'll marry you." Charley didn't want to be seen with some drooping petunia.

Charley was an accountant and Jane a Poli-Sci major, prim and proper. They moved in together and had the baby. "Now you must begin your diet," commanded Charley.

Some days all she had was a cup of tea. Others, she stared at an empty cup. Eventually, the weight came off. Charley was amazed; Jane had become a beautiful, sexy woman.

Other men noticed. A strip club owner offered an enormous sum if she'd dance for his customers.

Jane danced and lost more weight. The men at the club went wild when she shimmied down the fire pole in the middle of the stage.

Charley was jealous. He wanted this beautiful woman for himself. "I'll marry you now," he declared. "Let's go tie the knot!"

"Screw you, Charley," Jane answered. "I don't want to be seen with some boring accountant."

Charley came home to find Jane in their bed with the strip club owner.

Charley drove away angry, bitter. He'd done so much for her, he reminded himself. Got her to lose all that weight, after all.

GOD'S TOILET

I love to wander God's House of a Sunday,
admiring the luminosity of stained glass.
But most of all I like sitting
on God's Toilet
contemplating the Creation.

ALL THE TIME

I was dancing with tourists
and it was well before noon
at this grizzly Nashville bar
thinking of the grand and old
and the plane I had to catch
and a rebel cab driver
who told me he'd show me
outside, the streams and rivers,
the real wild Tennessee
as he shook his kiss my ass
shock of blue white hair and grinned.
I might have been from the south
with this attitude I got
he said sipping my whiskey
with the gravity of morning
and it tickled him no end
me twirling girls I don't know
and singing *old rocky top*
leaving all that smoggy smoke
and that cramped up city life
in the cab with my briefcase.
I sat down for a second
smiled deep and closed my eyes
and pictured how it would be
me just all catawampus
leaping around the mountain
gathering maypops for you
crazy mandala prayer wheels
wishing stars of the deep south
hidden in steamy ravines
I carry home in bunches.
And there in the soft twilight
nothing but a breeze between
me and your light cotton dress
wild as a mink
sweet as soda pop
It's been you all the time
with me up on rocky top
I still dream about that.

MORNING IN BABYLON

a bard and writers lament
beneath a mottled sky of
grey and dark and yellow light
hiding words falling like snow

gate of god whose swing cannot
contain or hold her own light
confusing in all language
and losing in all saying

so even the puffy man
behind the scratched half window,
uncle fester bald, eyelids
of brooding black and purple

where someone punched him and ran
as he fell on the platform
helpless and screaming in pain
only just the night before

looks up at me and smiles
as if to say yes I know
you have such nothing to say
only words and words and words

D. H. Melhem

JOHN UPDIKE AND MY MOTHER

I think you wrote those closing sonnets for us,
not for the page that held your rising wreckage
inches above the flood, before mere words
would claim you whole. You spent those few red leaves
of energy like autumn glimpsing winter
in a whirling gust, telling us how it is,
that we are not alone nor will we be
despite the final solitude, that one can
make the last throw on a potter's wheel
a formal taking leave, its strict release
gracing the turn that wrenches free of time.

     This is how I saw and see my mother,
who forty years ago slid past my clutching,
yearning fiercely poised to follow her.

                   But she had left
her spirit-breath, her loving bones for me
to introject the strength and beauty shed
to shape my legacy. Love comes from life
and from the quiet page. A cradle and a platform
where we launch our spirits, power we share,
deepening life, regenerating it.

PROSPECT

... and suddenly, singly,
> *mirrors which scoop again their outpoured beauty*
> *back into their own faces.*

THE SECOND ELEGY

> *... and these things that live,*

slipping away, understand that you praise them;
transitory themselves, they trust us for rescue,
us, the most transient of all. They wish us to transmute them
in our invisible heart—oh, infinitely into us!
> *Whoever we are.*

Earth, isn't this what you want: invisibly
to arise in us?
> —Rainier Maria Rilke, THE NINTH ELEGY, "Duino Elegies"

As if the bridges, islands could be lifted
by angels—steel, the concrete, stones and bricks,
the people in their speed and sorrows—into
a band of sunlight—cars and windows, each
revolving door, the trash and treasure, hope,
the Bibles, Torahs, Qur'ans, Buddhist scripts,
a thousand sacred texts, discarded with
computers and their screens gone blank above
a gutted theater, whose bare-gummed stage
faces the orchestra with seats ripped out
like a toothless mouth, while aged men in boats
lie still below a bridge. Lift them, lift
the young men and the girls who stare out windows
like blank-eyed caryatids in a building
whose highest floors are empty, tenanted
by angels sometimes seen with folded wings
as they lie asleep on carpets.
> Then descend

to the street, go down three levels of subway, down
by escalator through those ghostly spaces
clutching at dust of vanished streets and shops,
the ragged sounds of wheels on cobblestones,
the trolleys, milkmen, each remembered face,
drums of every parade and public grief,

keep treading into the chambers of the heart.

Keep moving. Rise, go out and up the street
to rooms with rows of empty lockers, names
in chalk to be erased at will or whim,
an island of standing coffins on a feathered
floor, where phantom birds abide, alongside
parakeets in cages that survey
the Public Library and people reading.
Lift the dreaming floors with all their books,
call numbers, references, the language-pillars
of the world. Lift them to sky, another planet,
to begin again. Lift to the forgiven past,
the judging present, future inspecting it,
funneled into ears as memorabilia
no one recalls yet holds aloft as trophy,
like the sound of a whirring rattle on New Year's Eve.

Cobbling out of thrum and clatter, yammer
of machines and people blasting rock to quarry
something durable and prime, we meant
to take some wisdom with us and denote
that we were here, we suffered, we endured,
and that we tilled a little while this tall
and tiny city, wounded at the tip,
and posed a wonder among exploding stars.

Robin Metz

CLEAR CHANNEL

In late night aftermath of birthday
dinner with a clutch of rowdy friends

(and gifts of Wenders' winged desire,
a house for wrens, and Cristofori's

haunted dream), my parents phoned
to wish me, shyly, many happy returns;

off-key, they sang the birthday song
and chanted cheerily our family refrain:

"may sunshine and gladness be given…"
regretting only their abrupt departure,

having packed their bags and fled
for home with little ritual or warning,

ghostly distances grown tenuous
in wake of five years mourning.

POSTCARD, BLOCK ISLAND, RI

You might be a fool
to view this seaward island
as a body meadowy and spicy,
anatomically replete, recumbent,
pungent, laving, languishing,
resplendent of salacious flesh
and ripe for taking, seasoned,
heady, ready when you're ready,
willing wooed abandonment…
or more the fool who fails to see
its cliffs and crevices, its clefts
and eddies, bluffs and breastworks,
scrub pines, salty marshes, surges
at the fringe of surf, its SE light
that rises like a nipple in the night
to succor all who've lost their way.
So one time, why not be a fool?

Edmund Miller

SOME APPLE

Watch the apple core
turn brown
right
before your eyes.
Eventually
it slows down
of course. But
it's
already too late
then
even
for the core
with the green skin—
it was McIntosh of course—
curling over.

THIS TIME

Wind drops,
and a heavy insistent smell
wrinkles the face up,
purses the lips.
You hear the quiet clear,
but you're never there
now that you've grown up,
so to speak.
Why waste time on such thoughts?
Because you could go do it,
but you don't.
You could try it,
but you won't.
No, it always comes as a surprise.
Troublesome cold damp lumpy hair
protected from the touch
is all around you.
And you are sometimes happy afterwards
for a moment,
getting lost and dizzy,
enumerating bygone realities—
babushkas and half-slips and dressing gowns—
and walking barefoot
and bareheaded
with a faceful of dark staring back at you.

GREATER TURKESTAN

Reindeer shepherds among the Samoyeds
Have rung litanies from their prayer wheels
That were writ in Sanskrit
At the dawn of rhyme.
And samovars have been in Samarkand—
and chocolate bars
And jelly jars.

WILD TREE

Tarnished brushstroke branches,
Undiluted-tempera greenery,
Flat-black trunk. The leaves
Are made of paper in the dark.
City tree, trippy tree,
The Art Nouveau in you,
By streetlight, at night.

Jesse Miller

YOU COULD HAVE BEEN THE BIRTH OF COOL

Your mother, when she was young, was a
dancer in a long black dress which
swum about her like a shadow borealis
hugging her waist where it dipped into her body,
letting her calves slip out at each step.

When she stepped out onto the street there was steam
rising from her body and her naked arms
glistened with sweat. On the ground there was snow.
She floated like a paper cutout or like
a cutout of snow underneath which was only
night sky. A voice
called out, unfamiliar:
a black man in a black limousine whose eyes had
followed her from the stage to the sidewalk.
She entered the car and it drove.

His apartment was filled with dark heavy things:
stones and old African masks with grim faces and laughing faces,
pungent curtains that hung folded like an unmade bed,
vertical, like a burgundy blues. They sipped bourbon
(your mother and this man with skin like her dress,
soft, dark and deep, and her skin like his teeth)
out of wine glasses and he let the groovefallen needle
scratch at the black veins of a record:

she loved Miles Davis
and he laughed his scratch-belly riverbed laugh and said
Same to you, so then she knew who he was
and stopped staring at his face
and started staring
at his hands.

He used his words few, said *Dance* and your mother
moved her dancer body about the room.
He took up his trumpet and played an unknown tune that lay
raveled up inside his head
curled, uncurling – your mother moved
close with him, with his notes,
her muscles clenched,
unclenching, and he stopped
to watch her and his notes thinned in the air.

He saved his breath for his song
but he said to her *Come*
like a road between them and he held out a hand
with its thick, dark fingers and its pale underbelly and
she stopped and stared
at his hands and moved towards him
body swaying heady and lost.
She could not touch him.

He took her hands in his hands and she
felt his dog-eared fingers, felt
his breath whisper, crack-lipped, sandpaper edges.

She had not known that his sound had substance, so she
pulled her hands away like brass plating or tin from a chocolate
and receded down the stairs, into the color-drained
streets where something like a bird calling could be heard
notes falling, lightly dampened in the snow.

Greg Moglia

AT THE SINGLES' DANCE FOR THE ALMOST DEAD

In a casual touch
At her waist I meet

Not cloth but flesh
And through me

All tomorrows run hard and fast
What a nice surprise I say

While in my head I shout
Keep it small, heart, keep it small

And she says *Another designer dress*
One dollar at the thrift shop

We laugh together and
She turns away

Towards the lucky one
Who shares the air around her

I left to walk the ache
But never to give away

The song
Of her skin

I AM IN LOVE WITH PAULETTE GODDARD

In love with that face in *Modern Times*
In love with her as Chaplin was in that movie
And her legs, the whisper of them
In her not quite ragged dress
In one scene, only one
She puts on a stocking
Her leg seen above
The knee
In love
Am I

Dead my friend says

   No, she's not I say
   I saw her in a movie

But that's only a movie she says
An old movie as well, she's gone… gone

   I can still be in love I say

   I can still be in love

IF I COULD
  for Felauai Iseula-Gebhardt

If I could
I would pick a thousand daisies
and carefully stick them behind your ear.
I would take black sand and rub it
between your toes and beneath your fingernails.
I would take the summer breeze
and bottle it for you,
so you would always smell like a tropic day
magenta streaks behind your brown locks.
I would wrap you in a Hawaiian sunset
and let the waves rock you to sleep.
Tears would turn into
butterflies and they could fly away with you
somewhere over the rainbow.

Annabelle Moseley

A TIME TO BREAK DOWN

An autumn afternoon, among the lanes
and bridges by the pond and stream— I stroll,
until I see the broken-down remains
of a grist mill. Its wheel is still. Each hole
and hollow in the wood, every carving
that blemishes the mill walls: names and hearts—
graffiti and the like, each is starving
for new paint, opportunity, new parts
to make the water wheel turn once again.
Imagine, as it circled, new and strong,
the grain and granules would be ground, and then
turned into powdered flour. Sorrow, wrong
and pain have stopped my walk, but as the wheel
of my break-down turns, I begin to heal.

A TIME TO BUILD UP

And not to rush the healing— breaking down
is an art: grain to flour, rain to flower,
but as I enter the guest room and frown
at my own sorrow, I pause. For what power
has arranged a picture of Glade Creek
Grist Mill in this bare retreat house room?
I have to laugh a little. Just last week
I found Roslyn Grist Mill on my walk. Bloom
of disrepair, it called to me, and now
this image of refining just confirms
wheat's harvest must be subject to the plow
and ground down before it is food. These terms
have helped me push my pain into a sieve—
I'll carry it sacked, lift it as I live.

Gloria g. Murray

IN THE HOUSE

where the widow dwells
weeds threaten
to strangle themselves
bushes bulge
like unwanted pregnancies
bees swarm the rotting pears

when darkness closes the slats of day
she still listens
for the sound of footsteps
a key twisting in the door
a snoring in the bed beside her

in the house where children
once climbed the Beanstalk
a husband banged his fist on the table
demanding a well-done burger
an un-crumpled newspaper

now everyday she contemplates
the alternatives
--a senior condo in Florida
a converted garage in her daughter's house
a dog who will lick her face, her arthritic bones
under the flannel sheets

or....there's always the gun
her husband kept in a drawer and bullets
that will enter her as he once did
suddenly, unexpectedly
exploding

THE DESK

I sit at the desk you carved for me
polished cherry mahogany
--so long it went from wall to wall--

a place for my computer
files of poetry, tape, a lamp—
nooks and crannies for everything

I place my face against the wood
remember your hand clenching the hammer
nails held between your teeth

this is the way you loved—
in splinters, in 4 by 4's
in paint that stained your fingers

in everything measured, leveled
anchored together

WHAT TO WRITE

I am told
'write what you know'
but I know so well

the taste of death
like too much black pepper
on my tongue
fear a red-eyed mouse
racing in its plastic wheel
the Scream of a Munch painting
how cupid's arrow
suddenly gets you in the back
the way the doors to the world lock
and I bang with small fists
to get in

and I know
how to write poetry
that moans and whines
and tells you everything
you didn't need
to know

Melanie Myers

TO ALWAYS REMEMBER

Do you remember the sunset
The blue, green, magenta hews
For they are breathless and enduring

They fade away as time progresses
The dark and starry sky looms up ahead
Scattered clouds hide the waning crescent moon

The brisk breeze that passes by
The sounds of the leaves rustling
This is a day of one's life

The cycle no matter if it is good or bad
Take heed in bad times and relish in good
See it all pass by like the stages of dawn

DROP OF MERCY

They say there's madness afoot in Winter
as if by barring the door to cold we lock out love

The birds are sleeping in today
all is snow covered, bleak as failed expectation
I huddle in my covers like the doves on the back stoop
I will not ski today
I am beyond Gulliver
pinned down by an army of a thousand thoughts
Lilliputians gone mad in a mind that seeks peace
but will not allow the change

I do not accept your kindnesses
I turn instead to my problems
feed them with doubt and fear
until they grow into the suffering I make
the way my mother made pudding
I am nurturing some pain planted long ago
in the soil of my delusion, in the fertile humus
of my desire to own then run from, to retaliate

I offer irate responses (in words I would take back)
to a frown I translate as disgust
and watch this anger grow on the time I give it
watch it expand, feed and flower
till I perceive it as a gorgeous thing and must pass it on
Stuck in the cycle of return, of reruns and rehashing
I miss all of the moments where beauty pours out at my feet
yet you come again

And all it takes is a single drop of mercy
to rain down on me
change everything to ahhhh
snow is no longer cold, birds awaken
the beauty you are is a deluge
Mind stilled, my heart is opened
to a glance, a word, curve of your shoulder
hand lifted in welcome
I finally see that I am gifted everyday
with life, breath and the nearness of you.

YOU, IT'S ALL YOU GOT TO LIVE

It's easier than you think
but you have to have food in your stomach
grace in your mind, air to breathe
and an Irish sense of humor
to pass thru the eye of this needle
weaving your tapestried life

Eating anger for breakfast doesn't work
so no talking first thing in the morning
and when you're tired, sleep
no speaking your thoughts aloud last thing at night
let it all fall away until there is just you
and the breath you rode in on

Be simply grateful for the sun today
it speaks of light in this sometime hell-hole of darkness
and figuring out when, how and why
you tripped and fell into it is a waste of time
you just did and here you are
dirt under you're nails and climbing out moment by moment

All the aphorisms are emollients
to make you feel better or your friends for you
you want something that sticks to your ribs
give up on the way you think it should be
and go with what is because it just is . . .
You don't have to change a thing for anyone else
you can't, just work on your own stuff
you're stronger than you think or feel
enter that place of beauty and laughter you know so well
and when you're tired of being told what to do
get over it -- just listen to your heart.

BUTTERFLY

This flurry in the garden
presents a puzzling sight,
two wings—or petals,
colored bright.
The blossoming is short,
more like a bloom in flight.
No song is heard,
it's gone within a quarter hour.
Tell me, are you bird
or are you flower?

MACHO

It's April in the greenhouse
and any amaryllis
that could
punched its eager fist
up through the bulb,
aiming for the sun's red kisser
(but any face will do),
adroitly turns its fingers
into megaphones
to get the brawny message out
in all directions.

THE WINTER OF NINETY-EIGHT

Instead of blizzards,
misty raindrops fall,
and dancing days
disarm the arctic squall.

Sun burns bright
as summer; clouds retreat.
I have the light
but not the heat.

In January,
daffodils appeared.
Where is this winter
I had feared?

Barbara Novack

FREE FALL

I wander the aisles
not admitting the purpose
eyeing the mirrors edging the ceiling
and the half globes of reflecting chrome
and the cameras mounted high
eyes
that I know
follow mine
watch my hands
read my mind.

I touch and fondle
the slithery deed
in book, pen, magazine,
candy bar and patterned hose,
nothing that I truly need
except
the need
to succeed,
a consummation that will be
like knowing all the answers
on *Jeopardy*.

I grab the prize.

And later
I will rationalize:
Sometimes you have to
free fall
to know you're alive.

SOMETHING

Reaching for something
that was of me,
I watch the sun set low,
washing me in its embered glow,
a cleansing I would rather
have not be,
sadness to fill the space between
where I am and where
I might have been;
something was
a part of me,
sadness fills where it used to be,
and I must pause
to remember what it was.

And if I could remember now
how it felt, those feelings now
would return,
some thing that I learned.
And I watch the sun set low
and I am bathed in its glow
and I've paused for the show,
but I would rather
not know.

Memory is a fragile thing,
crystal lives that will not ping;
they are not pure.
Memory is just a game
of illusions that remain,
and I'm never sure.

I am angling for that sky,
lavendered with day gone by,
leaning like a flower for the sun,
but it is done.
All that's left is me standing here
with feelings that are not as clear
as memory will soon make them be.
All that's left as I walk on
is the feeling that there's something
I should have done.

Tammy Nuzzo-Morgan

DANCING IN NORTH SEA

Golden fish eye gazes at my apple-blank stare
I fear I have lost the sun while seeking the path.
October leaves turn yellow, red, and brown
catch in the wind, land in a blond girl's hair.
Stars slip out for a dance with the moon tonight
I sneak out to join in. My neighbor walking his dog
spots me in my gown. My bare feet touch mother
I become grounded.

Bailando en North Sea

Ojo de oro viendo mi mirada fija
Temo haber perdido el sol durante la busqueda del camino
Las hojas del otoño se vuelven amarillas, rojas y cafes
Volando en el viento, aterrizando en el pelo rubio de la niña
Las estrellas salen a bailar con la luna esta noche
Yo me escapo a reunirme con ellas. Mi vecino anda paseando su perro
Y me ve en mi vestido. Mis pies descalsos tocando la tierra
Tomo mi terreno

Translated by Jeny DeJesus

291

MY SON DID NOT SLIP SILENT INTO THE DARK
for Michael Jason Nuzzo 1979- 1995

My son did not slip silent into the dark.
This young man battled. He put up a fight.
How can a summer walk snuff out his spark?

While crossing village street toward Hampton park,
could cause the death of my first born, my light.
My son did not slip silent into the dark.

I walk among the living with grief's mark,
where sunshine's swallowed, making day like night.
How can a summer walk snuff out his spark?

Across the river Styx my child embarked.
There are no words, no deeds to make it right.
My son did not slip silent into the dark.

No birds' spring calls can I hear. When birds hark,
I've nothing left, just poetry to write.
How can a summer walk snuff out his spark?

Oh, how the dogs of death do howl, do bark!
I bleed as their fangs sweetly nip and bite!
My son did not slip silent into the dark.
How can a summer walk snuff out his spark?

POEM # 1
for all the soldiers

If I could offer drops of faith to fill your endless need
I would open all my salty rivers, let them flow into your desert

If I could wrap our eyes in memories of peace
I would blind us both, blessed to grope

If I could morph these bloodied arms
into armored wings I would carry us up

Allow us just a bit of space to breathe, see more than the battlefield
Know more than the sound of the firefight, the smell of hope incinerating

Poema #1
Para todos los soldados

Si yo pudiera ofrecerte gotas de fe para llenar tu necesidad
Abriría todos mis mares salados para que corran hacia tu desierto

Enredaría nuestros ojos en memorias llenas de paz
Nos volvería ciegos, libres para buscar a oscuras y sin guía

Si pudiera cambiar estos brazos llenos de sangre
Por alas fuertas, yo nos llevaría hacia arriba

Denos un espacio para respirar y mirar algo más que el campo de batalla
Saber más que el sonido de la pelea de fuego
Y oler más que la esperanza desvaneciendose

Translated by Jeny DeJesus

ROCKET MAN

I want you to be my Rocket man.
Throw me in your space capsule
strap me down & tell me to 'hold on!'

I want you to be my astronaut.
Make me feel the sparkling of stars
taste the cream of the Milky Way.

I want you to be my Zoom-Away Guy.
Get my motor roaring as you shift gears
zipping us past the planets one by one.

Could you do that, put on jet propulsion boots
take me with you to the moon, the sun
& not get burnt or bored for one second?

Could you get us a pair of shiny spacesuits
so neither of us gets singed by the force
of bodies traveling at such a rate of speed?

Could you build us a ship to take us up & out
past the clouds and their sad-looking faces
past the pull of gravity and weight of want?

THE REPORT
after Schultz's poem "The Silence"

You always called with poems,
your voice in love with your work,
I, racked over birthing a line,
laboring for just one creation.

Today the local news reporter spouted
how your car spun out of control. You
were ejected, pronounced at the scene.
The cause, speed, the report said.
I knew it was the lack of poems in your pocket.

We met at a reading. Your voice shimmered.
Your poems flowed from a well they drank from.
I studied your poise, dissected every syllable.
I envied the way the gods touched your pen
and the way men swarmed to sip your honey.

Once we traded stories of our childhoods
like glory days of battle. "Top this one!
Bet your therapist doesn't help much,
but the pills do!"

Once I called to say I was checking out
I could not get past my past
You were half lit and slurred
"Take a 2-in-all and chill."

In the Russian Olive grove
in my yard you softly sang
Sappho, Plath, Sexton,
as if each note brought the sisters closer,
as if we women could make it all alright…

You knew there was no God
but you also knew there was
just as you knew he could not save you.

Thaddeus O'Neil

BROTHER

I am glad
to have never had
a brother.
I hear the viciousness of a pair
in the trailer park shower
next to mine.
The young one has peed in the shower,
as is a well and fine thing to do,
and the older is belting him for it,
the slaps crisp and resonant
on the wet skin.
The hushed whimpering coming now,
audible still
over the din
of old plumbing.
And just before this sin
of peeing in the shower
and its retribution,
the older said with a stutter,
say ne- neh- nnnay- ked –
say naked.
The younger
sensing something forbidden
would not.
And then, as we know,
Cain killed Abel
for peeing in the shower.
The naked skin
never forgiven.

PARADISE GAINED

the dead koalas strew
the bushland
like rocks –
the traces
of a long gone river.

the dead koalas lay
in the burnt out bushland
like their own tombstones,
baked hard and black,
while the magpies
eulogize
in skies
of permanent twilight.

the dead koala's stand
poised statuesquely,
Rodins still clutching charred sprigs of eucalyptus,
others embraced, with a keen gaze
into the distant clearing of green beyond the fires imprint,
or hugging the ebony pillar of a burnt tree.

And beneath these sarcophagi,
the worms circle nine times in the soil
panegyrically.
These true Charons
have no use for money
beneath the tongue,
they take all as they come.

And I cry as the story
comes to me over the cheap clock-radio
on top the refrigerator,
the tears coming
while I wash the dishes in the sink,
hungover, near naked, sentimental.

I don't mind the humans, I am thinking,
Take them. Take them all.
But the animals…

The paradise
was lost
with us.

THE BOOK OF THE WORLD

the book of the world
invites your mind
to the candle.

it asks only
for your wonder,
for your humble, curious *why?*

not the why at swords end
of ignoble inquisitors, but
the inimitable why
unrequited.

you do not need
the verses of Goethe's
Theory of Colours
to see, rightly,
the magnificence
of the mirrored twilight
in the bay
beneath the bowed
and sacred swan.

its words are cataracts
in the eyes.

and a Cartesian imprinting of them
by Kandinsky is no more spiritual
than a embalmed fly.

the wordless book of the world
invites your mind
to the candle.

stay away: poet, painter, candlestick maker...

it asks only
for your wonder,
for your humble,
curious, unrequited *why?*

the world
so greeted
echoes mantrically
in the mind
with everything
from science
to pagan delight.

its "answers"
blooming in the darkness of night
like shy cacti in a desert traffic jam,
an inchoate constellation,
culmination without end,
reason's ruination.

Linda Opyr

HAWK

Far above this beach, the dark suns
of your eyes follow your children,
their wings wide to the great new sky.

Whatever you can teach them
from the bare tops of these trees,
you will.

Whatever they can learn
of deep wind and strong water,
they will.

And these small circles from you, with you,
to you – sooner or later will grow into white
rivers of flight that belong to you alone.

But as for today, I hope that whatever it is
you make of my watching those small bellies,
those young hearts rising, rising, rising –

My friend, let it be good.

MARIA
for Gina and Lisa

When a washing machine is delivered
on a Friday, it never runs right.

Not while the box waits at the curb.
Not while the whites spin their white dreams.

Not while a Friday holds up a mirror
and lets you see yourself approving such a thing.

Even years later when night watches its watching
at window and door. Even years later

when memories have cleared the table and
moved to the living room to linger before bed.

Your daughters will find that machine and Friday
beside a basket of darks and a mother

who put her own needs aside as easily
as if they were Fridays and not for the living.

WHERE THE PRAYER BEGINS

This prayer begins with a buoy
borne on the white backs of waves

until the long arm of the wind
pulls its rope ashore just beyond

the reach of the sea.

Please help me to remember.
What was it I came to do?

Alicia Ostriker

3 HAIKU SERIES

AIRPORT HAIKU

Child at the airport
hugging his grandfather's legs
all the adults smile

CHESTER HAIKU

All night the peepers
singing around our small pond,
drunk men, happy men.

This haiku requires
that we fill our cups to the
very brim. And drink.

Drink, drink, and more drink,
then in the morning the poets
run around outside—

GRASSHOPPER HAIKU

A grasshopper leaps
through the meadow, escaping
the mower. This time.

I am so little,
thinks the leaping grasshopper,
why not let me live?

A PRISONER

The chickadee inside my
chest, next to my heart
imprisoned, but singing

and I, mostly not listening—
chickadee, forgive me.
Please don't stop.

BIKING UP PROSPECT

One of those blithe summer days that used to last forever
biking up Prospect Street for dinner and a movie

I say: the air is so tender it seduces you into believing
that a kelson of the creation is love

he says: we've evolved to feel good at moderate temperatures
such as this and uncomfortable when it is hotter or colder

I say: it appears we are actually coexistent with the universe
like salt dissolved in water

he says: maybe so
not being a reader of Whitman nor a Buddhist

We brake our bikes at a light
these days they go so much more quickly now

MEASURES

What is a voice anyway,
against the wind's wandering,
or the sea's persistent grief?

And what of a body's warmth
against the moon's cold fire?

Or lips, however full,
beside an iris in the rain?

SWAN RIVER LEAD

The frozen wastes of the bay
stretch south and east beneath
a dirty sky, but a dark
tongue of still water marks
the river's narrow mouth.

A handful of ruddies paddle
upstream through the lead,
heads turned back, half tucked
under their wings against the cold.

They have come a long way,
staked their lives
on this remembered coast,
and found themselves betrayed
by the far reach of the ice.

Tonight a hard skin will cover
even this gleaming vein,
and yet they swim calmly,
through the shadows of dusk--

as if they had miles
of open water ahead,
and hours until dark.

THE DEAD WOMAN'S THINGS

They put the dead woman's
things by the road. The broken
cupboard, the thin rug covered
with dog hair and dust, the tall
lamp with its yellow shade.
Now and then a car stopped,
somebody loading one thing
or another into a trunk--a bundle
of gauzy nylon scarves, a legless
ironing board–before pulling
quickly away. By evening little
was left, but for some trinkets
and a handful of misshapen shoes
lying like drunkards on the grass.
Though the next morning they,
too, were gone, as if the moon,
passing by, had gathered her
wayward children in the dark.

THESE DAYS

I do not think these days
of dead hawks nailed
to the sides of weathered barns
or of dead trees waiting for fire.

I no longer sharpen my knife
on the tongues of those who sleep
beneath stones splintered by frost.

Nor rise at midnight and spread
my fingers on the frozen pane,
pretending to touch the moon.

Joanne Pateman

CASA KANAI IN UMBRIA

Kiyoshi picked strawberries for dessert.
Zucchini and eggplant grilled over the ashes
Bread toasted to accept the tomato mozzarella
Drizzled with virgin oil from olives grown on silver branches
Guinea hens roasted in the open hearth.
Hours before they were pecking for worms and insects.
All washed down with house red and white
From his own grapes that he was learning to graft.
A walk into town with the dog to digest the feast
The town is quiet, in the bar, only the sound of The World Cup and
The echo of Italy's chances for victory.

The next day we visited the hen house and checked for eggs
The chickens mooch freely, lorded over by two roosters
Who govern with strong temperament and charisma (Kiyoshi says)
The walnut and almond trees, the plums, persimmons,
Lemons, peaches and two varieties of figs, a biblical garden.
We picked green beans for dinner and artichokes shot with purple.
Onions, leeks and garlic add to the recipe.
Two kinds of lettuce for the insalata mista.
I sit on the patio writing and reading and inhaling the heady jasmine.

Picked rosemary taller than me, oregano and lavender
To add to the summer stew. An Italian bouquet garni of memories
Bay leaves, the dark greenish-black have the most intense flavor.
Sage leaves under the chicken skin to infuse its essence
Oregano, still wearing its roots for tomato sauce.
Rosemary for remembrance and for grilling meat and fish
Lavender for drying, for its ghostly color and for its healing power.

So proud of his connection to the soil, so committed to slow food
When he took the freshly laid egg from the straw bed,
It was with a father's pride.
He caught his hand on the edge of the door
And the precious egg broke splat onto the dirt floor
Its saturated orange yolk stared up at us in defeat,
Never to be an omelet, frittata or torta.
"Oh, no!" he said in a plaintive cry.
He built the chicken house and fed the chickens every morning
He collected the eggs and he mourned the three chickens stolen by the fox.
The hens were traumatized by the tragedy and weren't laying their usual eggs
This golden egg a symbol of their return to fecundity and production
He scooped the egg up carefully and put it on the dog's pasta,
A fine sauce for the hunter.

JAM MAN

He's a jam-making machine.
Dices plums, juggles raspberries
Levels sugar in a measuring cup
Stirs in the pectin and melts the wax to seal the flavor.
Slowly he ladles the perfumey elixir into the hot glass.
Jars are gifts to special friends
Lined up like redcoats going off to battle.

And when I see him
With our grandson adhered to his hip
Pride surges as he
Draws roads to follow in the sand.
They giggle with complicity
Like two clams in the same shell.

Simon Perchik

AGAIN THE COLORS RETURN :THE SUN

Again the colors return :the sun
paired with their orbit, flower to flower
and the migrating winds
back from nesting on feathers
–from that distant snow
so many reds and yellows whose first meal
is the warm light and rain

–we drink this milk to begin each year
and our yard again head first
enfolds into that fertilizing song
these birds learn from their wings
from their caves in the ice and air

and we are returned windswept, matched
with the fire that knows only winter and winds
again house to house :this flower
carrying the Earth aloft
and under each soft wing more sweetness
not yet red or yellow or snow –each year
more petals –as if we were going somewhere cold

I hold your hand and the year
naked, wet, wading through tears
–the same small morning each Spring
we plant another circle, a song
over the small grave, count the blooms
sort the arriving stones.

THESE SHADOWS I GROW IN MY GOOD ARM

These shadows I grow in my good arm
cracked the ceiling, cross--. In the movie
gunners tracking the screen
freeze where its light is brightest

then fire. The plaster can't escape
--these shadows as every branch will sweep
steady the incoming sky

then squeeze :each leaf
lit, without a sound the sun
crashing into walls, the floor

--these leaves can't miss, the sun
dead and the shadow I grow in the dark
carries up a small bird in its throat
caught in the crossfire

where just offshore those planes
are lost and can't turn back
as sometimes a key --I'm not the one!
I'm not but the lock seals the way stone

and the key louder than feathers
louder than waiting, than the wings
left open on the ceiling
on the turn that once was safe.

THIS DEAD ROOT, ITS LIGHT

This dead root, its light
handed up --the sun
accepts the offering :mornings

are weightless and the stump up-ended
--what's in these bleached fingerbones
beside the shattered wind
frail as quivering moss
still aches for leaves --the sun

lets my yard lift
by the elbows --a child
hugged by uncles to cousins, aunts
circling on light, on warmth and overflowing

while birds blown around and around
and always the dead root
pulled from a kiss, another and another
clenching --the sun too

must have been slashed at the wrist
and these axe-marks
where the shade was struck
on its way to the ground, homesick.

It's dark half the time now, all night
my eyes left open, lit
so the Earth can see
will find the sun as once I was warmed

tumbled into orbit, taught around and around
a child how this morning star
exalted above all others
is the same Venus each evening looking off
the first to sight the darkness and goodbye

--the root dead and I
still move my hand over the stars
who at least have a name --the sun

now someone else's star
someone bravely, far off
who sees it first and alone.

311

Russell Cameron Perry

A DRAGON IN THE SKY

My grandson and I
just yesterday lying in a hammock
looking at the clouds blowing in from the harbor
and telling each other what visions we saw in them.

"Oh ... look Grandpa ... there's a dragon over there ... see?
See it Grandpa? See the dragon?"

"Where?"

"Just behind the *whale*, Grandpa!
Over there!," he said,
pointing to the sky with his tiny finger.
"Just behind the *whale.*"

"Oh yes! You're right Patton!
I see it ... it looks *just* like a dragon!"
He turned, looked straight into my eyes
and with as profound and serious a look as I have ever seen,
shook his little head and said,

"No .. *no*, Grandpa, it doesn't just *look* like a dragon.

It's *real!*

It's a *real* dragon Grandpa ... don't you see it?"

HAIKU

My grandchildren have looooong ears
ice cream truck

~

An egret
knee-deep in a tidal pool
a study in concentration.

STANDING IN THE RAIN

How I did love
to stand there
in the rain
and breath you in

such long deep breaths

such a sacred,
quiet time
for us,

such a sense of
Peace on Earth
that seemed to me
to last forever.

I wore the shirt to bed

something akin
to the fragrance
of sandalwood
still on its chest
called out your name

                even before I did.

MOVEMENT

Fingers reaching towards toes
head rolling down the anterior portion of body
flipped back up by posterior spinal cord vertebrae by vertebrae
until I am fully extended through my pineal gland to my feet that
      sink into to the earth's core
from which arms, legs and skull are diffusing.
Yet, magically held together by my navel
starting with my breath that feeds the systems of my body and opens the pores of
my skin to excrete everything that my senses cannot comprehend as I move
around in this temple

PAUSE

I hate this…
I see…staring at your chair, now vacant.
Looking out the window and
seeing the flowers that you planted last spring
Extra shelves you installed holds things we bought for one
      another
Going through papers and finding the notes you wrote…to me.
I loved the twinkle in your eyes when you laughed.
The scent of you…
The sound of your heart as we cradled each other in the
      deepness of sleep.
The 'Good Morning' I love you, as I woke.
Watching you sleep when I couldn't
Memories don't fade easily…time is slower.
What is my life now…just what was it then?

Susan Pilewski

ODE TO A JAPANESE HORROR FILM

These tales tell us the dead are all around
with little to do but stalk the living,
revenge their chief motive.

They appear as shadows and dreams, an untranslatable metaphor involving a
well.
No one believes the victim's pleas,
even as a finger extends itself from a cup of tap-root tea.

How to banish these visions? Pull out the phone
sleep with lights on, one eye open
make sure your husband didn't forget to mention how he bludgeoned his lover
from Kyoto.

This cannot end well, the marble bath will overflow
and spill down corridors frozen hard with snow—
as all shoulder the burden of being alive.

THIS POEM IS NOT AMERICA

We run a thriving leper colony outside the gates of Reno.
Inmate of renown, popular as hot Gazpacho
the Southwest light is fading as the evening flock returns.

We sought shelter after the cavalry arrived
10,000 huddled underneath a burning banana leaf
as the crowd cultivated an appreciation for all the lower notes.

Say it is war you crave, so be it.
Blood thickens in the veins like Baltic amber,
you'd be surprised what you grow used to.

No time for tear filled versions of goodbye
strike up the band, wipe out the noise.

CHINDERHARA 2

1
Wind on the oilslick
breeds bubbles
of reticulate neon,
later slime tracked by tires.

2
The bull quartered in my eye
turns slowly from his herd.
Now his tongue fights a nest of adders.
Stung, too late, he walks along the shore,
his head, a grieving moon, against the sea

3
In the dark all cats are the same color;
what color are they in a blinding light
All things are an expression of emptiness.
I study water for the forms it fills:

4
The dolphin harbored in the blood
races the coastal dragon thru riptide
around the east end archipelago.
Under the horizon the sea finishes the circle.

The last dance outside the skin no dance at all
but the breath of the dragon shuddering

5
A dive of a few fathoms
forces phosphenes to magnetize
& rotate; what you are seeing
is that other matter,
or zen. My friend David
dying from brain tumor
told me Rilke was right: beauty is the beginning of terror,
the end, he added, is how the gods felt
Before extinction

HEART SUTRA

Echoes of a golden bowl, struck thrice
fade flowers in an oaken floor
& return the undermusic
of the sea a field away,
the breastbone's hum fainting
inward with the light-
I breathe time
into eternity
& hear the last gull & goose call
Over drumlin & nauplii
then the white-throated sparrow lifting
a wild, indifferent lament
for no one at all

LOW TIDE AT SAG
1
Low tide at Sag:
dunlin & blackbellied plover
scouting the flats.
Snowy owl blinking
atop a duckblind.

Light comes on,
the sand retrieving hollows
the land slipping underwater,
the horizon hastening to contour the earth
one bright pearl, one deadly winter day-

Things are not what they seem.
Neither are they otherwise.

2
There is no order in the world
save what death puts in it.
Wind in the Japanese maple
mills to a standstill in it

3
listen to the voice of the wind
and the ceaseless message that forms itself out of silence.
Once for each thing. Just once: and no more. And we, too,
just once....But to have been
this once, completely, even if only once:
to have been at one with the earth, seems beyond undoing.

4
I sit in silence
Seeking the heart of stillness
While the gone retrieves the sound of groundswells
A half mile away

I succeed in silence
Or stillness, or nothing at all
You'll hear it from the wind

ONCE MORE IN THE COMPANY OF WOMEN

Once more in the company of women
      neither young or old, but full,
full of womanliness, I try my gaze
beyond them, & one
      turning in a mirror
inspects her dress.

Now, among spirits standing
      on my regard merely beautiful beyond the human
an angel peels away
      & I'm thinking if
I saw her awake & whole
      naked sometime after dawn
there'd be dolphins tossing me wave to wave
      till I danced christ beyond terror
terror of beauty

         & this one
turning
says how do you like it?

         Brought back,
still strange among women, to this one waiting---

Anthony Policano

BEFORE THE BIRTH OF COOL

I confess to what I did in the womb
I played with myself
Most of the time
There was no one else around
I drank blood from a fire hose
I trained to be an astronaut
Explored the darkness without clothes
Weightlessly drifted like a littleneck clam
Discovered God
Was a woman not a man
(although I couldn't tell the difference)
I pounded drum skins like Roy Haynes
Heard cymbals crash but couldn't duplicate the sound
Tried to open my mouth to laugh to cry but nothing
Came out
I was Buddha smiling under the shade of a banyan tree
Unaware of the banyan tree
Unaware of smiling
I developed the patience of a monk wanting to be a saint
Tolerated talk radio each morning
Suffered Pat Boone LP's in the afternoon
Desperately longed for Coltrane and Miles
I took a journey I never signed up for
Down a murky canal on my back without a paddle
I got stuck
Pushed like a tulip in the spring
Got nowhere
Pushed harder
Like a car salesman in the spring
I wrote a letter of complaint
And to my surprise, I was roughly exiled
From paradise

I AM NOT A CONFESSION

I am not a confession
waiting to slip from bank vault lips.

I am not the blue shirt on the bed
with lipstick stains after a business convention.

I am a burst of steam from a scalding iron.

I am the country music station playing nonstop on
your car radio the entire ride to Graceland.

The day after tomorrow is Easter Sunday.
I could have fasted much better than I did
this Lenten season,

I could have not eaten meat or cheese.
Not eaten anything but bread, lentils and fava beans.
I could have prayed with both my eyes closed.

What's done is done.

I shot a cow once in Reno
just to watch her die

then quickly lost my appetite (temporarily)
danced all night like a 300 pound Elvis on amphetamines.

This was a long time ago.

OK that was a confession. But don't believe a word.
Not a word.

A deal is a deal?

I promise never to write about my sins
if you promise the same about yours.

I'M GOING TO THE NORTH SEA

I'm going to the north sea
I've got a gilded framed picture of my sweetheart
Under my arm, just her and me.
The water's cold this time of year
And the sun is a stone,
The sands blow like Egypt
The streets crumble like Rome.

I found a digital camera on a boardwalk bench
Now I've got an instant family
For my blanket of thought.
Look, here are my twins
Wearing birthday cake and party hats
They just turned three.
I 'm going to the north sea
With my sweetheart and megapixel family,
It doesn't even matter that they don't look like me.

I'm going to the north sea without a novel
I'll be digging deep for my roots
With a dollar-store shovel.
Deeper than the journey I was led to travel,
Deeper than glass waves that rise and break in the distance,
Deeper than jetty rocks, lost hooks and lead sinkers.

Tell anyone looking for me
I'll be looking for my new home at the north sea.

Philip J. Postiglione

BETTER IN BLACK AND WHITE

Jump into another time,
a black and white movie,
detective drinking whiskey,
cheap grey suit, fedora cocked,
maniac murderer, slashing,
bare woman bleeding chocolate syrup,
swirling rings in the shower drain.

Check out the pin-up,
not a touch of color,
but a lot of stuff,
good stuff, real flesh on those bones,
I'm howling like a wolf,
as I fly over the moon,
saucer speeding, a guest of the Martians.

Look at the cowboy,
he is killing an Indian,
void of bloody bullet holes,
no red to match his skin,
some realities are better in black and white.

WITNESS TO THE LIGHT

Green ghost, translucent, not exactly whole,
or comprehensible, obstructed by smoke,
an image in the mirror, closing in around me,
another reality or nothing at all.

Sliding in and out of sickness, wandering sleepless,
no comfort from bed or dog,
only growling guts, aching head,
porous mind, a sponge for depression.

How wonderful it would be if I could witness the light,
following the beacon, till the tunnel ends,
and a new one opens inside a new host,
mother contracted and pushing,
waiting to introduce me,
to the same old, new world.

AN ANSWER FOR A BEAUTIFUL, YET DISILLUSIONED, YOUNG WOMAN

I cannot feed the hungry or stop a war
with just the strum of my guitar,
but this does not mean that it holds no pow'r.

I cannot change the world by
singing in the show'r;
but this too, my dear, can have its hour.

I can hold the killer of my daughter in my arms,
and heal old wounds, and this is how

I can hear again her laughter in each drop of water.
For me, my dear, it is every thing.

It is everything.

Single voices sung together become a chorus;
come together for a single purpose,
as grains of sand unite to form a land before us.

And if that song those voices sing bring solace,
then that, my dear, is Every Thing.

It is everything.

I can hum a lullaby to a hungry child
and hold her in my arms
and if that child should die before she wake,
after she should pray to whichever Lord
her small strong soul to take,
then to hers that song is every thing.

It is everything.

Elaine Preston

CHRISTMAS FLIGHT

At 3,000 feet, Fire Island sand streaks by below
like the trace of bullet in a gun-gray Atlantic.
We bank left 10°. The instructor's mouth
shoots out physics: *Highest wing, the right,*
stalls first! Push left rudder! Lower the nose,
add power! I cock the Cessna back--too hard,
too late. Like extinguished love, glare explodes
on glass, a simile of sun for failing fingers
on the yoke. Heart-thuds. Nightmare foot
on the wrong rudder. Beach disappears--
down is up--up, down--the plane plummets

toward an everywhere ocean the color of doubt

lingering when I've landed, walk by the harbor,
its darkened shore gathering red Christmas lights
seeping into water. Then an egret's white arc
leans into evening choked with coming storm,
syllables of snow on its crooked neck.
But its body knows without knowing the truth
of air. Its feathers whisper through last light,
trust the wind, surrender to marsh.
This bird, each easy curve, splits the sky,
descends like angelshot to earth,
a hot missive for wingless, hesitating hearts.

THE BLADE

After the men on tractors left at dawn
for dusty furrows each day, my grandmother,
ax in hand, set out, me at her heels.
She'd pluck up a bird in the coop,
carry it screeching and clawing to the stump
by her white-planked house stranded
at the end of a dirt Dakota road
where grit could suck out your marrow.
Holding its neck to the wood, she'd swing
the blade high, swoosh it down--
blood spouting, beak and comb and throat
trembling, thumping off, dying
the weeds red, wings flapping.

This kind of severance gleams in thoughts
before first sky cleaves though dark
and as sunset hisses into night's black folds.

Even so, come out, morning and afternoon.
Arc the long convertible through the streets,
top down. Be the girl, the boy in the front seat
seeing serrated leaves. Do not look back
but lunge wide-eyed ahead, immediate,
through the feathery tunnel of trees, face streaked
by the green world plunging against the windshield.

A TÊTE –À –TÊTE WITH MIHIR
"If I were *two-faced*, would I be wearing this one?"
                                        Abraham Lincoln

"Your father had Jew in him?"
He Indian, now American
I Caucasian, now Jew

remember our dismembered parts
with restive consecration
and little note

My locks curling at the roots
I braid them long
So they shan't perish

MONSTER BUTTONS
Dedicated to my grandfather, Albert Propper,
who was wounded in WWII.

Monster buttons
purpled onto your chest
gun bitten and worn out of fashion

Tomb wounds
chased with a silver,
or was it yellow, star?

Jew-badge made army-chic
stoned into utility's
right arm

We never spoke about the war
or about the gold crosses
pinned in my ears; instead

I'd fix onto your lap
and tap the skin dents
until we were both in stitches

JoAnn Proscia

THE GRIP

In your room at the nursing home
I tag your dresses so they won't get lost in the laundry.
You sit strapped into your chair,
clutching your matted-haired, glass-eyed doll, staring at it.
As I kiss you goodbye
you grab my hand, hold it tight and won't let go,
like the grip I couldn't get out of when I was a child
and we were standing in Grand Central Station
waiting for the train to take us to the Catskills.

SVEGLIATI (WAKE UP)

1
I speak Italian to no one in particular
amore, avventura, affetto
are words I like to use
svegliati, I like to say.

2
Two women in a row
read poems about dead brothers
and I realize I have never written one for you, *caro fratellino*.

Lying on the hard, cold table waiting to take my stress test
paura di morire that something might be wrong
I heard your laugh
You know, the one that mocks and chides me for being a "scaredy cat."

And at the beach, I looked up and there we were children again
digging for clams and catching killies
again I hear your laugh
all ticklish and giggly this time
as the young woman we both loved plays with us
and lifts you up over the waves and onto her shoulders.

3
Io sono proprio come mia nonna
I live in the same apartment as my grandmother did
88-12 Liberty Avenue, Ozone Park
right near the el
you could see it from her window
everything rattled.
I have the same lace curtains
listen to the opera on her radio and cry
select fruits and vegetables from the stand
with her careful hands
pray to Saint Anthony when something's lost
speak Italian to my friends.

Dominick Quartuccio

DUCKS WITHOUT HEADS

While cleaning the basement
with my old man,
I came across a burlap sack.
It was big and full and heavy.
I opened it and inside
were about two dozen
decoy-duck-heads.
I asked my dad about them.
He said they were made
by his brother, my uncle,
the one who
had died at eighteen.
Where are their bodies?
I asked.

He said,
Everybody loved your
uncle Victor.
He was killed in a car accident.
And when my father heard,
he went into the garage,
where Victor worked
on his decoys,
and he broke off
every one
of their heads.
He would have thrown
them all out too,
but I saved them.

I asked him why his father
would do that.
I don't know, he said,
that's just what he did.
He loved that kid.

What did you do
with the bodies?

I don't know, he said,
I just kept the heads.
I loved that kid.

I was seventeen at the time
and I wondered
if I were to die at eighteen,
what would my father do?
I had never built a thing
and hadn't written anything
worth a damn.

I looked into the bag
at the mess of bodiless duck heads,
their painted black eyes
starring back,
and they didn't look
like they could fool anyone.

THE FAT LIP

A fat lip, that's what you need.
That's what he says.
I'd like to see you try it, I say.
I close my eyes and point my chin at him.
I'd never dare him like this if I thought
he'd actually do it.
But he's in his seventies
and I'm much bigger than him now.
I could knock him on his ass.
But that fat lip is coming anyway—
fists balled up like boulders
or palms opened flat like pavement—
either way
the fat lip is coming.
His arm angles back.
It's like a hammer and a nail.
He swings down dead on.
The lip swells almost instantly,
fills up like a balloon.
The lip is about to pop
but it doesn't.
The lip expands,
eclipses my face.
The lip pushes at the walls,
rips open the roof.
The lip bursts outward,
comes crashing down.
The lip crushes us both
before anyone can apologize.

Barbara Reiher-Meyers

GREENWICH VILLAGE

slant-sided sidewalks hold heat
and strange discolorations
something gently rumbles underfoot

mummified plants gaze through gratings
doorways reek of mingled nations
string music – from an opening somewhere
scrapes along alleyways

beckons   come to consume
words hang vibrantly in low-light rooms
poets paint their pain with words
patrons listen,   suffer their own thoughts

LONG ISLAND DAWN

Slender clouds draw their fingers
across the damson dawn.
Purple pales to mauve
as night gives way to day.
Branch tips are muted by mist
that hovers; a shaken sheet
fluttering to rest on Earth's bed.

Sunshine pokes through the haze.
A plane banks; reflecting for a second
like a jeweled pin on God's lapel.
Half-remembered memories
shuffle in the semi dark,
awaiting sunrise to unmask mysteries.

MUSINGS WHILE MOWING

Grass grows relentlessly
I mow it down, and up it comes
like multimillion memories.

The sturdy oak in our childhood yard—
was that my mother, or my dad,
or someone else who gave me

shelter, away from angry thorns?
A stone hits the blade,
tosses sidewise shards at naked ankles.

I am as usual, unprepared for the attack.
Ivy encroaches upon the yard. It marches
toward the roses, intent on strangulation.

I choose to whack away at weeds
and trim the grass, then water it again
while every minute as I watch

it waits to mow me down..

Marie Emmons Wayne Reinstein

REFLECTIONS ON A *VICTORIA'S*
SECRET MANNEQUIN

The mannequins look different lately,
have you noticed? They
replicate the bodies of real women now
having discarded the mythical hourglass
and the fashionable twig.
Real women, yes,
but still, in undernourished
state. So now I sing—

I *had* that body—

and it too, was *almost* perfectly formed.
Sadly, I remember it only vaguely
now as I stand bravely full frontally
to the mirrors. Reaching out I lift my
right breast up by pulling its top muscle.
It is an action devoid of warmth,
it is crude really
and I see critically sadly curiously-
The outcome now is as it was
Before---but I do note
a wider deviation
of almost –
I will accept that of myself
and should I at some point ponder
some surgical interventions
I will pause
and reconsider this body of mine
whose Almost perfectness
was mimed for a mannequin

I *had* that body---

I'll remember the mannequin who emulates me.
I'll remember the mannequin who emulates me.

WANDERING THOUGHTS DURING A
COMPUTER VIRUS SCANNING

If I could but scan my memory for defects ---

the wonder of it (is)
my longevity in the spite-ing of my memory
wearing this face of nowhere, no time
        I saw things I guess ...
it is not clear
but I see my eyes
in those few pictures of/from my childhood:
vacant/vacuous blank/bovine.

When that same look appeared
in my child's eyes I cried
and fought and all the while
as a lioness or a she-bear ---

the wonder of it {is}
that I've lived this long only now to discover
there is a memory of my defect of memory
and why.
        Dare I pursue this?

Dare I ... from the strength of my everyday
happiness, view back- wards to that time of silence,
incomprehension --of fear.

What face will be revealed as the breaker
of me and the thief of my innocence?
I re-coiled at the evil, scarred anyway.

So in defense I wrapped up
and mummified that one child and all her hurts...
then made myself into a new one --
        One who suffered,
in night colored dreams stifled,
shaken and taken down;
while the other who learned
to turn ignorance into
blindness, could grow both in my stead.

MARIE

She brought out the best of me
i am driving to be better
daring myself to establish new ways to attach to my life
finding real reasons to care

she sought out the rest in me
i was striving; i let her
baring myself midst happy days by my Baby, my wife
minding our seasons to share

she caught hold of my heart
releasing deep shame and past pain
sensing so soon since the start
increasing, unceasing gladness to gain
to claim and attain
unwinding our love everywhere

i brought to her happiness
allowing her wholeness to blossom, to bloom
loving her deeply and purely and hotly
sweet smelling scents surrounding our room
twining two lives in laces of love, soft and rare

we had this small gift that we shared, creating our own time and place
the honeymoon couple that cared and who dared
blending family and friends in our space, with embrace
bonding two sweethearts in love, she and me matching pair

she's with me in daytimes and dreams
dressed up in dark dawns when I wake
mining memories of playtimes it seems
ardor adored and adorned we would make
bending bodies both beautiful and bare

sweetness sighed the night she was taken
purpose passing out days remaining…still
caring cried, bright light not forsaken
i loved my marie
marie loved her phil

SERENDIPITY

Serendipity
calls out to me
rooted in a mystery
occurring every now and then, when
good things just happen, unexpectedly
out of the blue
coherent harmonies---cohesive connections
to You

serendipity
generating direction, delusion
reflection, confusion
thoughts arise and i shine
yet all the while
eschewing emotional perception
contraindicating common sense
too old and so dense
stuck in some past tense
dwelling dormant in darkening domiciles of denial i do
smile...*this* is my trial

must i block the pain to go on, and on?
i am a survivor...so far

serendipity
its oddity audacity capacity
amazes me engages me
salient mystery synchronicity
outrages me unfazes me upstages me
startling sensation of "Gee"
obliging me to bended knee

minding the gap eliciting wonder
flash of lightning crash of thunder
phenomena resounding quite extra-ordinarily
bounding toward objectives BIGGER
serendipity reflecting in transparency
my undisclosed, unfamiliar identity...I was lucky once

1962

The PA chimes
three times

We all stand,
Then march silently
in single file
To our place
of practiced safety.

On my knees,
Cowering under my desk,
I see the crucified Christ
Dangling on the end of a chain
Next to sister's sensible shoes.

"Cover your head
in case of shattering glass,"
she commands.
"Cover your head
and pray"

Father forgive them
For they know not what they do.

A DAY OF GRACE

I will frame this day
and hang it on a wall
near a window
where it will catch
the morning's glow.

Then when I come upon it
after a long dark night,
I can borrow its light
until the sun rises in me.

PHYSICS LESSON

How polite
The particle of light
It waves
as it goes by

TASTE THE ROSE

carelessly picked
in the blossom of red
at your fingertip

WHY IT DIDN'T LAST

I made the mistake
of giving you an answer
when you asked
if your eggplant parmigiana
tasted as good
as my mother's

Ruth Sabath Rosenthal

TRANSITION

A longing for heart quiet,
end of further fall
into winter — short days of sun
forwarding to spring's
longer days, circling back
in the sameness of time —

heart-and mind-numbing time
with no respite. A longing to quiet
thoughts playing back
battle after battle, the failing
to even half-fill life's wellspring.
And in my darkest season

of discontent, convinced the sun
will no longer shine in this lifetime;
feeling that sting
as from a bee disquieting
green slumber, swelling to a fault
every damned day, slamming me back.

Season upon season, holding me back,
chilling me with doubt that the sun
warms body and soul without fail,
and without doubt, given time,
better times, rise with each dawn quietly
advancing into spring.

Fast forward, past spring
to summer, autumn, back
to winter, and round again, disquiet
ever more glaring under the sun.
Then, out of the blue, a glance, nod, time
stopped, my heart races falling

in love without doubt. No fooling!
Empty seasons done for. Spring
burgeons and flowers time —
a new lifetime. No looking back.
Past care and sounder reason,
my heart basks. Quiet

as snowfall, sun-bursting-through-
cloud-cover, springtime-sprouting
quiet, a kiss blown then blown back

Andrea Rowen

RED EYE RISING

I dipped my finger in your ashes this morning
Imagined smashing the case of our suffering
Into inconsequential bits just to choke them down
      it did no good.
There's been no food since the wind kissed the water good-bye.

I stirred my finger in your ashes this morning
Felt the velvet whisper of a peacefulness we never knew.
How I long for even one boring metaphor
  to tell you how much I love you:
      The clouds look like cotton; the ocean roars.
We are all so poor without you.

Our sweet candle melting from all sides
Never once did we think of exhaustion
How it would feel to warm our graying bones
By the incinerator's smoking coal.

I dipped my finger in your ashes this morning
To convince myself I was real
      it did no good -
We are nothing without the bubbling laughter of children
Tumbling down your fragrant hills.

SPRUNG LOVE

I know you know
He likes me.

You know I know
He's your man.

Why make dark times?
I'm resigned.

Keep your metal
& your fire.

Taking your man's
not my style.

Paul Rubin

INNER STRUGGLE

I see where we are and it's all too obvious.
A wedge of reality turned me into an "us."
Try as we may to savor each day,
This pain and disdain has caused a delay.

We try to find meaning in all of the gray evenings.
Battles of boy versus man have fractured our feelings.
The failure of family has left us on our own.
Marooned kings we have become, searching for our thrones.

A reunion of beings is what we strive for.
Only through change and discipline will we ever find more.
A storm of challenge churns as we watch by the shore.
Weather the storm we must, to find our mutual core.

We try to find meaning in all of the grey evenings.
Battles of boy versus man have fractured our feelings.
The failure of family has left us on our own.
Marooned kings we have become, searching for our thrones.

Oh what a gruesome battle we wage on this island of length.
Tedious yet cunning, demanding every ounce of our strength.
To see the face of our enemy would make our mission clearer.
A settling of dust reveals the enemy is only a mirror.

Alexander Russo

EXHIBITION OPENING

I hear the resounding pounding
Of hard rock a block away.
I enter and gaze around
at the swirling mob, can barely see
some paintings.

I can't shake the music,
and its insistent beat makes my feet
shuffle in rhythmic accompaniment.
My eyes dart from bobbing heads
to paintings and back again
like billiard balls.

I plow my way to the bar,
snatch a Merlot — all the while,
pow, wow, dip. dunk, wobble, wide open
throttle, everyone high on the bounce.

A few wander around like zombies.
Others sip drinks, nibble snacks,
greet others politely, or slap high fives.

Is anyone really looking at the paintings?
This is more like a happening,
a constantly changing kaleidoscope.

I decide to go with the flow, get loaded.
I'll see the show later.

HOW TO GET THERE

Discard any drags. Leave all arguments,
likes, dislikes behind. Don't pack worry
or doubt. Be prepared to disregard voices

telling you it's a hopeless journey.
Give up all habits, even good ones
until you're hollow as a reed.

Streamline yourself to eliminate friction.
Try running with the wind, look back.
If you see a cloud of dust run faster.

If you're successful
you'll be running faster than time and
will catch up with your former self.

Before it can trip you nudge it aside.
Keep going until you enter
a place of blinding brilliant light—

a metaphor for another metaphor
no one can explain —
but you'll know you've arrived.

BLOOD COUSINS

They were my cousins, but we weren't that close. Maybe it was because they were 100 percent. I wondered how long that bloodline would stay pure. I also wondered, 100 percent what? Were they 100 percent American? 100 percent straight? But the question had to do with their bloodline. The quality of nationality or straightness wasn't in the blood, or was it? No, the bloodline was more like a pedigree. Was my cousins' blood blue because it was 100 percent? Was my blood 50 percent—in other words, 50 percent red and 50 percent blue? Was my blood purple? Wasn't purple the color of royalty? Was that why I didn't live in the San Fernando Valley and my cousins did?

There must have been some kind of vetting going on, a testing of the components of blood. How far back did my cousins' 100 percent go? Back to the old country? Back to the Cro Magnon era? Weren't we all related if we went back that far? Maybe we were more than cousins; maybe we were blood brothers. I could definitely cut my finger and hold it to someone else's bleeding finger. I could certainly swap some blood for brotherhood.

OAK TREE AND CYPRESS

The oak tree and the cypress don't grow in each other's shadow. The oak is more of an upland tree, and the cypress is a swamp dweller. One of us is more like the oak; the other, more like the cypress. We both grow, but not close enough to cast a shadow on the other with our leaf canopy. We could be within sight, one of us looking up from the water, the other looking down from the hill, if "looking" is the right word. "Swaying" might be more accurate. One of us sweeps upward with tendrils waving, while the other bends downward. That is, assuming we have both achieved the same height. The oak might be little more than a sprout, splitting the shell of an acorn. The cypress may be a seed in a cone. Or we could both be fully formed, hundreds of growth rings old. We may have become brittle. It might be hard for us to sway and bend. No more snapping and whipping for us. We might be content to take it easy, keep the juices flowing, and let the xylem and phloem do what they do.

Wendy Salinger

APPLES

She is the one thing
that makes me brave,

whose round face
is sun-up,

whose cheeks
hide apples,

whose mouth first puckered
with the word *water.*

O round-the-clock face,
my heart skips
with the dusty swipe of the rope!

For her the rising sun
makes its yard:

the bars spread,
the bands swell--
the ribs of elation.

THE GREEN DIAL

Nick, the boy
with the name from *Gatsby*
and the bitter accent
of New Jersey,
took me out
the airport road
to see the night landings.

His headlights shone
like a moon on things.

I remember his radio,
his watch,
the slow phosphor
trails of the dials,
how in the dashboard clock
the chemical fish
of the minutes and hours swam.

I can still tell
the sharp fruit
of his cologne--
as if the evening
rose up off his neck.

The car window framed
the deep pile of night.

The flagellate
saxophone
lifted over Cleveland,
cut a broad swathe
like a locomotive
across the dark life
of North Carolina.

We sat past curfew
under the college trees
that let loose over us
such a sift
and dialed all the green
stations of the night.

UPHOLSTERY

Heavily upholstered
afternoon, too rich
for play.

Contusion of light on the
holly and magnolia leaves
like the light before a tornado.

The red wagon has overturned,
and she rides above it
on her high boat.

There is the highboy and the highchair;
high tea and highball;
the high, scratchy collar of her dress.

There is higher education.

There is the high window and behind it
her father's nap.
The Germanic gutturals of his snore

disapprove.
If he misses his sleep, he will die
or go sleepless,

lumbering all night around the house.
A crack of the floor
can wake him.

Sudden stranglehold catarrhs;
retching;
his reddening face.

The fountain plays luxuriantly
like the downspout of his urine
into the porcelain bowl.

There is the word *solution.*

There is a fever at the impasse,
a tantrum
in the back seat of the Studebaker.

Mother shapes
will attend her
with cool cloths.

Or else:
    the silence of transgression.
For example, when something is spilled.
Or the fork clatters to the plate.

Someone rushes from the table.
Someone says,
"Dinner is ruined."

Let the parents divide the child
and each can take the half he likes
to do with what he wishes.

There is company in the house--
scholars and refugees.
The spittle of their accents.

Seeing close up
the hairs inside the nose.
Then their hands inside your nice, lace panties.

If he wakes, the world will fold up
with a clap like cymbals
on the metal leaves.

The loss of the time sense.
The pendulum stops
or the swinging chain of his pocket watch.

In a clock tower
up a steeple of stairs
(like the one he took them to in Rothenburg)

the old century sleeps.
    A little man--
or a soldier or a pig--

comes out on the hour
and does a special dance
of some secret and hideous meaning.

She wants to grow up and spend her money
on something cheap,
like the rest of America.

She wants the loud music
he hates.
But her time will never come.

Afternoon like a too rich dessert.
She turns and turns the wagon wheel
so it scrapes in its socket--

a sound like the grinding of her teeth at night.

Darren Sardelli

A COLORFUL CHARACTER

My left leg is silver.
My right leg is blue.
My shoulders are yellow
and lavender too.

My right arm is turquoise.
My left arm is red.
I have specks of purple
and pink on my head.

My ankles are golden.
My belly is black.
My fingers are green
like my nose and my back.

My elbows are orange.
My forehead is tan.
I shouldn't have thrown
all this paint at my fan.

GALAXY PIZZA AND METEOR PIE

Those wonderful ladies have done it again.
Their meals are like magic. Their food is a ten.
They lit up the lunchroom and brightened our day
by serving hot lunch on an Orbiting Tray.

Their menu consisted of Jupiter Steaks
with Astronaut Apples and Milky Way Shakes.
Their Nebula Nuggets were something to savor.
Their Corn on the Comet was bursting with flavor.

My friends were impressed with the Cheese from the Moon.
We ate Lunar Soup with an Alien Spoon.
The ladies surprised us with Clusters on Rye,
a Galaxy Pizza, and Meteor Pie.

Their Mercury Muffins had Asteroid Chips.
Their Candy Cane Craters produced an eclipse.
The lunch in our lunchroom is rated five Stars.
I'm glad that these lunch ladies came here from Mars!

Robert J. Savino

BORDERLINE

you were happy only on the edge of uncertainty.
any fool can walk out into a wave,
look for the eye in the calm between wind howls,
not think of the undertow
and become strangled in the grip of seaweed.
i could have stopped you but i didn't.
i turned my back, let you follow wet sand
dreams through spirit mist into the sea.
and now you return to haunt me
for not trying to keep your bones
from being washed ashore with tidal waste,
when all I did was leave you to be challenged,
let you walk away without debt.

ODDS ON A GOOD POEM

I carry scratch sheets for thoroughbreds, on weekends,
never pick the favorite, everyone else does.
I play a long shot, not too long,
on an old gray mare or chocolate maiden.
She may not finish first or place,
but if she does . . . . payola!
I carry scrap sheets of words everyday,
of rivers and roadways
of sunlight and moonbeams
of tortoises and aborigines . . . .
on napkins and tissue paper
on business cards and boxtops
on white space of anything
or noted on the palm of my hand.
Spread out across the table,
I am determined to fit the puzzled pieces.
Yet at six to one odds
only one combination will make a superfecta.

TICK-TOCK THE THC CLOCK

A spring journey with Lewis Carroll
and I'm keeping time with Alice,
through summer, surrender
the Less Safe Dream to a backdrop
version, that begins black and white,
then embodies prismatic color.
Age doesn't relieve the anxiety
an angry Queen of Hearts bestows
upon my ticking clock.
A deep inspiration from the hookah
of a young caterpillar is breath-
taking after drinking burgundy wine.
Kaleidoscope colors implode,
racing to tea with the Mad Hare
and Mad Hatter; and the mystery
withdraws from sleep in a breath
of life that has become mine.
Winter colors begin to tone
blended seasons and pursue hands
of time, spinning the wheel,
each turn faster, with each
page of the book now magnified.
Everything becomes more blown-up,
a blur, outright obscurity.
Fear of falling through the floor.
Fear of being trapped in the looking glass.
Fear of the Cheshire cat who is only a grin!

Steven Schmidt

BENNY

Surprised that my stepson's
new room-mate was not
on a ventilator, I said hello.
Benny looked about eighty.
He just had to tell me
and I just had to listen,
slightly uneasy about ignoring Bobby.

About the guards who said
"You are the chosen people--
Where is your God?"
and always called him
by the number on his arm,
never by a name.

About eleven days in an open cart
without food and water,
pushing out the dead.
"I don't know how I survived."

About sleeping in the lumber yard--
the SS guard asked "How old are you?"
"My son is also 16."
Did not add to his punishment.

About his conclusions:
"I believe in God, but
I want to ask him why
he let this happen."
"Was six million our price
to get a country?
Without a country
you are nothing."

I didn't feel guilty
about neglecting Bobby
Or tell Benny
my last name.

CLOUD SPOON RANGE

street............... *Too Alike:*
Desperate to coddle the one I would win,
I make myself tough as St. Joan
and bend like a cotter pin.
Fancy runs guided by smell like an ant,
and burrows, no heed for tone.
Proud Daphne holds laurels, looks south, feet afraid
to root in one place like a chemical plant.
It's time for a love grenade.

ranch............... *Heavy Knit at Noon:*
Red hands labor, a green mouth to fill,
slithering dreams to pour out,
far from a home whose dead chill
forbids gluttony. Hands row, wash, climb.
Lush delta sympathies sprout,
nourished by sweat 'til their gazes expand,
eager to serve conjugations of time.
A love grenade is at hand.

vault................. *Universe for Two, License Null:*
Fantasy and oil now warm;
Hands, eyes, and nerves still hot.
Shattered endearments swarm,
harmonize distraction, stoke
a hug that binds to one spot.
Brief gust of fear, no cough,
no ring of sulfur smoke--
our love grenade has gone off.

MAY 21, 2008

Memory seems random.

Red garage-sale spinet, garish tone.
Working on a canon in maqam lami
that never fit together.
Then Jean sat to my left.
I scanned the Beethoven she read,
watched her forearms brace
firm arpeggios.

One year ago, we last made love.

Jean came home on hospice
with fentanyl patches and lofty pills,
nausea almost under control;
After a week, refused ativan
and could grow memories again,
write poems;
Said "We could *do* something, y'know."
And, for a month, we did:
Spacious melisma,
Moderato e espressivo--
ritenuto--turn up the oxygen--
Adagio sostenuto--

Ripe love, fresh tang.

Mary McGrath Schwartz

PARACHUTES AND CATERPILLARS
ACROSS THE HEMPSTEAD PLAINS
With thanks to Maxwell Coryden Wheat, Jr.

Words float
aspiring
to catch the wind.
Milkweed's ephemeral parachutes waft over
Blue stem, foxtail,
Clamoring in wild profusion below.

Once, *Spirit's* engine
Drowned *Cricket's* hum,
Meadowlark's song,
Rustling *pheasant*
Whispering instruments in the orchestra of nature.

Lindy flew into
wide blue yonder.
Leaving behind small blossoms;
Bird's Foot Violet and *Blue Curls*
Nestling in the waving sheaves of grass

*My caterpillar words crawl across the page, across wagon ruts, under
blackberry vines tromping on grey-green Lichen and British Soldiers, brushing
past Wild Indigo. Words lumber on to celebrate the preservation of this space,
this living heritage and we come to stroll through grass.*

Now *Mustang* engines
Speed and power
Roaring causeways of speed
Meadowbrook Parkway - Northern State
Bright flash, gleaming metal flashing past.

Words hover above
Blowing grasses
Protecting the elusive
Sand Plain Gerardia symbol of hope
In the rescued golden prairie.

THUNDER AND LIGHT

Our small boat charts across the bay.
Enclosed in a deep v
We are in our bliss.

The storm approaches as you pilot toward land,
Black clouds close in - air is electric.
I sidle close while you steer.
Eyes scan water, sky, harbor.
White, hot heat sears the sky -
a crack in glazed pottery that evaporates
and reappears again
and again.

Cormorants, gulls find safe harbor,
Egrets, swans nestle low in grass,
Invisible forces thunder around us.
We seek our shelter.

Closer still
You are my safe harbor
And you are my storm.
Surely you guide us home.
Together.

Ron Scott

RECKONING

When footsteps fail to be heard
When children's laughter no longer resonates
When change becomes the enemy
Visible is your smile.

In the face of intimidation
In the face of life threatened
In the face of loneliness
Visible is shared resolve.

After outer accoutrements
After flesh reverts to earth
After the skeleton succumbs to time
Visible is the soul.

THE DO NOT LIST
In memory of Robert Dunn

DO NOT leave home without that 1st cup of coffee; Caution: coffee
holder is not a laptop.
DO NOT use the HOV Lane with a dummy (plaster). Otherwise,
dummies have the right-of-way.
Hands Free DOES NOT apply to steering wheel (the cell, dummy).
If you succeed in your commute, DO NOT confuse your secretary with
your wife. Both will take offense.
DO NOT invest in stock recommended by your brother-in-law.
DO NOT reaffirm your mother-in-law's first impression.
DO NOT believe all is forgiven if you tell the truth.
DO NOT fly if you can't carry your own bag (bag is a test).
DO NOT enter into a political or religious debate expecting to win.
DO NOT embrace any of the above if you wish to test the water, the
warmth, the chill, the excitement of the next wave; always ready to
answer Saint Peter's question: What are you doing here?

Alan Semerdjian

CRUSH

I once had a crush on the word
          reconciliation
how it moved in and out of my life
          its slippery *cil* rounding corners

and rubbing up against the hard *con*
          how I misused the word
     on more than one occasion
          meaning almost clear

at once here and never here
     there but never somewhere.
     It was about love and it's always
          about love

this forever balance of stretching
     and returning, push and pull
     like some sad scavenger hunt
          or tug of war

the soldier never quite back
          and her always here.
     And time makes a gray postcard
          from him to her

boots heavy with memory's lead
          in one bed, the need
     to *reconcile* in the other, and me
          still in love

with a word
     she's trying
so desperately every day
          to say.

IN HIS HEART IS HER BOMB

In her heart is
      a mouse
that laughs at his jokes,
that circumnavigates
the entire world.
That makes her laugh
and tickle inside,
      in her heart.

In his eye is Alaska,
in his chair, his ass,
in his back, his pain,
in his mind, Alaska.

In her apartment there's a frame and
      in the frame there are sisters and
      in the sisters there is love.
There is love in her sisters.

In his car there is music,
in his music there is a song.
Sometimes many songs
make up music
in his car.

In her mouth are words
that are other people's words
with her words, in her mouth
there are conversations
about words and his words
are in her mouth too.

In his ear is an echo
that gets further away
from his ear when he thinks
about Alaska.

But in his heart is her clock
and in her clock is his tick
and other mighty human ticks
with little human hands
he hears every night.

Not Alaska.

In his heart is her clock
that ticks mighty ticks,
mighty human ticks
with little human hands
every night, her clock,
her tick, his heart.

WHICH CAME FIRST

Which came first, desire or the story of desire?
Which came first, melody or the word behind the sound?
Spring or the fountain? Rain or water?
Heaven or this earth – old and impenetrable
Orb – or something that revolves around something else?
Which came first, my wanting you or *you* itself?
The idea of you, misshapen? Happenstance?
Or no coincidence, this longing, or this short breath?
Which came first, this letter or this story of tiger?
These endangered things or reconnaissance by fire?
This hunger, this old and impenetrable hunger,
Or the sustenance around us not enough, not ever.
Which came first, the hyperlink or the need to move,
Or to be so guided by motion that you're standing still?

BRIDGETTE'S DAUGHTER

I see her in a dark rental on a street where the hydrant runs all summer long,
soaking the kids' torn t-shirts and Salvation Army jeans, tossed
knots of hair agleam with municipal water.

Bridgette's daughter watches from her second story window,
wrists crossed on the chipped-paint sill, the room dim as a cellar.

She hasn't played by the hydrant this summer.

Reaching to tuck a strand behind her ear, half of it falls
away in her hand. She shoves the hair into her pocket.

Every day there is a little less of hair, of her;

the patched dress hangs from her shoulders like a used parachute,
folding around itself after its fall from the sky.

Bridgette's daughter rubs the stent in her chest:

she's been taught not to scratch it, has grown
accustomed to the dull itch, tolerating it like a rich kid
learning to suffer the discomfort of braces.

Soon, her mother will bang up the stairs, home from work,

a tiny sack of groceries in her backpack: apples, coffee, milk,
and a box of dry crackers for her daughter,

the kind pregnant women nibble to keep the nausea down.

THE SCISSORS OF MY MOTHER

Five or six times every year we'd re-enact the tragedy of haircut,
where Mom squints over my magazine example,
a Pall-Mall dangling from her apricot mouth,
asking for details she somehow never used.
"That one will be beautiful on you, it frames the face,"
she'd say, as if hair could frame a person somehow else.

The scissors of my mother committed atrocities
like high-water bangs and pointy sideburns,
her sloppy layers like a lopsided chessboard
decades before buzz and fade became styles.
Sobbing in the aftermath, I'd have to hear
how much her customers love the way she does their hair,
the nicest way she knew to call me stupid and ungrateful.

In the magazine still open on the table,
a babe in a feathery shag tosses her head.
I tear out the page, wave it in Gloria's face:
"You said you would do *this*."
"Don't holler at your mother," she tells me,
"I've got more two-dollar tippers than anybody else in the shop."
I had no way to know if that, if anything she said, was true.
And I had no way to know, then, that no hairdresser
could give me what I wanted.
Not the magazine model's gleaming cut
but the mysterious face that it framed.

Neil Shepard

FEAR IN NORTHWEST HARBOR

I knew the eagle was coming because of the crows.
I was reading Cormac McCarthy. *The Road*. The end
Of the road, really, post-literate, that ends
At the ash-gray, iodine-smelling sea, millions of fish
Washed up and decomposed to fish-scales –
And the crows told me with their wild caws:
Eagle. They don't fear osprey, only
The eagle's omnivorous appetite.
I looked up from my book, straight up.
Thirty feet overhead, the eagle's
Yellow talons and cruel yellow eye.
Its domineering gaze was, indeed,
American, a sun tied to extinction
blazing from its eye, a world viewed
as ash and gray domain. In the novel,
all the birds are dead as well.
None can fly high enough to pierce the nuclear
clouds born of the light of a hundred suns…
None can reach the one life-sustaining sun.

MEADOW COVE, DEER ISLE, MAINE

Last year I came alone, to finish a last draft
of a book with no deadline, the beginning
of late middle age, the eagle shriek
overhead for my ears only,
the bay-wind rustling birch leaves
for my clouded eyes.

Last year taught me this year I've produced
nothing worthy, except for a *family*:
a daughter singing *Chim-Chim-Chiree*
in the shower, the happy gush
of water, the fruity scent of her shampoo,
a wife outside in the Adirondack chair,
reading *her* great-grandmother's journals.

A shared agenda for the day –
coastal hike to an island reached only at low tide,
forager's picnic of blueberries and edible flowers,
and late-day swim in a bay of red granite.

Last year, I watched for hours the osprey's
gyroscopic motions, the flash of talons,
the fish whose fate had come to an end,
the flat rock where it flew to devour its meal.
There was a certain tree where an eagle
fed fish to her fledglings. Binoculars let me watch
her tear meat with a yellow beak and
a measured, bloody eye.

I've heard that eagles mate in mid-air,
copulate as they fall, and in the mad rush
of such feathery clasp and company, sometimes
seem to forget their solitary natures,
orgasm, swoon, and crash into the sea.

SOUTHWEST HARBOR

Tire tracks on the beach
fade in rising tide.
The sandbar to the island
disappears. But I can see the flash
of field glasses from the mansion,
the billionaire at high water
approving the sea's separation:

how it closes the circle around his home
and keeps it safe from beachcombers,
who stand and gaze across the high-tide bay
and wait for whatever washes up on the mainland,
a drifting piece of wood, an empty shell, a polished
shard of broken glass, to keep or sell.

A lone loon spies me and dives,
surfacing far off. Harbor seals laze beyond the breakers,
on rocky shelves. I wander far down the strand –
hoarding my privacy –as close to the vanished
sandbar as the tide allows.

How can I hoard what I don't own? How can I condone it?
I watch seagulls circle the lobster boats, squawking for a claw
or pulpy bait, the boats floating over fished-out waters.

UNCLE GEORGE

Uncle George made a million bucks selling real estate,
back when a million bucks meant something, girls in Vegas and
Wayne Newton winking
from under his falsetto and pencil mustache.
If Uncle can do it, I can can.

Uncle says the secret of success is rising whenever you wake and
getting right to work.
You'll have time to sleep later, he says, when you're dead. I can do that, can rise
and write as early as I want with my wife sleeping like a hibernating minx. No
problem.

Uncle bought a lake out of boredom. An Arizona lake. Spent millions on a wave
machine. Surfing in a god damn desert, on an undulating wave. I can do that.
Machinery of the gods is my specialty, surfing on every swelling phrase.

Uncle lost his shorts. At the bottom of the lake. It had something to do with
words.
Heated words with an engineer, arguing physics and asymptotes. I can do that,
write without shorts, naked as God's Adam before the naming of animals, and
just after –

Uncle found new threads for another deal in the "real" Caribbean.
Bought an island from Howard Hughes. Howard didn't want it. It offended his
sensibility. Namely, it had nothing on it. I can do that, every poem like a desert
isle, until I build the bridge

between stanzas, scatter a few huts, and people it with wry creations. Or cry
like Uncle George, cry uncle, and throw in the towel. In his case, he threw it on
the beach and lay for a long time, admiring the sun. That's how *I'd* like to end.

John L. Silver

DRUMS ALONG THE POTOMAC ARE LEAKING

no empty hollow horse
can swim this Styx
when mouths of lesser beasts unveil
a dome of white
spews fogs of night
from where these brigands hide
Their new old wars
won't ever fix
until enough have died

some in camouflage
did beat and leash
young prisoners to and fro
while other twice born armies pall
with shrouds of media snow
they too, as of old,
would stake and burn
what "heathen" science knows

compassion truth and justice
lost in tankers sleuthed below
a flotsam slick
reveals their trick
of those who kill our free

in jetsam words
conveyed by birds
(a flock their "act" can't tree)

this bottled note a scrap of hope
adrift in the oil dark sea

PETALS
for August who returned whole

numbered days are now as then
since we who walked with rifles
in morning's heaven
day's only peace
we scattered horizontal
each a glareless mirror
to mix with earth's terrain
except perhaps to orchids
those special ones neither red nor white
we saw them glowing there
in precious jungle dawns they grew
between sleep and terror's wake
how could such beauty then exist?
always just before
a smell of powder and cracking guns

where once we waited breathless,
for those spinning blades
our truest petal friends

transparent in rotation
existing on and between colors

wind blown dreams of sky cut rescue
to drone and lift us
from a blood born geography
we chart this memory of a flower

TWELVE STREET

walking past discarded mattresses
on Ave. A
early morning brings
with it wind

billowing blue tarps
on the corner
lift out from a roof repair

sounds of straining ropes
and flapping plastic
draw one's eyes up
from the flow of people below

Sahid Sahid struggles to open
his little newsstand

some local kids have deftly filled
the large chrome locks with crazy glue

"I lose sixty dollars", he says,
"and soon I will need locks for locks"

with hammer, bar and hack saw
these locks retire along with their
chains
one by one

blade skaters whiz by
on their way to the 10th St. bridge
and the East River beyond

Cathy Silverstein

A WAKENING POEM

I keep dreaming you poems of love
Crisp as newly laundered grass
Peeper chorus strong
Ice bright
and colorful as a mandrill's ass!

PORTAL

I wake up
as the chipping hits of sleet
attack the window
like a memento mori.
This thin glass sheet
the only defense
against an invasion of
my sleep warm nest.
A candle of clock light
shadows the cat
snoring in beat with the storm.
I yawn.

Hal Sirowitz

HOW TO GET FROM HERE TO THERE

Dorothy in 'The Wizard of Oz,'
father said, sings 'Somewhere
Over the Rainbow.' Each time
I hear it, I think of your mother's
traffic directions. She wants me
to take her to a new store. 'Where
is it?' I'd say. 'Somewhere in
that direction,' she'd say.
'And which direction is that –
North or South?' I'd say.
'North,' she'd say.
'North of what,' I'd say.
'All I know is that's it's north,'
she said, 'of where I had the conversation
with the woman I met who went there.'

LOOKING FOR FOOD IN THE WRONG PLACES

I look down while walking
my dog and notice she has
half a waffle in her mouth.
I couldn't find waffles the last time
I went to the supermarket. Yet,
she finds them on the street.
I gave the command, 'Drop it,'
which has been used by dog owners
for centuries. It didn't work.
She closed her mouth, chewing faster.
I pried open her mouth with my fingers.
The waffle no longer had squares.
She had ruined its geometry.

Marcia Slatkin

AFTER EIGHT YEARS

I pray that if you
alive in lighter times
excavate our ancient graves,
you'll pity the cuts
that furrowed our bones,
note our huddled contortions,
and ask how we survived it –

how we withstood a daily assault
of lies violent enough to maul,
to slice, until our minds
resembled bodies turned inside out,

veins dangling, arteries
spurting, the poor exposed heart
heaving as it tried to pump
against a violent wind,
and the dry puckered skin
lumped in the center,
longing for air and light.

I pray you'll know
there was no soap, no
scrub, no way to wash
clean, no glue to make
us whole. Our legs
were stained to the thigh,
our lungs were forced
to breathe the sour
dough rising round our chest
as our feet sloshed their muck.

The future might ask
what we did as we listened
to their spin – did we
laugh the dry chortle of the cynic
and go back to our beer,
did the way our gut constricted
make us wretch, could we stay
numb -- or did our fall
to their subterranean sewer
make us weep?

NOURISHMENT

Both my parents visit me now.
Though my mother's not yet dead,
they choose the same route,
strewing my sleep with freesia, –
jasmine, lavender, scents
that soothe. My mother's hug

is honey and walnut stirred in wine,
so rich it burns. "Sweetheart," she cries,
leaning toward me, her voice
a saxophone wailing love.

My father is more reserved.
Sometimes he visits
while I'm on cafeteria duty
in the high school.
We sit on the long scratched
tables, student obscenities
covered by our outspread fingers.

"I work here, dad," I tell him
as he looks around, dubious
that any good can come
of such a job. "I close
the door to my room
and fly." He smiles.

So both of them
feed me in this unlikely way.
And I who in youth spat out
all they put on my plate,
am now healed and open
to their balm, a bird
with spread beak, eager
for their pungent worms.

OUR JOB NOW

We are hurtling
toward a cliff
few seem to see –
                    past the dying
                    children of Rwanda,
                    their bone-thin mothers
                    in dusty robes,
                    homeless, huddling
                    in the sand, weeping;

                    past the hacked up
                    bodies in the Congo, or Kenyans
                    caught on the wrong side of danger.
                    Past the keening folk
                    in Louisiana, their parlors
                    mud-stained three years after.

Neither shown
on an HD screen,
barked at a circus
by a clown, or clearly
shouted by God,
many are still deaf
to the veiled clock's tick.

                    The scientist
                    studying the ice
                    on the Greenland shelf
                    knows, but his voice
                    is thin, no match
                    for the will of the mob.

It will not be easy
to illumine the cliff, enlarge
the clock, photograph
or film its deadly progress.
But that is our job.

Justin Slone

MAN'S VIEW ON POETRY

I am a poet.
I scribble a verse onto this literary canvas,
punctuate each statement for properness.
I inspect letters A-Z.
Does it rhyme?
Letter "A" goes with letter "B?"
 1 + 2=3 ?
This goes with this,
and that goes with that?
But that is not poetry.
Not the poetic verse I wish for you to hear.

A TRIBUTE FROM A MOTHER TO HER DAUGHTER

Lonesome nights.
Eighteen months of an endless plague.
We would walk the streets beside bomb sirens.

I can remember
combing the strands of my daughter's hair,
singing melodious tunes into her brittle ears,
feeding her a piece of my heart,
she needed rhythm to stay alive.

I shall never forget
sounds of bomb sirens and missile launchings,
these nights of the plague.

It began late December.
frost on the ground,
man disguised as beast;
grappling to escape the casket.

We sought the help of an honest man.
Daughter and I would sing ourselves to bed

each and every night of these eighteen months.
We would walk the streets beside bomb sirens.

And I would touch
the porcelain skin of my daughter,
whisper God's verse into her ears,
She needed faith to stay alive.

Mahtob is my daughter's name.
She was five.
I was the age of a haggard begging for bread.

And I will never forget those tormenting threats how
"...Women will be separated from their daughter's forever!"

"Not without my daughter!"
                        A knife punctured my chest
                        Venom poured from my cheeks.
"...What's a mother to do?"
And from that point on
Mahtob and I feared the plague.
We feared death.
We feared life.
We feared separation.
We would walk the street beside bomb sirens.

And I will never forget,
wiping the tears from her eyes,
whimpering God's verse to her frail ears,
feeding her whatever heart I had left
she needed it to stay alive.

Searching through a seemingly meaningless universe,
on these nights
eighteen months of an endless plague.

Callie Jean Slusser

PLUCK THE STRINGS UNTIL THEY SNAP

Body language speaks secrets
the mind is yet to know
in the waking hour.

Breath short.
Heartbeat hard.
Tear-moist skin.
Mind pulsating truth
through screamless cries.

Shadows on the wall
keep safe damages past.
Regret pushs pressure
onto shoulders
hold hostage the release to dream.

Barbara Southard

RIDE

Families are such tumultuous storms,
soaking rain, wind, tossing us
in a salad of fate, or decisions gone wrong.

We start out thinking we have full control
—teenagers behind the wheel of a car—
yet end up like new-born mammals
seeing the world through unfocused eyes
holding on tight for rides through rapids
where eddies swirl around rocks
at the edge of clear pools,
small fish swim in circles above pebbles
far below the surface,
sky changing from azure to sapphire, sun's rays
grazing the water through a lattice of leaves
ruffled by a soft breeze.

THREE-YEAR-OLD

She watches snow land on the sleeve of her coat
as if each collection of crystals
is a wondrous baptism of her expanding cosmos,
searches the sky for its source, not yet knowing
how they float from clouds above, collide,
grow branches like trees, each flake as unique as she.

Still the center of the universe, she wears shoes
that tell her where to go,
is certain she flew with the sparrows
when she first jumped on the trampoline—
each day filled with mysteries waiting for a name.

The ground she walks on is worn and torn
from constant aggravations, but she is new,
still believes in magic crayons and buttons,
stars above glowing just for her pleasure.
Her head tilted toward the skies, she feels
their diamond-light wash down over her.

TWO-YEAR-OLD

At what point in time does a child say no.
I am me, not you, mother of my birth,
all-knowing father. My path, not yours.
Mine, to travel—chosen acquisitions, my own.

Everything new to the eye:
stairs at the aquarium,
a new mountain to be scaled, not once
(There, I've reached the summit,) but again
and again, each time, my hand held
less tightly, until the shake of her head,
(No, no, no,) leaving me reduced
to following behind to break her fall.

She stares intently into the eyes
of children passing by, as if she's deeply
in love, prefers running back and forth
in the tunnel, to standing in front
of brightly-lit displays, until
strands of undulating seaweed
catch her eye long enough to pause,
then back to the tunnel, glancing back
to check she's not entirely alone.

AS

as love smiles in the dark
        come only for a moment
        to go away even much sooner

as truth is
        much more real
        than light

as all goes on
        no one knows if I may find the rope
            and all those needed

Aşa cum

Aşa cum iubirea zîmbeşte pe-ntuneric
        venită doar pentru o clipă
        pentru a pleca chiar mult mai iute
aşa cum adevărul este
        mult mai adevărat
        decît lumina
aşa cum merg toate
        nu se ştie de voi găsi funia
        şi cele necesare

BEING DISPOSSESSED OF APPEARANCE

I consider myself a human being
I breathe
        and I am not surprised
        at those who go to hell
I know lucidity and the song
of the flute of vanity
there is still something left for me

in the everlasting fall / of things
        the embodiments break
as logic describes and understands
                only afterwards

Deposedarea de chip

mă socot un om
respir
        şi nu mă mir / prea tare
        de cei pe care îi ia dracul
cunosc luciditatea şi cântecul din
flautul zădărniciei
cîte ceva mi-a mai rămas

în veşnica surpare / a lucrurilor
        se sparg întruchiparile
cum logica descrie şi-nţelege
                abia după

TAKE THE ROAD

awaiting the eve/awaiting the morn
before the sea
        man
his eyes watching the sky and the waves
knows
that there will /never/happen
          anything
there will come night/it will have your look
and all silent we will descend
          in the furrows of water
tearing the sewing between the soul and the body

ASTERN-TE DRUMULUI

aşteptînd seara/ aşteptînd dimineaţa
în faţa mării
        omul
cu ochii la cer şi la valuri
ştie
că nu se va-ntîmpla / niciodată/
nimic
va veni noaptea / va avea privirea ta
şi muţi vom coborî
          în brazdele de apă
      rupînd cusătura dintre suflet şi trup

All three poems translated by *Olimpia Iacob from the Romanian version*

HOLY SMOKES

He leans against the wall of the candy store, His long, dull robe cinched with a coarse rope, a leather-sandaled foot flat against a yellow-stucco wall. He exhales. Smoke lingers in His beard a moment, then rises through His long, lank hair.

He raises His chin to heaven and snaps off a smoke ring, pierces it with a second smaller yet quicker one. They rise and become haloes for passing angels, who giggle, then flit away.

A puffy cloud of text fades in at the bottom of the screen. "What would Jesus do?" then fades out as the question is answered with another cloud: "Jesus would have lit up a Holy Camel."

The camera closes in on Smoking Jesus, who turns to it and winks, blows a smoke ring that dilates into the message: "Buy Holy Camels, a Christianly inhale of heaven on Earth."

THE MEMORY OF WATER

I'm in the bathroom at the mall,
standing at the urinal
to the right of an elderly gentleman.

I finish my business, zip, flush,
and I'm on the way to the sink,
when the old guy steps back
and turns towards me,
his erect penis pinched among
his thumb, index and middle fingers,
And I think, *Here we go, some old perve...*
when I see his face and realize...

Alzheimer's.

I watch him squint,
trying to focus on something behind him,
his penis, a compass to nowhere.

I turn away, have to leave.

I can't even wash my hands.

WHILE EXAMINING YOUR SAUSAGE

In the dark of night
I am huddled, hunchbacked at the table
beneath a pyramid of light,
working the corpse,
a Creative Writing student's
poemplaystory.

I am slashing its flesh,
red ink spraying the pages,
an unclamped artery.

I am a madman, eviscerating,
pulling intestines up into light,
dangling them, twirling them,
the light glistening off the sausage of their dreams.

I drop them on their desks

one

by

one.

And as I walk away
I see my own intestines
reeling out from
the last student's desk to the next.
But I pay it no mind.

This is our last class.
Next semester — fresh meat.

THIS DAY

A man holds the hand
of his small daughter, other
daughter in tow,
waving, smiling.

The rhythm of his speech
takes our breath,
forces us to hope
when some had given up.

> *America of thee I sing!*
> *O beautiful*
> *for spacious skies!*

Words we believe in again,
the echo of other
voices, Robeson's baritone,
King's evocation

of a dream he had,
at least for this day,
come true.

LOUSE POINT

A mother osprey floats down to her pole-top nest.
Like her, a woman migrates to this Point

each summer, ready to cry aloud,
contemplating the brevity of a life span,

living with heartbreak, stretching her body
and wringing her hands, staying to watch

the small islands at low tide
rise from the bay's wetlands

until a pink hush turns into a blaze
over the water. Then just her,

like an exhausted bird, nearly finished
with the wind and the wild grasses.

PEACE

A shy, polite man, his soft voice escapes
the sound system, muffled, unheard.
His all-white audience suggests,
Move around, project, as he reads

about crawling through the jungle
into rat-filled tunnels, booby-traps waiting
to explode into the heavens, fallen parachutes
hanging from trees like death. Later, we dip

blue corn chips into hummus and drink Chardonnay.
Beyond the swimming pool in August dusk,
migrant workers stoop to pick tomatoes.
from Long Island farmland that's disappearing

like the poet's childhood
of gorging on sweet pulpy Southern
muskmelons. I hope he will recapture
his voice. That it will rise above the bulldozers

turning over earth. He signs my paperback,
"Peace."

Mario Suško

HOMEWARD BOUND

I remember tomorrow, that was all
I said when I set out on the way home,
though, by the way, if there were a way by,
tomorrow must have already happened or I
would not have remembered it, which meant
even if I had arrived where I was supposed
to arrive, back home was there no more,
for I would've made it only to yesterday,
and wouldn't that have been the very day
when I said: I remember tomorrow -

still, I followed the rusty railroad tracks,
thinking they'd have to get me somewhere,
although they were overgrown with weed,
only here and there a meager looking flower
I hopped over or walked around, often losing
my step, until I came to a gate, a spider web
iron gate with a lock shaped like a heart
on a chain around someone's neck, but there
was neither a fence nor a wall at the right
or the left of it, except two track ruts going
on and fading into a breathing shimmering haze.

I stood there, to see whether another day,
the one before or the next, was on the other
side of the gate, but then a child appeared
as if he stepped through a curtain, jumping
unsteadily from one invisible sleeper onto
the other, from time to time flapping his arms
to maintain the balance, and he came to me,
his cheeks all puffed up, took a key
out of his mouth and unlocked the gate.

I could have gone around, I uttered, but he
smiled and said: Walls and fences are not absent
Because we don't see them, but you remembered
Tomorrow, so you can pass and go home with me.

he turned around and jumped onto the first patch
of scarred dirt, and I followed, the sleepers
getting farther apart, our leaps ever more daring,
and I waved my arms, and he flapped his, as if we
were going to leave the earth and fly up, still
two playful kids on their way home, not to be
caught out too late, overtaken by darkness.

IN THE CLASSROOM

the night slowly chokes the light
around us   and she closes the book
her hand hovering above the cover
History Primer: A Short Guide

we look at each other
    as if trying to remember
each other's face before it becomes
    its own shadow

the building's roof's a charred skeleton
the classroom floor littered with textbooks
notebooks   the village half burned
deserted   except for one donkey

braying in the field   as the two of us
came down the road   two animals approaching
warily from the opposite direction
    trying to sniff each other out

she placed two hand-grenades
on the desk   that now look to me
like overgrown exotic pears
    we are going to feast on

History is supposed to teach us
something but it never does   she
almost yells   I look at the blackboard
    and make out its message

TELLING STORIES

where do I go from here if where I
came from turned out to be nowhere

and how do I tell you that now
when unscripted deeds lord over words:

for the sake of bare survival I traded
instincts for second-hand reflexes

but there are only so many ways to breathe
and read the trajectory of the past

what to hold off and what to hold on
as zero degree defines the angles:

could that have been the reason
I left you in another story: to save you

or to save myself and come to this
point wrapped in your frayed army

coat stained with blood I don't
remember whether yours or mine

as if to see how much space there is
left before we run out of time

before the stories run out of words
and we end up with nothing to tell

having been devised by someone else
who may have already rewritten the future.

Douglas G. Swezey

#507 (NIGHT TERRORS)

The whole of me
Is as good as half of you
Endless nights slept beside you
Your warmth against me in the same bed.
Yet still, I miss you so much of the time.
No time for talk or play,
Just the hypnotic REM
Between work and work again.
Unconscious midnight ramblings
Dot my existence with you.
I wish it were more.
Maybe a waterbed
Would be better.
Or a bed of nails,
To keep us up at night.

#543 (WATCHING ONE WATCHING SHARON OLDS)

Her legs were poised
Grey, but pinstriped
Crossed, but open to me
Sitting next to me
Hands clasped
Around the paper label
Of a bottle
Of water
Of the clarity
Of life
Soft novelty socks
Adorned about ankles
Too, poised
One raised in the air
Over the other
But solemnly so
Her head tilted
So as to better understand
By the view
Of words floating past her ear
Until true climax is reached
Apexing peak
Is visible on her sweet face
When the smile rises,
Eyes become small
And the laughter of
Knowledge exudes

#583 (YES)

With Thanks To Gloria g. Murray

What ecstasy is there in "No"?
I find none.
It is confusion
Abandoned sanity
Wanton bliss
Spread out wide
Across the abyss
It is "Yes" over and over
With little discretion
Or discrimination
Screaming ruby wild
Sapphire green
Flailing silly
Aching arms
Scratchy throat
Heaving breast
Longing for breath
Pangs of pain
Prodding my side
It is the pleasure
Of after
Of reflection
In letting go
Forgetting regret
There lies
Ecstasy

Patti Tana

THE SECRET OF LIFE

Watching my dog sleep beside me
I discover the secret of life: Air
rhythmically swells and shrinks
her whole body — a bellows
    pulsing with life
        inspired by air.

This ubiquitous elixir
fills our lungs, aerates our blood,
bubbles in our brain.
Asleep and awake
    we ride the waves of air
        as long as we live.

As long as we live we breathe
this invisible essential,
and we pass it on
one being to another
    this anonymous gift
        this blessing that keeps us alive

WHAT REMAINS

I wish I'd saved a wisp of her hair,
a white curl to keep beside her picture.
I still hear her voice rising with endearments,
dark chocolates hidden in the drawer,
still see her smile, the smile she raised me with
and the peaceful smile she left on her pillow.
Today I placed an envelope with money
by her picture for her to hold for me
the way she always did.

Mama, when you motioned for me to hold you
I slipped beneath the thin
white blankets of your hospital bed.
Pointing to the window you asked
What's going on out there?
Thinking of the storms that had washed away so many
I said *You don't want to know.*
For a long time we laughed together,
my body curled around your body, so small, so light

HARD WIRINGS

I

Along the jagged ruts and slants
in my approach to the cornered home
newly fenced, with new faces,
new belongings purling an undersong
spilling over and through the shiny
spaced stakes, each so elegantly
mounted with a little hatted light,
as I jog by a few times a week,
I've seen in piecemeal, an extended family,
an unsharpened strangeness in
the old man's wound turban,
the old woman's draped head and body--
I've welcomed the comprehendible tongue
of the children's catch-me, catch-me frolic,
and then that tilt of the old man's head
when I dared wave into the strangeness,
to an Omar Sharif ardor in his dark, aged eyes,
a bloom of smile when I pushed off
the 911-Iraq-terrorist track,
and eased into a solace underneath
my own feet, feeling the level ground.
So smile and gesture became our idiom
leading us back to a knowing country,
and when he pointed to the sky at my wave,
I knew he was praying to a god I couldn't access,
as I knew we'd come from that same native place.

II

Does nature hunger to destroy?
Could that be why two little hats were awry?
Just that small a slant cut off their lights?
On my next jog by, the fence was fixed.
But within a week, one light was missing,
and one was hanging by its exposed wires,
while the wind's poker face brushed it back
and forth, back and forth, like my assuming mind--
wired prankster goblins or gobbling blind hate
yanked by wires to darkness like wooden heads?

On my next jog by, the fence was fixed.
But within two weeks, a stake was severed
from their ground, three hats were skewed,
and one light was smashed beyond repair.
On my next jog by, the fence was fixed.
I kept looking for the grandfather, though I knew
he couldn't tell me what hunger for darkness
struck again, and again, till torn light-veins were left--
The fence was never fixed again.
And I never saw that man again.
Just jogging by, today, I was thinking
how more people say they'll vote for Obama,
but that their friends will vote for McCain.
What strange forces decapitating lights
lie hidden, like the little curled up dimensions
where our invisible strings vibrate?
Peace to the man who prayed outside.
Peace to his family, his garden, his fence.

MUCH ADO

Next day, as I jog around
the ring-shaped route I've known
some forty and some odd years,
the gusty wind piles up leaves
much as our marital moods get
swept up, suddenly, along my purview
as I go treading through--last night
how our tenderness was leafing out
and toward each other, drawing in
upon our shared colorful day,
the gripping, long-running Broadway play,
blowing our diets with potato pancakes,
pastrami piled on triple deckers,
crunching up Kit Kats and a meshwork
of amassed anecdotes we reshaped
and cracked-up over on a sunny bench
right in the heart of our bustling lives,
in bustling midtown, our afternoon off,
so there would be love-making
we knew from all this gathering fullness
pressing us, flesh to flesh, in our bed,
buoyed by the same rocking springs
of our long, shared story upon each other,
but where we rolled apart last night,
some sudden gust scattering our dreams
into separate corners, the covers piled
on each, on a separate side of the bed,
mighty forces reshuffling our seasoned colors,
inexplicably, just as they would roll us each
toward each, next night, or the one after that.

Peter Thabit-Jones

A GIFT FROM SAG HARBOR.
LONG ISLAND, U.S.A
for Vince and Annie Clemente

A whaling-seaman's whistle,
The size of a man's finger;

A serious, ocean toy;
A warning in weathered wood;

A pocket, blank totem pole,
Its shrill narrative sleeping.

A relic of the ocean,
Smooth as beached stone in my palm.

I blow for notes of the sea,
The call of an unknown bird.

I hear a command, a plea.
A picture of me, a boy.
Sails my waves of memories.
A cadet in uniform,

Cold on a ship off Mumbles,
Tipsy legs longing for land.

As water bashed starboard side,
As one crew man piped my fears

And loutish gulls tore the sky.
The frantic call to duty

Of a glinting whistle's scream.
The water wild below us,

The spit of spouting salt spray,
My Grandpa's house on Kilvey

Shrinking, shrinking: and Ahab's
Nightmare breaching in my mind.

401

BLACK WINGS

Black wings of death
Over my dying child,
Folded wings of my love
That cannot save his breath.

Black wings of death
Whirring through all my thoughts,
Folded wings of my soul
Weeping feathers of breath.

Black wings of death
Cover my shining prayers,
Folded wings of my grief
That choke my words, my breath.

Black wings of death
Stopping the starry night.
Folded wings of his heart
Bearing boulders of breath.

Black wings of death,
Folded wings of my world,
In the silent corner
All the angels of breath.

STARS
in memory of Terry Hetherington, Welsh poet

Stars shine,
flowers of broken glass
on the mind's black carpet.

The prayers of gods
solidified,
romantic notes

written by time's
slow burning.
They snag

the deadened eyes
of the loneliest
of men.
The night's burrs,
frosted codes
of the earth-palaced

kings of Egypt,
how they scratch
the stares of silence,

wound like fine dust
the emptied-out soul,
the universe of being.

Snow cobwebs
of shining thoughts,
brooding

with eternity,
unfinished elegy
on the page of the sky.

THE MASSACRE OF THE INNOCENTS
*(1630-2) a painting by Nicolas Poussin in
Musée Candé, Chantilly*

It is the foot on the baby's throat
That really hits home,
Reaches the parent of any child.

And the wild sword held
To decapitate the pure head,
The face as pale as snow.

Oh the kneeling mother's
Anguished face,
Shocked with the fear,

Begging and struggling, oh silently
Crying forever
In the moments of one man's madness,

The freeze-framed
Killing of innocence.
One masculine hand grips

Her hair with violence,
Prevents the intervention of love.
The terror of a soldier,

Ordered by Herod to murder
The helpless hope of the future
In an envious frenzy of blood.

Aeronwy Thomas

NIGHT WATCH

I am the watchman waiting for dawn
through the night
I see the stars and moon
pasted on the backcloth sky
lighting familiar shapes
to gross shadows.

I strain to see the brook
running behind the copse
fingers of light
shaken by wind
flicker.

Dawn will surely come
the brook and the birds on their trees
return
I sit and wait
all the night
hours.

PAINSHILL POETS

You blend into autumnal colours
red, orange, yellow and brown
sweeping boughs of trees
conceal you.
Your voice cannot be heard
above the wind
the crunch of dead leaves
the thud of chestnuts.
you fight to read
your words flutter
through ruins, follies, lakes, vineyards
but leaves and poems
colours and sounds
will have their way.

PARASOL

Today I saw you
on the sunny side
of the road
smiling and waving
until a pedestrian jostled you
and you scuttled across
to join me the other side
a pool of gloom –
shouldn't have spoken
about Mother's death –
until you remembered
an urgent appointment
escaping in the nick of time
from the shady side,
to enjoy the rest of the day
in full sun,
your sunhat to protect you
from its overpowering rays.

PUNTA LOS LOPOS, CARMEL BAY, CALIFORNIA

Seals look like dead
matter on a sandfloor
brought there in a burp
of a sealion wave.

We've battled through
stinging oak to get here
to hear the bark
of a seal

waking from slumber
ready to slip sleek
into a wave of foaming white
rhythmic, inevitable.

A cormorant dives for fish
emerges yards away
by islands of seaweed
the waters peacock blue.

We've battled through
stinging oak to get here
to hear the bark
of a seal.

Two seagulls perch
on a seabound rock
chat amongst themselves
preen

letting the seals
seawolves
predate the fishy waters,
prowlers.

Coated and mufflered
I'm waiting here
on the cliff
away from the crumbly edge

crunching needles of
Monterey fir

stripped by the winds
to a petrified marker

the end of the world
the smell of yerba nueva
and wild lilac
in the undergrowth.

We've walked through
grey mauve blooms
on our way here
to the edge

of a seaworld
seals and birds
los lopos marinyas
gabbing gulls.

I am looking and laughing
in the salt-laden air
as I loose my footing
and the cliff disappears.

SWIMMERS

Angry sea
we are swimming
one east one west
splashing overarm
to calmer waters
away from the swell
with words sinking
into swirls and eddies
sea weed or fish
sliding slippery
out of grasp.

Already
you're so far away
always a good swimmer
the tide turning
the words said
floatable, reachable
between heavy strokes
despite fatigue
and reluctance
to grasp again
what was said.

As my feet touch ground
in the shallows
words surface
on a rippling wave
covered with
the oil of tankers

of scum
and clinging animal life
the last words
you said to me
let's end

and I tumble on to the shore
to watch you waving
far out
at sea

Juanita Torrence-Thompson

DRIVING ROBERT DE NIRO
—A SESTINA

A young cab driver from Brazil
Drove Robert DeNiro
The famous actor
In his private taxi
One night zipping
Through the busy streets of New York.

The driver was new to New York
And the streets were different in Brazil
Where it's easier to zip
Through crowded streets. DeNiro
Hopped into the front seat of the taxi
When the driver didn't recognize the actor.

Don't you go to the movies asked the actor?
I don't have time to go to the movies in New York
I'm too busy driving my taxi.
I drove a cab in Brazil.
What do you do when not hacking asked DeNiro
I go home, eat watch TV and eyes zipped

Shut for 10 hours. Ten hours your eyes are zipped
Shut asked the actor?
This is hard to believe said DeNiro.
You're a young man in this great city of New York
and you just vegetate like a Brazil
nut. You live to drive your taxi

12 hours a day! I drove a taxi
in the movie "Taxi Driver" and I zipped
through streets. If you were in Brazil
what would you be doing now, asked the actor?
Having fun with friends. I have no friends in New York.
Don't let that stop you, said DeNiro.

Look, you have a friend, I'm your friend, Robert DeNiro.
You need to enjoy life. Get out of this taxi.
Turn right, take the second left. There's plenty to do in New York.
You're going to have fun and zip
With me, whom you've never seen act
In movies, not even in Brazil.

Stop at this nightclub. You're DeNiro's guest. Forget the taxi.
I'll pay the taxi and tips, me the actor
You've never heard of in New York or Brazil.

STRANGER IN THE WILDERNESS

For years he trod familiar streets after sunrise and returned before sunset. Today he ate oatmeal, then dressed -- one blue sock, one grey. His wife made him coordinate. He laughed his nervous laugh; slid on two grey. He longed to go to work, but his office had shut down.

Every day he took his thermos of hot chocolate, his attaché case, boarded the sleek blue bus, got off at Grove and Spring Street. Every day he walked by the brown brick building with a FOR SALE sign, hoping to see former co-workers. Every day he sat on the lower wall watching school children file into class. At noon he walked the block to O'Malley's Restaurant for lunch. He talked to Katie, the redhead with a hairnet and too much makeup. "Spanish omelet?" She asked. He smiled. Nodded yes.

Today he did not take his thermos. He walked past the bus stop to the park and sat on a jade wooden bench. It began to drizzle. The drops pelted his alabaster hair, which needed a trim. He wandered the streets for hours, then remembered his house was 22 Rose Avenue. He peered through the window. His wife was crying. He rang the bell like a stranger. His grateful wife ran down the hall, flung open the door and hugged him for a long, long time.

TURN DOWN THE SUN

Today golden sprinkled
through our lacey curtains.
Down the clay road
Near Tompkins' old barn
A stranger squinted,
Rang Jeb Tompkins doorbell
Which played "She'll Be Comin'
Round the Mountain"
Not a plain chime,
But a silly song selected
By Jeb's new wife Laurel Lee.

Always putting on airs
Trying to be different
From us plain folks.
Sashaying about in her
Designer finery
Best worn at Buckingham Palace

But Jeb needed a woman
To help run his place
And keep him company.
His money was legendary
Which drew her to old Jeb,
Who was meaner than
A fox on a trampoline.

The man began plowing
Jeb's alfalfa field.
Laurel Lee came outside in a
White virginal dress to
Hang up her personal laundry
All the while smiling and nodding
To the muscular stranger.
With a tattoo. At least it looks
Like a tattoo on his arm
through these binoculars.
It's none of my never mind.
I'd best get to the canning.
Can't wait to hear the gossip
Tonight at Johnson's barn dance.
My Lord it's sticky.
I'd better turn on the fan.

Edilberto González Trejos

DNA

Egyptian Smoke
of an Atlantis Fire
Ashes of mine:
Mayan Embers
still burning.

ADN

Humo Egipcio
del Fuego Atlante
cenizas mías:
Brasas Mayas
(que) aún arden.

FEARSOME

A lifespan wasted in fear
a quest for revelation,
only dim lights outside
in the Pilgrim's Night;
Romancing the Stone
even when dreams
seem to sink like a paper boat.

TEMIBLE
Esta vida se me escurre entre temores,
aquella búsqueda por la revelación,
apens luces pálidas afuera
en la noche del peregrino;
Batido en el cortejo de la piedra
aun cuando los sueños
parezcan hundirse cual bote de papel.

MAGNETISM

Within the urban labyrinths
you find sharp corners
fields charged of electricity
Treacherous Magnetism?
Electric Surprise?
The sidewalk silently shelters
the secret sacrifice
of rubber and flesh.

MAGNETISMO
En los laberintos urbanos
encuentras esquinas punzantes
campos cargados de electricidad
¿Magnetismo traicionero?
¿Sorpresa eléctrica?
La acera resguarda silenciosa
el sacrificio secreto
del caucho y la carne.

MOON SONG

Tonight
the moon sings
I drink its light
through my pores
like an Electric Broth,
wild and erect
in a Moondance
I fertilize dry dreams
of an Old Soul.

CANTO LUNAR

Esta noche
la luna canta
sorbo su luz por mis poros
cual brebaje eléctrico,
salvaje y erguido
en una Danza Lunar
fertilizo sueños secos
de un Alma Vieja.

Jack Tricarico

A BEACHCOMBER'S STORY

I am a multicolored comb
That braids rainbows
Or a glass eye
Sunbathing on sand

I was erased by love and now
At the end of a long story
Who am I, really? Every thought
Is a door. In an instant I'm here
And in another I'm someplace else

There's no order in this
Whoever I am
I have to make a decision
Should I go back to beer?
Or follow a straight line
That may never end anywhere?

These mind altering salads
Are for graduates in madness
And I am only a little off key
With an atonal gong in my head
And my fixation on circles
Which is just nauseating

I was informed by a sandbar
The shape of a toad outlines the sun
This may imply that the sun is the child
Of a toad or vice versa. Implications
Are self-generating. I don't trust them
If I imagine a pot of gold
I feel cheated. A watch, a ring or a shoe
May tell stories and one day even recover
A life, like my own

When nothing comes up on the beach
I sit by the waves and listen
Waves have a language
Like someone mumbling in their sleep

And the cries of the gulls
Looking for something to eat
Clouds fall from the sky
Like crumbs brushed from a table
And night always arrives with a thud

ORGANIC ART

The shape of a bird
Formed by a bubble of spit
The branch of a tree
Shaped by a gesture of awe
The chasm between one foot and another
When indecision divides us in half
A puddle of rain
Suspended in air
Interrupted by your outline
Against a lit window
In the dark
Only another clue
About the mother of everything
But why meddle
In universal comparisons
If we are enough
At the end of a truly successful night

Martin Tucker

HOOKED

What made him do it?
The first time, needy. The other times
the headiness he felt
when nothing happened,
no one cautioned about it.
Months later a phone call.
He forgot calls were taped.
When did he know tomorrow
would not only be different
but would never lead again to yesterday?
And when must he have known he had been set up,
he who was the master of such techniques.

Some men have time to grasp their fall,
others have moments to prepare their loved one.
I, who have secrets, wonder what he felt in that moment of knowing.
Perhaps there is a satisfaction
in being caught in one's lair of hiding.
Perhaps having nothing more to hide is the gift of peace.

RAISIN SCONE

A raisin scone disappeared this morning.
I bought it at a hefty price in Grand Central.
Such scones are valued in memory of warm kitchens
and their presences on mellowing tables.

My mother did not bake scones--
but approximation counts.
We called the blond mounds coffee cake
and ate their fuel like cars driving down hills.
That's why I'm searching for the raisin scone I bought this morning.
I'm sure I took it on the LIRR train with me.
I think that's where I left it,
though why I should abandon such a loved one,
homeless and living in a brown bag,
consumes my passion now.

I've been looking all day in all my corners,
finding letters I've not answered for years.
I'd search the Internet if that would help,
but baked items don't smell on the screen.
It's discomforting to know a comfort anticipated--
the elevenish repast of blooming flour--
is burning my day by a no-show.
Worse, the yeast in me is rising, I fear,
to remind me forgetting things is an oven
I no longer can shut down.

TEEN-AGERS OF ALL AGES

Going to a movie is half the picture.
One needs as well the ticket of an arm,
not so much to lean upon
as cushion appraisals coming from the aisle.

WHY I TEACH THE HOLOCAUST

I teach the Holocaust to wear beneath my clothes
an awareness of skin beyond casual wear.

I have many skins.
I am far from the core of my onion.

I teach the Holocaust
to touch my deepest skin.

BENEDIZIONE
for Chloe Ellen Lyga

Wednesday, October 8, 2008,
the Roman sun is shining on a throng
of thousands of parishioners and tourists
who flank Saint Peter's Square at the Vatican
waiting for him to arrive, to pass by,
right hand waving his *benedizione*,
his blessing, to all assembled.

You're there, Chloe, but you won't remember
what we will never forget. You're 6 months
and 4 days old and you're wearing
a lavender outfit, shirt emblazoned
with purple flowers. His driver approaches,
you're taken in capable hands and held
until his driver slows, then stops.

It's 12:26pm, Chloe
you're lifted to his hands, which cradle
your head as he kisses you, and the crowd,
thousands of the blessed cheer for you, Chloe,
cheer for him as his driver carries him along
bestowing his blessing as his Popemobile
moves on.

Yes Chloe, kissed by Pope Benedict XVI –
his general audience began with *In nomine Patris,
et Filii, et Spiritus Sancti Amen*, and ended
Chloe, with you being kissed by the Pope,
a blessing reserved for angels-in-the-making ...
so not really a surprise, Chloe
as you're already an angel-on-earth.

CURVE IN THE ROAD

There is nothing reckless about it

a friend is rattled that he may have hit
a squirrel as it scampered across the road
in front of his car, nothing he could do
nowhere to go on a single lane road
not speeding, not sunblind this cloudy day,

nothing reckless about his driving

but his concern for the squirrel
had him turning around to drive by
to see what he wouldn't/couldn't
– I assured him – shouldn't describe –
the squirrel was dead.

There is nothing reckless

about a squirrel on a November roadway
crossing over to gather a store of walnuts
for snow season approaching,
a car approaching as he reaches his destiny
crossing over to an eternal field of acorns.

There is nothing reckless about my friend

who goes home, collects himself and returns
to the squirrel, through his open window,
ground tobacco offering tossed in blessing
as an American Indian tribute to the spirit
of the squirrel, representing a gathering of wealth.

There is nothing reckless about it

to not abandon the squirrel, whose essence
will remain in mind and spirit long beyond today;
my reaction to my friend's actions is a blessing,
a reaffirmation of a caring soul gathering the wealth
of the universe, an undying respect.

FLASH-CARD FREDDY

It's harmless
We meet a few times a week at a red light
on Hillside; initially a coincidence but I've seen him
slow his big-rig 10-wheeler down to a crawl

to let a Corolla or Benz slip in front of him,
to wait for the light, wait for me to catch up so he
could line up beside me, peer down through my sunroof.

He's got rectangles of rough-cut cardboard
stacked on his dash, marked with black Sharpie
messages he flashes to commuters ... or is it just me?

Flash me, Freddy
it's Monday blues on a Thursday morning
no hot water for my shower, the milk went sour
I'm late for work and my cell is dead

Flash me, Freddy
flip through your bold cap phrases, pretend a passion
for me, print me a fantasy I'll never experience
pay me a compliment I don't deserve –
    nice legs
    gr-8 smile
    give me a wink
    blow me a kiss
– perhaps you've added to your flash-card collection
been late-night writing on box flaps, composing
poeticizing to woo me in silent plea ... or is it not just me?

Flash me, Freddy
crash the doldrums of driving alone
crack the reality of red-yellow-green
break the boredom of white lines on black macadam

with the ruptured roar of your mighty engine, your rigid lines
on rugged tires – don't reveal your real name, don't say a word
don't burst the spell of commuting, communicating, flirting
        with Flash-card Freddy

GLOBAL WARMING

Apparently, December didn't get the memo
about tropical winds sweeping heated waves of swelter
across our planet. It seems like yesterday, meteorologists
were forecasting hundred degree days for today, tomorrow,
next week, month, all year every year. I'd say, global warming is a lie,
a grand falsification, a prevarication of misleading misinformation
meant to make us worry about the increase in anthropogenic
greenhouse gas concentrations.

Yeah right; it's all a whopper of steaming delusion
because it's Big Freddy frigid outside, boulders of snow
big as a Mack truck and twice-as-mean-frigid,
so freaking frozen cold that Frosty can't feel his carrot nose;
he's booked a flight to Bermuda in the morning.

So numbing glacial that icicles shiver from phone lines
too cold to take calls, frozen shingles of asphalt on rooftops
that turn Santa's runway into a downhill ski slope
not meant for sleighs. Ice Dagwood-sandwich-thick
on sidewalks so slick, the dog skates to the fire hydrant
with me in tow but he's too cold to go, and we both go
tobogganing on our butts into the street where SUVs
boogie-woogie from curb to curb like a pinball off bumpers.

It's so frickin frigid, man, that words hang in the air,
the wind frozen in place, not even Ernie, our mail carrier
can stand it; he's sitting inside our blazing fireplace with Frosty
who can't fly from an airport that's a frozen rink of jet skaters
and there's nothing globally warm about that.

Yeah, it's bad, my nose is packed with freon,
teardrops leak and freeze on my cheeks,
my ears feel like a pair of Moscow ice sculptures,
what isn't frostbitten won't move –
we've entered the ice age,
and they say beware of global warming –
Hey Al Gore,
Melt this!

Kempton B. Van Hoff

A GOOD CAPTAIN KNOWS

Struggles of brothers and sisters last
good feeling lasts the first I see you
amidst risen rain departing veins of green sunset
on me and we are crazy skin turning alabaster
thoughts to run down feelings nearing
bitter portions of cords lengthy for the living.

Dredge Drudgery.

Sail my pride on out through harbor and river mouth and sink it.

Taking action many made able
in fables spun to clarify in
rising beauty of what's fact lost in lyric fearful
potential teachers squoze control and rose different phoenix
leaning heavy on every kid who couldn't hold tight the lunch money
wading in afternoons of this with grin up and chin set
thin and topping off flowing air with sodium.
Yes it's me – me is him.

Dredge drudgery.

Sail pride on out through harbor and river mouth.

Sink it.

Swimming.

MESSAGES HOME (I)

When I am confident
clear beauty is wrapped safely
in a blanket of my words
the hunter watches me away
where gospel through branches
is frozen truth teaching
warm heart tonight
I laugh with Isaac
this almost whole day
before the feast we
ladel our salt stew
laden with all of the pieces
of the beast others would never eat
when we were confident enough
we had to take home to clear-eyed dear ones
we looked at the backs of our eyes' lids and
quickly through dream prepared us
and with hunter watching
we struck from fire another morning
light heralded by stealing away
through brittle skeletons stunning only as the safe ones we laughed for
who graced those aft surfaces of Loving lids through those
      impressions
      in the other pieces of our living.

ON SEEING SEASON

This western sky is consuming the atlas
crafted in the interior of atmosphere
can hear you here cotton slate and indigo
these growing days
teach alone the vibrating branch
signals that original significance
sees me back here sending messages
weathervaned, touched with paint
from spear tip the listener can hear you here
these growing days bring Equinox'
solitude birthright gift
throwing weapons down
today allows passage to land
over polar energy cradle reins
the light in these growing days
with collected vapor
hours chill ground
softens as the worn is birthed
over older gray and greet someone
at the end of this day
                            growing

Kausalya Venkateswaran &
Pramila Venkateswaran

MOUTHING GOD

I love the word seed
in Sanskrit—*beej.*

I roll it in my mouth:
It travels from my pursed

lips to stop short
of the roof.

My tongue barely holds
it before it vanishes.

Seeds are magical;
how they sprout

an entire pantry
to feed a world

created from
an original.

This sound I
pronounce

is the first sound
that holds millions

of facsimiles,
multiverses, theories.

It feeds its singular syllable
to this frivolous verse.

Translation from the Tamil by Kausalya Venkateswaran

கடவுளின் சத்தமில்லா ஒலி

விதை என்ற வார்தை
மிகவும் பிடிதமானது

சம்ச்க்ருதத்தில் "பேஜ்."
வாயில் உருண்டு பயனம் செய்து

உதட்டின் மேல் சிரிது தயங்கி
பிரகு நாக்கில் நழுவி உள்ளெ மறையும்

விதைகள் மந்திர கோல்கள்
முளைத்து விளைந்து பயிராகி

உலகனைத்தும் பசியாற்றுகிரது
சுயமாக விளைகிரது.

நான் உச்சரிக்கும் முதல் குரல்
கோடிக்கண்க்கான வர்களின் குரல்

இதுதான் உலகமனைத்தும்
அடிப்படை தத்துவம்

உலகோர் பசிபோக்கும் இரட்டை அக்ஷரம்
நான் பாடும் அற்ப பாடல்.

429

Pramila Venkateswaran

UNBURDENING THE CAMEL

Burdened we are,
Camel and I, as we carry our load
            through history.

Unyoked, often, from the caravan,
                we sway down
            onto to gravelly sand
to rest our knees.

        At some point before this poem
ends, or after, you may decide
            if this analogy is
            unfortunate.

Under a cold moon,
our bodies, color of desert
            winds, blend into the road
                well-hewn or erased
            from memory.

Our hunger at bay,
            we count past moments of
                fulfillment as we lean back
                into the night sky and
exhale: Flesh and earth join
            reverentially.

Rest--our sweet panacea--ease
            the length and breadth of us,
right up to our restorative
                        humps.

Ah, now let the earth carry our burden.

VISITING ALEPPEY HOUSE

My mind is dark, too dark to entertain
shadows of the Aleppey house as afternoons
give way to roadside lanterns, bugs rising
out of the gutters, fireflies limning mango
and chikku trees that have taken over the yard.
A couple of doors, a shuttered window, some inches
of faded wall ponder the former vastness--
three magnificent entrances, nannies, gardeners,
cooks, and maids entering and leaving, kids
playing hopscotch or swinging on the gates,
women drying their hair by the window,
the hurry of the day, the sound of the seasons.

Time decides that only a fragment of the family tree
will live in part of the house to preserve fading memory.
Ah, irony! This house shakes awake that which I would
like to stay hidden, thunderous footsteps, the patriarchal
decibels ranging from critical observation to commands,
the suddenly silenced singing, the hush after a storm.

Let the voices fade into the undergrowth. Better the bean
vines and the summer scents overwhelm the brick and tile
than my ghost joining ancestral expeditions.

VRIKSHASANA – TREE POSE

> Urdhva mula madha shakam/ ashvattam prahuravyayam
> The ashvatta tree with its roots above and branches below
> --Bhagvadgita Ch.13

Are my roots above
or below?
Do my roots
snake into the earth
to drink from the well
of *nagas*,
or do they reach
higher and higher
into invisibility?

Only this torso signals
my presence
on this planet where my sisters
and brothers are cut down.

Can you hear their screams?

I hold my torso,
unwavering,
my arms closing around
my matted hair,
palms in prayer,
enduring this massacre.
No trial.
No judge.
No jury.
Plenty of witnesses.

Balance is hard
even when the winds
die down.
Storms rage within
threaten to uproot me.
My roots above aim
toward the clouds.
Looking back at earth
would mean vertigo
and collapse.

Sattva, sattva, sattva,
my mantra keeps me
upright, upward reaching,
my gaze locked
in the seed of this sound.
rescuing me from inertia.

Nagas = snakes
Sattva sattva, sattva = Absolute Goodness

George Vulturescu

DEATH AND READING

Nothing more unchanged under the sun
than the birds that come to the corpse of the horse,
than the eyes that come to the books, ever others,
                    to spread the letters.
          Death and reading are ashes
                    beneath which the corpse is ever identified

Moartea şi lectura

Nimic mai neschimbat sub soare
precum păsările care vin la hoitul calului,
precum ochii care vin la cărţi, mereu alţii,
                    să răsfire literele.
Moartea şi lectura sunt cenuşi sub
                    care hoitul e mereu recunoscut

GOLDEN HORA*

Today   I have seen
a heap of stones on the way.
Among the screes
they've looked like deer muzzles.
They have almost seemed to follow me,
as if a flock close behind the shepherd.
You need to wait,
I have said to them. Someone else needs to show up,
another man, so that
I am stoned to death.

Aurea hora

Azi pe cărare am văzut o
grămadă de pietre.
Între grohotişuri păreau
nişte botişori de
căprioară. Aproape că
se luau după mine,
ca o turmă după păstor.
-Trebuie să aşteptaţi,
le-am zis.E nevoie să
mai apară altcineva,
înca un om, ca să mă
lapideze cu voi.

* horă: Romanian round dance

THE FENCE

I practise the place of the letter like my father in the garden:
first he struck the acacia stakes into the earth
then he brought wattle and wove between them the fence

the following morning I was agog to leap over there
in the orchard of Old Achim, for cherries

now the loops between the letters are your breath,
reader, you eat the cherries for me
never mind, but leap first over the fence to steal them.

Gardul

Exersez locul literei precum tatăl meu în grădină:
întâi bătea în pământ ţăruşi de salcâm
apoi aducea nuiele şi împletea, printre ei, gardul

în dimineaţa următoare abia aşteptam să sar dincolo
în ograda lui Moş Achim, după cireşe

acum buclele dintre litere sunt respiraţia ta,
cititorule, tu mănânci cireşele pentru mine
nu-i bai, dar mai întîi sari gardul şi fură-le

All poems translated by Olimpia Iacob from the Romanian version

Lois V.Walker

THE SHELL

The shell I pick up
is now my shell, yes
the swirls of hardened
matter repeat a pattern
the pattern rises and falls
over and over again
while pinnacles appear
to protect a soft ooze
that has disappeared
devoured by unnamed
creatures or has left to grow
a larger house
but I will never
ever know for sure
simple fact
it remains a hard
object in my hand

THE UMBRELLA AND THE RAIN

In this fairy tale
the red umbrella
with a carved handle
rests on an iron bench.

Not raining now
but it will

Its handle is a black snake
with ancient flakes
of mica cut, set in wood
flashing patches of light

Not raining now
but it will

The prize can open for her
even give shelter, but first
her hands must touch the snake
grasp its strange coldness

Not raining now
but it will

Abandoned there the umbrella
gives off a hard cold light
but she doesn't claim a cover
from the rain   But it will come.

George Wallace

AGES OF A MAN

seven is chasing butterflies with a wooden sword
thirteen almost chokes to death in salt water
three is patting its red rump with talcum powder
who can even remember two or one?
eight is coloring eggs with an apron on
six is a shaving brush with big fat soapy bubbles
fifteen is a brown spider in the woodshed
five took me to the movies and held my hand
nine has a halloween hangover again
four is holding scalded milk on its tongue
twelve has fingers the color of nicotine
what is fourteen hiding under the bed?
sixteen will not write a thank you note
seventeen drove the car into a wishing well

eleven is hotter than a kid with mumps
so is ten, it's been eating firecracker soup

INTO THE DEEP GRASS OF AUTUMN

her mother had
the arms of a dowager
she has the arms of a pin cushion
tripping through the rainy streets of chelsea
like a punchdrunk merchant marine
like an old cubist with plenty
of time on his hands
and no new ideas
she moves like a bride moves
through placid water
she floats like a boxer floats
into the fateful ring
she flows like yellow light flows
out of her sculpture studio
into the arms of
a fool tsunami
she's got no friends
she has no lover
she is like a helicopter
hovering over new orleans
she makes no waves
she moves easily
through influential men
diamond bracelet women
all the worn out critics in town
applauding like a letterbomb
it does not please her
the opiate of fame
it does not please her
the smoke and dope of opinion
only this audience
with death
pleases her

she moves like
a georgia breeze moves
over swamp water
into the deep grass of autumn

IT IS A MAN'S WORK

it is a man's work
but it boils like a
bubbling pot of
witches oil --
caulking tar
sitting on a rock
waiting for the tide to
come in, waiting for
the one who will come this morning
to repair the hull of
an overturned
coracle -- then,
under the cold irish sun,
someone like a child
saunters by &
curiosity
gets the better
of him --
he reaches
in, burns the skin
off his right
hand

TOO MANY WORDS

too many words cross the boulevard
without looking both ways. too many words
enter the recruiting station with
empty hands and come out carrying a gun.
too many words leave their sons and
daughters behind or their parents
or their wives or husbands.
too many words
sit in front of a television screen
watching the twentyfour hour news for
twentyfour hours. too many words stuff a duffel bag
with fists of sand. too many words go blind.
too many words come home without
their legs on, without their helmets
on, come home without their
buddies or their minds.
too many words stay at home
and write about things they don't understand.
too many words die crossing a desert
that never asked to be crossed.

Richard Walsh

BERRYMAN MID-FLIGHT

Berryman, Berryman, mid-flight,
Did you try to fly? Too sudden a
Thud? Bounce or just implode?
A whim or a performance,
Metaphor galumphed? A final, futile
Deconstruction? You old coot,
Was it Henry you saw that last
Spacetime, maybe Mistress Anne?
Not Mr. Bones, all cackle and coal?
Oh, I know—it was clots of Dad,
Wasn't it? Then?: Did Hart hit on you
Or just enumerate the ironies?
Any keys to Weldon (I couldn't
Resist)? Did Sylvia mean it?
Just another elaborate masque?

So, you sorry sack of syllables,
Fill me in, did the crazy make
The poems, or the poems the crazy?
Truthbeauty, beautytruth—mere
Marginalia; the dancer become the dance;
Language exhausted, gods pinwheeled;
Must we fear high things?
        Was it too much
Dark or too much light tripped the switch?
Did you get what you wanted from the ice?
Should the cirrhotic poet sip away
Until inspired, or will a jingle do?
Life? Synecdoche or just punctuation?

SCUD STUDS AND HOLLYWOOD TRUTH

the TV War, the nightly living room event—
watching scuds over Baghdad, blazes in the
distance, with Arthur Kent and was it Wolf Blitzer—
my wife's co-workers in their
Israeli owned company receiving daily
reports of hits and near misses.
There is something soothing about a missile,
something reassuring about a newsman on top
of a quivering hotel reporting on casualties
and chance encounters with security forces,
his fear palpable yet controlled in the name
of Pulitzer or some such—a living color war,
replete with shaking cameras and unscripted terror,
no need to imbed here, to die like David Bloom,
who was real. Yes, I'll take it—there was a sense to it,
something you could dig your teeth into,
hope of a bizarre sort of victory—
unlike the sudden click of a roadside bomb
or terror taped to a uterus.

THE EAGLE ATOP THE STEEPLE OF ST. JOHN OF GOD

The eagle
often perched
atop the
Cross on
the steeple
above the
Saint John of
God Church in
Central Islip
is really
a seagull
Although when
seen in a
certain light
it can seem
A raven
or a dove
or most typically a hawk reluctantly eyeing its prey
Even though I live across the street from the church
and try to
gaze upward
as much as
possible
never have
I caught the
miracle
of swoop or
ascension

Muriel Harris Weinstein

AT ISABELLE'S ON THE WEEK-END

Mornings she rises, hums through rooms
opens windows, squeezes paint tubes
on her palette, and lines up
burnt sienna, ochre, raw umber,
and cadmium yellow.
Filaments of gauze and mesh tumble
from paper bags, veils for collages
to create mysteries, maybe miracles.
She fingers the photo of her husband,
traces his bearded face,
the man with sad eyes, long gone.

Nights she descends, tongue thrumming,
eyes shut, calls him up from the dead.
"You didn't understand," she says, in her sleep,
"You said I was wrong. Remember, and you got angry."

Her voice, plaintive like a dove's
then words sticky with burrs.
Fired by his response her words shoot flames
ricochet against the blades
of the ceiling fan, and with a strength
I never heard in her voice,
she resurrects their old argument
alters the old dialogue.

But one night she sobbed
I, deep in sleep, sucked into oceanic dreams
two rooms away
half wakened, thought of running in,
to calm her, cradle her,
but my feet were sewn to the sheet.

Next morning she rises, says nothing
I tell Isabelle I heard her arguing,
demanding a replay of an old fight.
She says, "I know,"
then opens a window and hums
as she spills paint tubes on her table
lining up burnt sienna, ochre, raw umber
and cadmium yellow
planning to paint miracles.

EVERYONE IN TOWN'S HOLDING A FUNDRAISER FOR YOU

Forgive me, Barack,
but I can't have a fundraiser for you.
My apartment's not big enough
and I'm lousy at making canapés
and terrible at mixing drinks
and if there's a lot of drinking
I have only one bathroom
and the line for it would be so long
I'd have to keep my apartment door open
and then the super would come up
and give me hell for breaking a fire law
and the neighbor downstairs who's for McCain
would complain to the Management
that I'm disturbing the peace
and then I'd get so angry at her
mainly for not voting for you
that I'd run down and throw a pie in her face
and race up with her husband in chase
and he's a big muscular brute
so you see, Barack, I think you'd
make a great president, so is it enough
to say I'm voting for you?

ICARUS IN THE ICU
winter '95

You are airborne again
fleshless arms flail like wings
loose fitting bones slip and clack
your wings dip and soar
trying to fly from hospital bed.

Stiffened by fear & sedatives
your head jerks from side to side
assessing air currents, turbulence.
Eyes squint, detects traps
collisions with the Russian Squad
the Stiletto Mob
their fingers' nails suck your blood
lust to nurse on your neck's gargoyle.
You're still trying to fly... into any sky.

Drop your demons. Let go. Fall free.
You'll float easily. I'll catch you.
Or is your anguish dimming my vision
and your flailing arms are swimming
in some boundless sea
swimming from doom,
sweating and cold
swimming from Stygian snakes
as you spit sludge.

You're safe. You don't have to fly away.
Float. Float down to me.
My arms are strong...they're open.
I'm waiting. I'll catch you.

Daniel Weissbort

FLOWERS

I glanced into the room where we'd sat
with mounds of papers
sorting through, reading Yehuda's English poems
making our selection. So many,
where there'd been a mere half a dozen thirty years ago,
the couch was pushed aside,
the floor covered with wreaths.

Note: When I went to Devon for Ted Hughes's funeral, I was struck by the fact that the sitting-room of his home where he and I, not so long before, had made a selection of Yehuda Amichai's poems, was now filled with wreaths and bouquets for Ted's funeral.

GUDEA

High culture is what you worshipped: order, justice,
a ruler who warned of the danger from without,
the barbarian at the gate: chaos and destruction.
You sought examples of this primal struggle,
of this battle with the forces of disintegration.
at an exhibition of Cartier-Bresson,
pausing before a portrait of Camus,
noting the intelligence in that face,
as in that of Sumerian Gudea,
when, painstakingly, you assembled an epic poem
on his resistance to the Guti,
You championed time-honouring truths
against the new, visionary, experimental,
which was not justified, the stakes being too high.
You were convinced justice was an attribute of intelligence.
to be protected from assault, expecting no reward.
You who, like Gudea,
should have an honoured niche.

Note: Gudea was the Sumerian priest-king of Lagash.

450

THE PROMISED LAND

If this is the end or beginning,
my reflections are singularly unimpressive,
but was I trying to impress e.g., some future reader.
Or I may imagine him,
and the illusion will be so real,
nothing for it but to let the dream extend its sway.
He's no longer there, they'll say: This is my Promised Land!

YIDDISH

If almost happened!
She was there; I was there.
And I knew how to do it.
But somehow, I wasn't sure I knew.
And somehow, she didn't realize I *was* there.
And I fell into a reverie.
And then she vanished.
Yiddish is harder than that.

OLD WOMAN & THE SERPENT
  "We will rock you, rock you little snake.
  We will keep you snug and warm. "
  (*Genesis* – "Supper's Ready")

I do not desire to be pulled under,
among the subterranean hot spots
where all the sinners collect their wage
in an unending line which stretches into
eternity, only to transect a tear that glistens
in an old woman's eye, who is startled by
the sudden appearance of a serpent in her lap.

This old woman who swallowed a spider
to swallow a fly in order to abolish this ancient lie
that family tradition insisted she keep snug and
warm and take to her bosom each night.

She does not shuffle, stammer or limp
but is now transformed into a sweet child
of innocence, who dances like there's no
tomorrow into a glorious new sunrise where
every single soul who has ever lived and died
or is still alive now celebrates the triumph
of humanity over its greed and headlong
plunge into global genocide. *

She motions for us to brave the difficult miles
into an alternate destiny where death holds no dominion
as the old woman who was once this sweet child
only a moment ago, now clutches the snake
in her lap with one hand and with the other
swiftly sews its jaw shut.

- Excerpted from *the Choice: Global Domination or Global Leadership by
Zbigniew Brzezinski*

PEA SOUP

It's raining pea soup from turquoise skies
as Squatter Tompkins kneels in the deep
green mud and begins to weep.

Squatter suspects that this must be
the first day of the Apocalypse as he
notices that instead of bacon, carrots
or bits of ham, the only things that stretch
into the distance are the sundry sun bleached
artifacts from all the friends and family
He has ever known.

He believes their spirits are no doubt
safe with God as a fearsome cloud
of vultures, enthused over the prospect
of a hot lunch, squawk and screech
just above Tompkins' head.

It's been raining pea soup since only
God knows when and still the feathered
Freaks return to have their fill and swap
stories of our downfall yet again.

Tompkins realizes that he should
have quit while he was ahead but
then wonders why it always comes down
to who's grabbed the greatest goodies
in the end.

Then, with a grin wider than the horizon,
he slowly rises from the steaming green sludge
and begins his eternal trudge into the sunset
where endless treasures await his greedy touch.

453

ORION'S SWORD

December evenings, Orion,
grandest, bravest of Greek hunters,
uniformed with belt and sword,
each jeweled with three stars,
assumes command of the eastern sky.
No longer is Orion risen for the kill

Look with binoculars
at the sword's middle star--
Theta Orion, in glow of haze,
"The Great Nebula."
In telescope, flame-like cloud,
twenty-five Light Years in diameter,
celestial manger for birthing of stars

Christmas Eve,
all you men and women of war,
gaze up at mighty Orion,
think about his sword,
his heavenly plowshare for peace

RITUAL OF ZERO
". . . several times {under microscope}
I have seen a volvox {one-celled animal} die.
Usually his activity slows down and then stops. . .
What was alive is dead."
Joseph Wood Krutch
"The Great Chain of Life"

They follow order:
the bishop, celebrating Mass, "Book of Common Prayer,"
the warden, carrying out the sentence, "Execution Protocol"

Month before
Jamie Lee Sherman is segregated from the others,
secured in solitary cell in X Wing.
"Completes process of breaking them down," says the warden.
"This way, they go quietly."

Hours before
Jamie Lee Sherman is moved to "holding cell,"
his sacristy,
absolution from the priest

"It's time," the warden announces,
appearing at cell door
three minutes after the hour.
The small processional--
Jamie Lee Sherman
enveloped by his escorts
could be carrying a Cross

In the chamber
the high gurney.
Clean white pillow,
last few seconds of comfort
or convenience for strap-down guards?

"Avoid eye contact," they are told.
Each man assigned a body part,
stares at what he straps down,
leg, arm, head

"Qualified medical personnel"
inserts intravenous line,
no swabbing with disinfectant

Sluicing of elements
sodium pentothal
pancuronium bromide
potassium chloride
collapsing consciousness, lungs,
halting the heart

Five to seven minutes

Claire Nicholas White

SILENCE

It slips between
the constant growth of sound,
rarer than sleep,
than grace.

It flows like water,
like the blood in veins.
It has no pulse or pain.
It pales, contaminated by
a constant increase
of names and nouns.

Some sounds are silent,
caresses and the blinking stars.
Listen to taciturn trees.
Books keep words to themselves
and the language of dreams
drowns in the quiet deep.

THE DANGER OF LIVING

is the danger of loving
too much or too little
on slippery sidewalks
where passing faces
demand recognition

There is danger in loving
delicate children
in miniature shoes
who need a hand to hold
and mock our oversized
balancing act

The danger of living
is to be blind to snow
to the blue of Vermeer
to crotches of trees
that freeze and glisten

It's the danger we court
the edge of disaster
Come ride with me
through the wind that topples
houses, while shoes float
down frozen rivers

ASSET CLASS
(I, I, ME, ME, MINE)

Money Is A Tool, Money Is A Drug
Money Eats A Hole In Your Soul Only Money Can Plug

subsidize me, supersize me, I'm entitled to bet
play both sides, buy and sell, offset losses, pile on debt
what can go wrong working my ass off to join the jet-set

Growth the world's growth industry, metastasis what we get

free enterprise is free if you know the inside story
structured right debt doesn't have to be obligatory
get credit risks off your books, shuffle and scuffle for glory

It's a zero-sum game, zero for you and some for me

Money Is A Drug, Money Is A Tool
Money Buys Things You Don't Need, Getting And Spending The Rule

greed, recklessness, fraud virally link economic ranks
go long on stocks and oil, short the dollar, screw the banks
global finance an engine momentum primes, pumps and cranks

Rack up profits, make enough, never have to say please or thanks

leave it to the markets, they will ferret out the best deal
undervalued, overvalued, worthless, polish up your spiel
inexhaustible drive for a bargain, better yet a steal

Stocks tumble, currencies fall, bulls and bears rally, pigs squeal

Money Is A Tool, Money Is A Drug
Money Eats A Hole In Your Soul Only Money Can Plug

you need to have the instinct, risk-adverse need not apply
borrow money where interest rates are low, invest where they're high
wheel and deal for 2 and 20, no way to indemnify

Win-win for me, win-lose for you, wave your life-savings bye-bye

everything in life is a trade-off, don't look so dour
money makes old men attractive, young women dig their power
count their husband's death benefits in his final hour

Silver spoon, gold fork, diamond knife, let the luxuries shower

Money Is A Drug, Money Is A Tool
Money Buys Anything You'll Ever Want, That's The Platinum Rule

CHARACTER + CHARACTER ACTOR = ...

Punster, funster, quipster, hipster
done the Robert Dunn way
your references arcane, oblique, unique, sneakily funny
on countless occasions irreverent and flippant
delivery defining the meaning of droll

I don't believe, though I'm not sure, in reincarnation
or an afterlife but If I'm wrong and heaven has a
gate you surely showed up, hat on your head
most definitely not in your hand

You checked out at around the same time as Paul Newman,
coincidence just made for you to note, I imagine you
having quite an exchange with Paul who after all could also deliver
a line with expressive facial and body language
to match
        But he's not known for writing dialogue and there you
could give him some pointers. With a little preparation you two could
put on quite a show though Paul might well be upstaged

(Apparently Paul's always been self-deprecating about Newman's Own Salad
Dressing
but he hadn't met you yet)

Or if reincarnation is perhaps a fact you and Paul could come
back in combination maybe your souls could coalesce in spontaneous
generation

Dunn man...Newman...Deadmen...Redoneman

Sandy Wicker

SHE COMPLAINS…

She complains,
like a discordant flute--
harping on what used to be
or should have been
not hearing the vibrations
pulsating through her room—
the cicadas raucous warning
of summer's early death.

THE ROAD MORE TRAVELED

Two helicopters hover
over Southern State
monitor the traffic
backed up from Hempstead Road
as I sit disconsolate that
despite my early rise
I'm stuck with other motorists
listening to the estimates:
20, 30, 40-minute delays…
until I see the crumpled hood,
about-faced SUV--
ambulance leaving the scene.

Ginger Williams

NINE WOMEN

One whose hair blows green across springtime.
One who forgets why she hides in shadows.

One whose skirts are of velvet and silk.
One who remembers rape in an alley.

One who dances on tintop roofs.
One who weeps for the loss of her children.

One who sighs at the new crescent moon.
One who drowns below waves in the ocean.

One who stares and stares at the hot desert sun.

THAT YEAR I WAS A LEAF IN THE WHIRLWIND OF THE ORDAINED*
    *after a line by Derek Wolcott book length poem *Omeros (p.* 217 line 5)

While they walked slowly, balancing
I blew through their midst
while they were measured
I was a-twirl and a-twist,
in the midst of their saffron
I, blue-jeaned and light-footed,
wished myself unseen
but they were of clacking beads,
half-closed eyes, of chant and drone
I of trembling karma, small merit
was of blither, bumble and stumble.
So I sat alone
my mind a race across random plans,
but they were of mantra, and meditation,
of moments and mountains
and that year I was a leaf
bouncing, blaming, beseeching
the great Buddha for even one small blessing
even one sliver of grace.

John A. Williams

LOVE POEM
for Ginger

The poem to say
'I love you'
is hard to write,
the landscape
littered with attempts,
the words worn
and threadbare
from too much use.
Then can my poem be
in the silence, all
those expected words
trimmed off, to reveal
something never
seen before—
like an old Chinese
woodcarver, who whittles
until he sets free
the bird hidden
inside a piece of wood?

A SIMPLE MAN

Just like the translation of his
Hungarian surname, that's who he was.

Although we had worked together for
a few years, I believe I learned everything
about him during our first cafeteria lunch.
For there was not very much to tell.

He hailed from a small town outside of
Buffalo, which offered no opportunities other
than his late brother's job at the near-by paper mill.
So, he left to come to the Big Apple –
as he loved to call it – sometime during
the mid '60s, fresh from high school and
with large brown eyes full of astonishment.

During his first employment agency interview,
a nasty woman asked him how he would ever be able
to get a job, if he had no experience.
Left disillusioned by that recurring Catch-22 question,
Uncle Sam soon helped him with the answer,
as he found himself a few weeks later in the downtown
induction center and then off to the Mekong Delta.

Although the war left him homesick, he was delighted
to carry a rifle – something he had missed from the
duck hunting weekends with his father and brother.
When his papers eventually came through, his combat buddies
thought he'd return to that two-bit town once he was stateside.
But, no. Now that his father was also gone, he had no reason
to live with an invalid mother who received care from
an estranged sister.

During the next decade, he learned the banking trade,
first as a lowly teller, like many at the time.
He then bumped into the right man, at the right time –
in an elevator – who offered him a junior desk job.
That made him rather happy. And, that's how I found him
when we originally met in that posh midtown office.

I learned that his needs and interests were rather simple,
but somewhat dated for a then young, eager buck like me.
Without fail, he'd question me each day about where
I bought my office clothes and especially about my shoes.
He also was amazed that I gave them a high polish
without too much effort, whenever that was necessary.
And, he questioned why I regularly went to the movies,
as he confessed that he was too paranoid to sit alone in the
large city theaters.

Following a round of pay raises, one day he sheepishly
asked me if I'd accompany him at lunch time to the
post office to buy the newly issued Duck Stamp.
That was a new experience for me, a true city slicker.

While waiting on an endless snaked line, he mentioned
that he had recently bought a new rifle and with the
new stamp, he'd be ready for the upcoming season.
But, he begged me not to tell anyone at the office,
because he didn't want them to get the wrong impression.
His comment puzzled me, but I never had the chance
to ask him what he had meant. I was transferred the next morning
to another department in a building downtown.

On that morning, as I headed to the elevator with my box of
desk supplies, he asked me if I had a girlfriend – which I did.
And, then he told me that he had been forever fearful to go on
a date, because he believed he could never afford to have a family.

Once the elevator door closed, I never saw him again.
Yet, all these years later, I remember his broad smile and
I remain struck by that lingering comment.

LET ME

Let me be your drug of choice
your warm bath water
seeping under your skin

Let me be your bungi ride's arms
cradling your fall
the smell of thunderstorm lightning
breaking a dull night gray

Let me be your desert
drinking each tear until it turns to song
steeped with the sustenance of your mind's
womb and breasts

Let me be your skeleton bones
carrying your flesh like womanhood's miracle
the bower upon which you climb

Your father and mother
your sons and grandchildren
casting lines upon the future
their lure to you by pain and sunlight

let me be the ram at your back
the pleasure and boy-toy under you
let me fill your lips with maleness
caress you under your skin

let me be your mirror
sighing memories of first and last forevers
let me be the juices of hope and succulent ripening
fragrant lipstick kisses and strong arms

let me be your death
so I will hide myself away
until you call

let me be your soul
so I will
never lose you.

LOVE

Can love break
(he wondered) under
the weight of dreams?
or dreams unfilled?
(Can dreams break
under the weight of love?)

Can skin and flesh sustain
the weight of years
like waves
lapping
into waiting
sand?

And what
of words
having their own
life resembling shadows
and bridges of cumulus
clouds?

And smiles …
what of them?
The years
of smiles and tears
and your warm
hand touching mine.

REINCARNATION OR DREAM PART 1

when he became a lion
reincarnated or in self-defense
fashioned in sleep he could not tell
but he walked through the forest
sensing all sentient life

some he heard like the caw of birds
the wing thrush of forest owls and eagles
some he heard like the soft scurrying machines
of small eatable weasels and mice
some he saw rushing to hide like beetles
and ants and katydids

the bluff of howling monkeys overhead
the flashing ghosts of white-tailed gazelle
all like wind clouds streaking with life
he could smell them sweet as lioness musk

the world was all soil and flesh
and the leaves and trunks of dead trees
in which things hid
little gifts if he could only surprise

and damp mushrooms and ferns
on wet earth to boot
he could fill his lungs
and swallow them whole

But the river
he was in love with the song
she sang to him each night
and the song with which she ushered in
the forest mornings light

and he saw her leave once
in the shape of a flying fish
luminescent scales of purples and blues
silver and grays a thousand mirrors reflecting
the fires of forest, water, sky
and when she returned
slipping back to her home
she sang to him only him

Walter C. Wojcik III

BEFORE HER MARIGOLDS

I am thinking of the mystery of the bones
That shapes the face I long to see
At the end of each of the sun's golden rays
Spread out like a peacock's tail.

My finger traces the angular grace of her jaw
In the space her face just pressed itself against
While thinking about peaches or sailing
Or her lover's chest.

I find myself looking for her nose
Wondering why it is not an ear or a shell
Or a charm I could wear around my neck
Like a shark's tooth or polished moonstone.

The broad plain of her brow is fit for the horses I keep,
I see them munching on the sage brush that grows
In clumps around the sleek cheekbones I scale
With the hooks and ropes of my eyes.

I sink into the spring tundra of her cheeks
And cast my hopes into the sad canyons of her eyes,
And linger on the shore of her chin listening to the waves
Wash over the red sea of her lips
That I may learn to open her head like flowers
And release the sun that made me love her.

But for the bones, the bones, the bones
And the beauty of their making
I am powerless before her violets,
Before her marigolds.

EMPTY SPACES

I cannot save you from the empty spaces
That make you invisible,

My hands cannot find your cheek, your lips, your waist

Like tumbled stones across a dry riverbed,
I have yielded to the sun and sky
        and have forgotten your water in my thirst

I cannot negate your eyes from our old photographs
Or seal your ears from the simple sounds we shared,

My heart cannot warm your heart, your belly, your feet

Like the flower whose head has gone to seed
Surrenders to the eddy of the wind
        I keep within me the blossom of my first

I cannot save you from the empty spaces
The sulfurous flash of memories that burn like sparklers
Through the roots of your breath—

I REMEMBER

I remember your hands.
Thin fingers, rings, bracelets.
Franklin's key awaiting
Lightning's strike.

I held your hand
Again, for the first time
Closer than my blood
To the self I hide.

I remember your shoulders
In a blouse that stole my breath
As you slipped off your cloak.
Pale skin grazed so softly
By gold and copper hair.

I kissed your neck
Not believing
But accepting precious surprise.

I remember your eyes.
Though at first I could not recall
The colors of wood and earth.
So far did I see into caverns of
Rich brown hue and quiet paths.
So far did they see
Me falling.

WHY HIGH SCHOOL SUCKS... SOMETIMES

So, I was the boy chosen last for every game
Drawing the attention of the strong only
As a target for the stinging, maroon dodge ball
Lobbed with malice aforethought
Across center line of the gym floor.

God knows, I tired of that...
The litany of their scorn,
Scraped on the rough surface
Of a darkness I carried...
Outsider, loner, geek, freak
It's amazing I didn't climb up something tall
Take a bead on those poor outraged bastards.

It didn't matter that I was smart,
That I wore my heart well out on my sleeve
That I wanted, God-help-me,
The same things those jackals wanted
That I was Boy-Scout loyal
That I could be trusted.
Or maybe I couldn't.

There was nothing I could do or say or be
That could gentrify me out of loserdom
Until the clock and the calendar
Dragged my ass, almost unaware, past that ill-lit exit ramp.

It was lunch hour in the cafeteria,
Annette stopped me -
Appearing in my path, unavoidable,
A sweet, misplaced Jersey Barrier
Gazing over her third-year French text.
Her smile, like her schoolbooks, adorably askew
Voice hesitant with the kind of fear I now understand,
Screwing up all the gumption earned in an entire
Sixteen year life of shyness and longing to ask:

"Would you marry a Catholic?"

Acknowledgements

Richard Bronson:
"DOC BLADES"
Appears in *The Pharos / Winter 2005*.
"THE DINNER PARTY"
Appears in *Long Island Quarterly*.

Michael J. Bugeja
"PLATH ON PRIMROSE HILL"
Appears in Michael Bugeja's 2000 collection, *Millennium's End* (Archer)
and originally appeared in *Anthology of Magazine Verse and Yearbook of American Poetry*.

Graham Everett
"APOLOGIA"
Appears in *A BOZO'S BON VOYAGE BROADSIDE, No.: 04*.

Pat Falk
"VESTA"
"VIRGO"
Appears in *Crazy Jane: Poems* (Plain View Press, 2008).

Ray Freed
"MOOM"
Appears in *Backstreet Editions* in 1979.

Christine Gelineau
"ENDOW"
"PICKING PEACHES"
Appears in *Remorseless Loyalty* (Ashland Poetry Press, 2006).

Roberta Gould
"FARIDA A. WILEY LEADS A BIRD WALK
TO OYSTER BAY IN HER EIGHTY NINTH YEAR"
Appears in *IN HOUSES WITH LADDERS* (Waterside Press).

George Held
"FEEDING CHICKADEES"
Appears in *Winged* (Birnham Wood Graphics).

William Heyen
"A POETICS OF HIROSHIMA"
previously appeared in *Great River Review*, in *The Seventh Quarry* (Wales),
and in *A Poetics of Hiroshima* (Wilkesbarre, PA: Etruscan Press, 2008).

Tony Iovino
"ECHOES"
Appears in the Fall 2008 issue of the print and on-line literary magazine *Stellar Showcase Journal.*

D. H. Melhem
"PROSPECT"
Appears in *New York Poems* (Syracuse University Press, 2005).

Paddy Noble
"DROP OF MERCY"
Appears in *Long Island Quarterly,* 2009.

Barbara Novack
"FREE FALL"
Appears in *Slant: A Journal of Poetry.*
"SOMETHING"
Appears in *Nassau Review.*

J R Turek
"FLASH-CARD FREDDY"
Appears in *Grassroot Reflections, Vol. 10, 2/2009.*

Notes on Contributors

Hassanal Abdullah is a Bangladeshi-American poet, Editor of *Shabdaguchha*, and the author of 13 books. He has been translated into French and Spanish. He works for the NYC Department of Education as a High School math teacher.

Bart Allen is a High School English teacher in Richmond Hill, New York. He attended SUNY Geneseo and has a Masters of Science from the University of Edinburgh, Scotland in Creative Writing. He has been published in Poetrybay and the PPA, and is currently working on a novel.

Michael Ambrose writes, "I'm a little bit of everything. I enjoy listening to metal which in my opinion is extreme poetry. I love Edgar Allan Poe's work."

Debby Andreas is a native Long Islander and a newcomer to the world of poetry. She enjoys writing in free verse, but her heart belongs to form. She is married and they have three children, who are now young adults.

Philip Asaph was working as a furniture mover when he was offered a free education at NYU on the basis of a ten-page portfolio of poetry. He also won a Stadler semester at Bucknell University and a grant from the Vogelstein Foundation. His poems have appeared in local journals. Philip teaches poetry, fiction and creative nonfiction at The Long Island High School for the Arts.

Susan Astor has worked as a poet-in-residence in the public schools for over twenty-five years, also conducts poetry workshops for adults. Her poetry has appeared in myriad magazines and journals. She has won several poetry prizes, including the C.W. Post Poet-in-the-Community Award, and is the author of *Dame* and *Spider Lies*. She was named 2008 Poet of the Year by The Walt Whitman Birthplace Association.

Dr. David B. Axelrod has been published in hundreds of magazines. He was the 2007 – 2009 Suffolk County Poet Laureate. His seventeenth and newest book is *Deciduous Dreams*. He is the recipient of three Fulbright Awards including his being the first official Poet-in-Residence in the People's Republic of China. He has performed for the UN and has been translated into fourteen languages.

Sybil Bank is a retired Early Childhood Administrator, a writer of poetry and prose, and a member of the Poet's Circle at the Graphic Eye Gallery. Her work appears in numerous literary journals and anthologies.

Bob Barci is a lifelong resident of Elmont, Long Island, and began writing poetry in 1974. He discovered open poetry readings while attending Windham College in Vermont.

Stanley H. Barkan is the editor/publisher of the Cross-Cultural Review Series of World Literature and Art, that has, to date, produced some 350 titles in 50 different languages. His own work has been published in 14 collections, several of them bilingual, his latest is *Strange Seasons*. In 2008, he hosted "A Dylan Thomas Tribute Tour of America" featuring Aeronwy Thomas, the poet's daughter, and Peter Thabit-Jones, in consultation with poet Vince Clemente.

Diane Barker defines herself primarily as a prose writer but keeps dipping her big toe in the poetry waters. She is an award-winning poet and is a member of the LIWG and the FCWG.

Bill Batcher considers himself a poet under construction. A retired teacher, he leads a writers' group in Riverhead, NY. His poetry has been published in magazines, anthologies and online collections, and has won several awards. He has a book of Easter poems, *Footsteps to the Resurrection*.

Leslie Brooke Bell is an award-winning poet whose poetry has appeared in numerous literary journals and anthologies. She is a native Long Islander who retired after thirty years of government service. She is a member of TNSPS, PPA, and LPS.

Linda Benninghoff is an award-winning poet whose poetry has appeared in numerous literary journals and anthologies. She has published two chapbooks, *Departures* and *The Street Where I Was a Child*.

Byron Beynon lives in Wales. His work has appeared in numerous publications. He has read his work at the Edinburgh Fringe Festival, the Hay Festival, Cork (Ireland), and The Dylan Thomas Centre (Swansea). He has been Co-Editor of the poetry magazine, *Roundhouse*. A sequence of his poems appeared in a Painters and Poets exhibition in London, inspired by the work of Vincent Van Gogh. His most recent collection is entitled *Cuffs*.

Janice Bishop is a resident of Manorville, NY and has published poems in journals across the USA, in Canada, Ireland, Wales, and England. She has been a featured reader at Walt Whitman House, and radio host at Adelphi, Stony Brook, and LIU.

Cliff Bleidner Haiku poet, formalist poet, PPA cofounder and coordinator, retired scientist, former long distance runner and substance abuse counselor. He is one of the 2009 honorees **of TNSPS's Recognition Award.**

Andrew Boerum is 35 and a native Long Islander who writes poetry between life and chores. He is also Co-Editor of *Good Japan Press*, purveyors of progressive verse and poem.

Sharon Bourke is a writer and visual artist who was born and grew up in Brooklyn and now lives in Central Islip, NY. Her poems have appeared in numerous literary journals and anthologies.

Mel Brake was raised in Philadelphia, PA. He graduated with a BS from West Chester University. He has written poetry as a method of healing. His works are in numerous literary journals and anthologies. He published his first CD/chapbook entitled *Adoration of The Sol*.

Thomas Brinson has been writing poetry for the past 43years as self-meditation against cynicism and nihilism, despair and abject hopelessness. He is an ardent NY Poet-Activist since returning home from duty in the American War in Vietnam, landing in Washington, DC's National Airport a couple of hours after Martin Luther King was assassinated on April 4th, 1968.

Richard Bronson works at the SUNY Stony Brook medical center, where he is Professor of Obstetrics & Gynecology. He is on the editorial board of *Xanadu*, the literary journal of the LIPC and is the recipient of the 2003 Prize for Poetry of the American Academy of Physicians and the 2005 Poetry Prize of the Institute for Medicine in Contemporary Society. His first collection of poems is *Search for Oz*.

Michael J. Bugeja is a National Endowment for the Arts fellow (1990, fiction) and has published verse in *Poetry, Harper's, Kenyon Review, Georgia Review, New England Revie,* and many others. He directs the Greenlee School of Journalism at Iowa State University. He is the author of *The Art & Craft of Poetry,* Writer's Digest Books.

Margaret Garry Burke is a Reference Librarian in the Joan and Donald E. Axinn Library of Hofstra University. Burke is the subject specialist for Women's Studies and in this capacity over the last 7 years has conducted readings at Axinn Library to celebrate Women's History Month. She has written extensively on the Irish poet, Nuala Ni Dhomhnaill.

Fred Byrnes continues to live in his hometown of Huntington Station, NY. He holds a degree in Communications from SCCC, Selden Campus, and a BA in English from Dowling College, Oakdale, NY. While at Dowling, Byrnes taught Creative Writing at the Hausman Center for Disabled Students. *1969 and Other Poems* is his ninth collection. Byrnes writes what he feels, a bit of advice given to him by the late professor-poet Dan Murray at SCCC.

Louisa Calio is the Director of the Poets' and Writers' Piazza for Hofstra University's Italian Experience. She is an internationally-published author and award-winning writer. She was recently honored with Alice Walker, Gloria Steinem, and other *Feminists Who Changed America(1963-76)* at Columbia/Barnard. She was cofounder and first Executive Director of City Spirit Artists, Inc. and in 2008 and 09 curator and participate in exhibitions of her photos with poems in *A Passion for Africa* and *A Passion for Jamaica* at the Round Hill Resort in Jamaica, West Indies where she lives part of the year.

Paula Camacho moderates the Farmingdale Poetry Group. She is an award-winning poet whose poems have appeared in numerous literary journals and anthologies. She has published *Hidden Between Branches,* and two chapbooks, *The Short Lives Of Giants,* and *November's Diary.*

Vincent James Carbone was born and raised on Long Island where since childhood he has gained a deep appreciation and interest for music, theatre, dance, and writing. He is currently a senior at SUNY Brockport with a double major in Theatre & Communications. He is a member of Drumcliffe School of Irish Dance. He would like to thank his mother Tammy Nuzzo-Morgan for the opportunity to appear in such a great anthology.

Edgar Carlson is a lifelong resident of Farmingdale, NY. He is currently enrolled in an MFA program at Adelphi University. He has three grandchildren.

B J Cassidy is a lifelong Long Islander, currently living in Northport. She raised two sons, helped run the Huntington Poetry Cafe at the Conklin Barn 1993-9; participated in the LIPC workshop for many years, was a founding board member of the Northport Arts Coalition, has coordinated "The Kerouac Connection," performs on the "Northport Celebrates Jack" CD Tribute to Jack Kerouac, and won a PPA Award. She has been published in numerous literary journals and anthologies. She published a chapbook, *Leaving Port.*

Fran Castan's poems have appeared in *Poetry, Ms,* and *Confrontation.* She's received five Pushcart nominations and The Lucille Medwick Award of the Poetry Society of America.

Sultan Catto is a professor of theoretical physics at the CUNY Graduate School and at the Rockefeller University in NY. Two books of his poems, one in bilingual edition were published by Edicion Godot in Argentina.

Jay Chollick writes, "no bio-boredom please; just read the poems, the only credentials that count. many thanx."

Clarity (Michael Cannatella) is an independent poet/emcee from Suffolk County, Long Island. He spent most of his early performance career behind various open-mics in and around the LI and NYC area understanding his abilities and finding his voice. Clarity has performed at many local libraries, high schools, and has participated in several writing workshops, working one-on-one with students in an academic environment.

Vince Clemente, a SUNY English Professor Emeritus, is a poet-biographer, whose books include *John Ciardi: Measure of the Man, Paumanok Rising: Long Island Figures in a Landscape*, and seven volumes of verse, one of which, *A Place for Lost Children*, is a text taught at University of Wales at Swansea. His latest volume is *Sweeter than Vivaldi*. His poetry has been published in numerous literary journals and anthologies. He is a founding editor of *West Hills Review: a Walt Whitman Journal*. He was the 2004, the first, recipient of **TNSPS's Recognition Award.**

Jonathan Cohen has prize-winning translations of Spanish American poetry. He is Editor of Ernesto Cardenal's *Pluriverse: New and Selected Poems, 1949-2005.*

Lynn E. Cohen was nominated for a Pushcart Prize. She is an Associate Editor of *Long Island Sounds*. She was a student of Stephen Dunn's at Syracuse U. Lynn teaches writing at Hofstra University and literature and writing at SCCC. She has published a chapbook, *Lone Star Days.*

Lorraine Conlin is a US Customs' Broker at Kennedy Airport, and a National Park Service volunteer in her spare time. Her poetry has been published in numerous literary journals and anthologies. She hosts "Tuesdays with Poetry" for PIN. She is the initiator of *The Long Island Poets for Darfur*. She is a breast cancer survivor.

Victoria Cooper is from Cold Spring Harbor, Long Island. She's spent the last three years living in Amagansett, gaining both sand fleas and ample editing experience as the Coordinating Editor of Dan's Papers. She likes to write about our on-the-edge culture and is currently pursuing her MFA in fiction. She loves photography, sad music, and her bike, Le Orange Crush.

Yolanda Coulaz is a poet, photographer, editor, and founder of Purple Sage Press. She edited and published the anthology *For Loving Precious Beast*. Her first book of poetry *Spirits and Oxygen* is being used in an advanced course in poetry at SUNY Stony Brook.

Lisa Cowley of Jamesport, NY, is the author of the poetry book, *Noah's Dove.*

Walt Dawydiak lives in Remsenburg, NY with his wife, and their three poet children. Walt is a professional engineer, attorney, and adjunct professor in the field of environmental health. His love of poetry began in college, where he was first published when he won the NJ Collegiate Poetry Competition.

Jeny De Jesus is a 17 year-old high school student, who speaks both English and Spanish. She enjoys playing soccer, and loves to listen to techno, rap, R&B, and bachata. She helped translate work in *Finding our Voices* for TNSPS as a translator and here as well for Tammy Nuzzo-Morgan's poems.

Cassandra DeMario is an aspiring 19-year-old poet born and raised on Long Island. She was inspired by her high school English teacher and has been writing ever since. She is currently studying literature and writing at LIU.

Joan Digby is the Director of the Honors Program at C. W. Post, is author of the poetry book *A Sound of Feathers* and several poetry chapbooks. She is also author of *Peterson's Guide to Honors Programs in American Colleges and Universities*, co-author of *The Collage Handbook* and co-editor of *Permutations, Food for Thought*, and *Inspired by Drink*.

John Digby is an internationally famous collage artist. His poetry books include *Fluttering with an Attempt to Fly, Incantations, Miss Liberty, To Amuse a Shrinking Sun, Sailing Away from Night*, and *The Structure of Bifocal Distance*. He is also co-author of *The Collage Handbook*. We are sad to say that John has passed on; we will miss him greatly.

Camillo DiMaria was born in Bushwick, Brooklyn to Sicilian parents. He attended Hunter College and Brooklyn College. He is Editor of *Freshet*, the anthology publication of the Fresh Meadows Poets.

Arthur Dobrin is the author of more than 20 books, and is Professor of Humanities at Hofstra University and Leader Emeritus of the Ethical Humanist Society of LI.

Kathaleen Donnelly is a graduate of St. Vincent's School of Nursing, and is currently a Nurse Practitioner in Cardiology at Stony Brook University Hospital. She earned an MA in Philosophy while working 12 years in the Surgical ICU. She is a single mother, a member of the Sweetbriar Photography Club, with published/awarded poems.

Walter Donway is a poet living in East Hampton and NYC. He is the author of *Touched By Its Rays*. Until 2005, he was editor of *Cerebrum: The Dana Forum on Brain Science*.

John Dotson is an author, editor, artist, and educator. Born in Kingsport, TN, he now lives in Carmel, CA where he was the first poet-in-residence of the Robinson Jeffers Tor House Foundation. His poetry and prose are translated and, along with his illustrations, published internationally. He has written two produced plays, is a sculptor, and also works in several performance arts and media. He teaches integral philosophy, psychology, media studies, and creative process.

Peter V. Dugan is a resident of East Rockaway, a graduate of The New School in NYC, a member of the Rockville Centre Poets and listed in P&W. His first book is entitled *Medusa's Overbite*. He has taught poetry workshops and classes on form and style. His poems have appeared in numerous literary journals and anthologies. He is the Grants Coordinator for TNSPS. His newest book of poetry is *Members Only*.

Robert Dunn is a writer/artist and is the author of such books as *Zen Yentas in Bondage, Horse Latitudes, Baffled in Baloneyville*, and *The Sap Songbook,* plus the poetry/music CD, *Sickly Minutes.* He is the editor of *Asbestos Poetry Journal* and has served as Editor of *Medicinal Purposes Literary Review and The New Press Literary Quarterly.* Mr. Dunn's poetry has appeared around the world, which is more than you can say for him. His comic strip, *Knish & Carob,* currently runs in *Street News.* Mr. Dunn was recently been named the Poet Laureate of Pluto. We are sad to say that Robert has passed on; we will miss him greatly.

Desmond Egan was born in Athlone, Co Westmeath. He founded the Goldsmith Press and edited *Era.* He is the Artistic Director of The Gerard Manley Hopkins Society International Summer School, which is in its 21st year. His collections include: *Midland, Leaves, Siege!, Woodcutter, Athlone?, Seeing Double, Collected Poems, Poems for Peace, A Song for my Father, Selected Poems, Peninsula, Elegies, Famine*, and *Music.* He has also published *Medea*, and a collection of essays, *The Death of Metaphor.* He has been awarded the US National Poetry award for his *Collected Poems.* He lives in Co Kildare.

Carolyn Emerson has poems published in numerous literary journals and anthologies. She is a founder of the Euterpe Poetry Group.

Duane Esposito is Assistant Professor of English at NCC in Garden City, NY. He has an MA from SUNY Brockport and an MFA from the University of Arizona. His work was selected for an Academy of

American Poets Award; he was nominated for a Pushcart Prize. His poems have appeared in numerous literary journals and anthologies. He has published two books of poetry, *The Book of Bubba* and *Cadillac Battleship*. He lives on Long Island with his wife and daughter.

Sasha Ettinger is a former diagnostician and Special Education teacher. She is a participant in Taproot workshops of the former Nassau County Poet Laureate Max Wheat, and Hutton House workshops of former Suffolk County Poet Laureate George Wallace. She is a founding member of the Poet's Circle at the Graphic Eye Gallery in Port Washington. Her work has appeared in numerous publications.

Graham Everett is a poet, publisher, painter, and professor. He currently teaches in the General Studies Program at Adelphi University. He is the lyricist with Middle Class, and the author of over a dozen books of poetry, the latest being *That Nod Toward Love*. The founding editor of Street Magazine and Press, he was the 2006 honoree of **TNSPS's Recognition Award**.

Gil Fagiani co-hosts the monthly open reading of the Italian American Writers' Association at the Cornelia Street Café, and is the Associate Editor *of Feile-Festa: A Literary Arts Journal*. He has published *Crossing 116th Street: A Blanquito in El Barrio, Rooks*. Gil is a social worker.

Pat Falk is Professor of English at NCC. She is the author of four books, including *Crazy Jane*. The recipient of several awards and fellowships, she is also the author of *In the Shape of a Woman, It Happens As We Speak,* and *Sightings: Poems on Discovery*.

Johanne Farmer (Veroflame), a Canadian accountant living in the Montreal area, started writing poetry in 1998. She writes in both English and French. Involved in her community, she has contributed her accounting skills and her poetry to different organizations, such as prevention and intervention for the sexually abused and drug addiction prevention.

Kathryn M. Fazio was named Poet Laureate of the College of Staten Island CUNY where she won the first Ed Rehberg Prize for poetry and was awarded the Ferrara Scholarship from the Performing and Creative Arts Department. She is the author of *A Taste of Hybrid Vigor: new poems of War, Passion, and Social Significance*.

Harvey Feinstein was a resident of Southampton for 40 years, before moving to Greenport, in April 2002. He has been writing poetry since 3rd grade. He remembers his first poem, "Cat In A Hat, 20 years before Dr. Seuss. After retiring from business he took up writing again and was a scholarship student of the late David Ignatow. He is a member of the East End Poetry Workshop, and the Writers Workshop in Amagansett. He has been published in numerous literary journals and anthologies. He is president emeritus of the Southampton Rose Society, a Master Gardener and Rosarian, past VP of the Southampton Artists Group, a docent, and Council Member of the Parrish Art Museum, and a director of the Horticultural Alliance of the Hamptons.

Thomas Fink is the author of five books of poetry, including *Clarity and Other Poems* and *No Appointment Necessary*. He is also the author of two books of criticism, including *A Different Sense of Power: Problems of Community in Late-Twentieth-Century U.S. Poetry*. With Joseph Lease, he is co-editor of *Burning Interiors: David Shapiro's Poetry and Poetics*. He is a Professor of English at CUNY—LaGuardia.

Maya Diablo Mason (Maya Fink) was published in The First Hay(na)ku Anthology. She is a high school student who plans to pursue a career in drama, visual art, or writing.

Adam Fisher's poems have appeared in a wide variety of publications. His two books of poems are *Rooms, Airy Rooms*, and *Dancing Alone*. He is Poetry Editor of the CCAR Journal.

Diane Frank is author of five books of poems, including *Entering the Word Temple* and *The Winter Life of Shooting Stars*. She has mentored hundreds of writers at San Francisco State University, City College of San Francisco, The University of VT, and the Professional Writing Program at MIU in Fairfield, IA. She lives in San Francisco, CA – where she dances, plays cello, teaches writing workshops, and creates her life as an art form. She is also a documentary scriptwriter with expertise in Eastern and sacred art. *Blackberries in the Dream House*, her first novel, was nominated for the Pulitzer Prize.

Ray Freed's poems have appeared in publications in the US, Canada, and UK. His most recent chapbook is *All Horses Are Flowers*. He served as Poet-In-Residence at the State University of NY at Stony Brook, and currently lives on the Kona Coast of the Island of Hawaii.

James Friel is Professor Emeritus at Farmingdale College. He is Editor of *Humanities Magazine* (in its 35th year). He has been published in over 75 magazines. His longest poem is a 50-page poem in honor of the artist, Miro. He has been running the poetry and essay contest at Farmingdale College for the Multicultural Committee.

Celeste Gainey is a lighting designer who lives in Springs with her partner, Elise, and their two dogs, Alfie and Max. She is attending the MFA Creative Writing Program in Poetry at Carlow University

Christine Gelineau is the author of *Remorseless Loyalty*, winner of the Richard Snyder Memorial Prize, and nominated for the LA Times Book Award. Her other works include two chapbooks, *North American Song Line* and *In the Greenwood World*, as well as *French Connections: A Gathering of Franco-American Poets,* an anthology she edited with Jack B. Bedell. Her work have appeared in numerous journals and anthologies, including *Prairie Schooner, Connecticut Review, The Iron Horse Review, Green Mountains Review, Georgia Review, American Literary Review.* Her poems have twice been nominated for a Pushcart Prize. She lives on a farm in upstate NY, and teaches at Binghamton University, where she is Associate Director of the Creative Writing Program and coordinator of the Readers' Series. She also teaches poetry in the low-residency graduate writing program at Wilkes University.

Gail Goldstein has been a Special Education teacher in NYC for 30 years. She acted as faculty advisor for several student publications. She is an ABA therapist for children with autism. Before becoming a teacher, she worked for McGraw-Hill Publishing. She has finally returned to her love of writing with poetry. She belongs to a women's African drumming group.

Kirpal Gordon writes for speakers, entrepreneurs and small businesses as well as for literary journals and jazz bands. His latest book is *Eros in Sanskrit: Lyrics & Meditations 2007-1977* and its companion CD, *Speak-Spake-Spoke*, a jazz/spoken word project with the Claire Daly band.

Roberta Gould's ninth book, *Louder Than Seeds*, has just been released; previous books include *Dream Yourself Flying, Not By Blood Alone, Pacing the Wind,* and *Only Rock.* She has appeared widely in the small press and has edited several literary publications. Aside from poetry, she studies ping-pong, and piano.

Leonard Greco is still alive and hopes to continue that state of being into the foreseeable future. He has been a poet for so long that he is now as old as dirt.

Geraldine Green collections include *The Skin* and *Passio*. Her poetry is included in various anthologies in the UK, USA, Italy, and Scotland. She has read widely in the UK, Italy, Greece, and America. She runs Creative Writing workshops, and is a tutor for Continuing Education at Lancaster University. She teaches

Undergraduates at Cumbria University, organizes poetry readings, is an Associate Editor of Poetrybay and Co-Editor (UK) of Poetryvlog. She lives in Cumbria, UK, happy among sheep muck and rain, and is undertaking a PhD in Creative Writing, Poetry at Lancaster University, and is currently working on her third book.

Russ Green is a graduate of Hofstra University with a BA in English. Trekking through the Himalayas, wandering through Europe, and driving across America, together with his marathon running and practice of yoga and Eastern philosophies has formed the foundation of much of his poetry.

George Guida has published two collections of poems, *Low Italian* and *New York and Other Lover;* as well as a volume of criticism, *The Peasant and the Pen;* and a chapbook of fiction, *The Pope Stories.* George is Associate Professor at NYC College of Technology and co-producer of the Intercollegiate Poetry Slam.

Chao Guo-Hui is a bi-lingual poet, Bible scholar and associate professor. He teaches at Guangdong University of Foreign Studies, China. He served as writer-in-residence in Edith Cowan University and University of Melbourne and University of Sydney between 1995 and 1997. He was anthologized as one of twenty contemporary Australian writers by the Cimerron Review in USA. He has nine books published in and out of China, five of them collections of his poetry and two concerning Bible philosophy.

Russ Hampel, lives in Wading River, NY, and credits the wooded trails of eastern Long Island as well as the cool waters of the Long Island Sound for his spiritualism, recreation, and inspiration. His introspective poetry has a penchant for passion, pain, and revelation.

Billy Hands is a lover of writers and a fighter of words, twisting them into positions that they just can't stand. A writer of poetry and song lyrics, Billy's work has appeared in many collections of poetry. He is the author of *You Can't Trade Up.* Billy lives in Orient, NY with his wife and three children.

Barbara Hantman has her MA in from Teachers College, Columbia University and had served the NYC public schools since 1982. She is Corresponding Secretary for the Fresh Meadows Poets. Her four poetry books include one that is fully bilingual: *Capullos Del Alma: Soul Buds.*

Patrice Hasbrook enjoys writing and painting from her home in Sag Harbor, NY. She received her education at the University of Minnesota-Minneapolis.

Meredith Hasemann-Cortes writes poetry, fiction, and drama. Her work has been published in many literary magazines and newspapers. Her poem *Tacqueria* was nominated for a Pushcart Prize by the Higgensville Review. She teaches 8th grade English in East Hampton.

Deborah Hauser graduated from Stony Brook University with an MA in English Literature and has taught at Stony Brook University and SCCC. Her poetry has appeared in numerous journals and anthologies. She is a poetry reviewer for *Sotto Voce* Magazine. Her academic writing has been published at *MP: An Online Feminist Journal*, and she has presented her academic work at national conferences.

MC (Mary) Healey is a member of the FCWG and the FPG. She is also a member of the PPA and TNSPS. She hosts the PIN poetry event the first Friday of the month at the Village Bookshop in Rockville Center. She has been writing poetry for three years and loves it.

George Held has been published widely across the USA, Canada, England, India, and Algeria. A five-time Pushcart Prize nominee, he is the author of six chapbooks and a book of poems; he is also the editor of the anthology *Touched by Eros* and the literary journal *The Ledge*. His most recent publication is *The Art of Writing and Others*.

Frane L. Helner is a Brooklyn-born, LI-raised, poet. Her book of poetry is entitled *Onion Juice*. Her poetry has been published in numerous literary journals and anthologies.

Gladys L. Henderson's poems have been published in numerous literary journals and anthologies. An award-winning poet, she is author of *Eclipse of Heaven*.

William Heyen was born in Brooklyn, NY. He is Professor of English/Poet in Residence Emeritus at SUNY Brockport, his undergraduate alma mater. His MA and PhD are from Ohio University. A former Senior Fulbright Lecturer in American Literature in Germany, he has won NEA, Guggenheim, American Academy & Institute of Arts & Letters, and other fellowships and awards. He is the editor of *American Poets in 1976, The Generation of 2000: Contemporary American Poets*, and *September 11, 2001: American Writers Respond*. His work has appeared in over 300 periodicals and in 200 anthologies. His books include *Pterodactyl Rose: Poems of Ecology, The Host: Selected Poems, Erika: Poems of the Holocaust*, and *Ribbons: The Gulf War, Pig Notes & Dumb Music: Prose on Poetry* and *Crazy Horse in Stillness*, winner of a Small Press Book Award for Poetry, *Shoah Train: Poems*, a Finalist for a National Book Award, and *The Confessions of Doc Williams: Poems*, and *The Rope: Poems, The Hummingbird*

Corporation: Stories, and *Home: Autobiographies, Etc.* Carnegie-Mellon University Press has recently released his first book, *Depth of Field*, in its Classic Contemporaries Series. His new book of poems is, *A Poetics of Hiroshima*.

Joan Higuchi was a first place winner in the PPA 2008 contest; she also received an Honorable Mention in TNSPS Poetry Contest and from Princess Ronkonkoma Productions in 2007. Her poetry has been published in numerous literary journals and anthologies.

Barbara Hoffman was the 1st runner-up for 2008 Bordighera Poetry Prize. Her poetry has been published in numerous literary journals and anthologies here and abroad. She was the subject of WLIW Channel 21 show – Originals – Arts on Long Island series. She was awarded Fellowship to Virginia Center for the Creative Arts, Amherst, VA, and to Stony Brook National Writing Project.

Martha Hollander is the author *The Game of Statues*, which was awarded the Walt Whitman Award by the Academy of American Poets. She is also the author of a chapbook, *Always History.* Her poems have appeared in numerous literary journals and anthologies. She is a professor of Art History at Hofstra University, and lives in Jackson Heights, NY with her husband and two sons.

Tony Iovino is the founder of the Summer Gazebo Readings, which raises funds to send underprivileged kids to a summer camp operated by the NYS Kiwanis. He is a native Long Islander, received his BA in History and Economics from the University of Richmond, and JD from St. John's University School of Law. He is the lead litigation partner in an eight-person general practice firm. His essays and reviews have appeared in *USA Today Magazine* (the Journal of the Society for the Advancement of Education, not the newspaper) and assorted on-line blogs; his poetry has appeared in numerous literary journals and anthologies and he has been a feature reader for PPA.

Lisa James has been published widely. She has won numerous prizes for her poetry, and has been nominated for a Pushcart Prize. Currently, she hosts PPA's monthly reading at Barnes & Noble in Huntington.

Mike Jenkins is a poet, novelist, and story-writer who writes for both adults and children. He lives in Merthyr Tudful, in the South Wales Valleys. His latest poetry book is *Walking On Waste*. He is co-founder and co-editor of *Red Poets*, in its 14th year.

Evelyn Kandel is an artist-poet. As an art teacher, she received a Fellowship award from Skidmore College. Her art is in private collections and has won numerous awards. She originally began writing poems to put in her constructed sculptures. She is a member of Taproot and Poet's Circle. She has taken workshops with George Wallace, Billy Collins and Marianne Moore. She hosts poetry readings sponsored by PPA. Her poetry has been published in numerous literary journals and anthologies.

Rita Katz is the author of five chapbooks. She is an award-winning poet who has been published in anthologies and journals. She is a member of Graphic Eye Poet's Circle and Taproot. She is also a member of Art Advisory Board-Port Washington. Her art work is in the permanent collection of NCC.

Bobbie Kaufman has been writing poetry since childhood. She has been a member of the LIPC and is a current member of the East End Poetry Workshop. Her poetry has been published in numerous literary journals and anthologies. She resides in Southampton, NY.

Nancy Keating has participated in workshops with Brooklyn Writers and Artists, Manhattan Writers and Artists, and Amherst Writers and Artists. Her work has been published widely. She curates the poetry-reading series, "Poetry in the Village" for the Babylon Village Arts Council.

Kate Kelly is active in the arts community both as a visual artist and poet. She has published her work in numerous small press magazines and on-line publications. She is the author of *Barking At Sunspots and Other Poems* and many chapbooks. She is a featured poet on the CD, inspired by Jack Kerouac, *Northport Celebrates Jack,* with music by David Amram.

Ann Kenna is a third generation Long Islander. Her poetry has been published in numerous literary journals and anthologies. When she is not writing, she can be found on the beach walking her dog.

Teri Kennedy is a member of the EEPW. Following the death of Francisco (Paco) Sainz in 1999, she spent countless hours in his studio cleaning and organizing and ended up inheriting art supplies from his studio.

X. J. Kennedy's *In a Prominent Bar in Secaucus: New & Selected Poems* was a 2008 Notable Book of the American Library Association. In 2009, he received the Robert Frost Medal from the Poetry Society of America for his life's work, and served as Poet-in-Residence at the Walt Whitman Birthplace in Huntington, LI, NY.

Kay Kidde lives in Westhampton and is the founder of Kidde, Hoyt & Picard Literary Agency in NYC. She was Senior Editor at New American Library and Harcourt Brace Jovanovich and also a schoolteacher. Her recent books of poems include *Home Light: Along the Shore, Sounding for Light,* and *Early Sky.* Her poetry has been published in numerous literary journals and anthologies. By invitation of the Suffolk County Community Council, she became the 2008 Long Island Woman of the Year for her work with Maureen Haven, a shelter for homeless women.

Alan King's fiction and poems have appeared in numerous literary journals and anthologies. A Cave Canem fellow and Vona Alum, his work was also part of Anacostia Exposed, a collaborative exhibit with Irish photographer Mervyn Smyth that showcases the life and energy of Anacostia.

Brendan Kirk of Southampton lives with his mother and two brothers inside a house upon a hill. He is 17 and shaves every two to three days. He would like to think that everything is happening for a good reason, but finds it hard to believe when ancient shapes lick secrets inside his ears and he never snaps out of it.

Denise Kolanovic is a poet and a Language Arts Teacher. She has published one poetry book, *Asphalt Sounds*. Her poetry has been published in numerous literary journals and anthologies. She co-edited several editions of *Eve's Legacy*.

Beverly E. Kotch is a holder of Scholarship Key in history from Phi Alpha Theta. She is Director of Program Development for the LIWG. Her poetry has been published in numerous literary journals and anthologies.

Lynn Kozma is a retired registered nurse, served in World War II. She is the author of two books of poetry, *Catching the Light* and *Phases of the Moon*, and one poetry chapbook, *Great South Bay*. Her work is included in *When I Am an Old Woman I Shall Wear Purple* and *If I Had My Life to Live Over I Would Pick More Daisies*. She is listed with P&W.

Belinda Kremer holds an MFA in Poetry from the University of Michigan, Ann Arbor. Her poems have appeared in numerous literary journals and anthologies. Some honors include a Hopwood Award for Poetry, a Meijer Creative Writing Fellowship, and a NYS Council on the Arts grant for a neighborhood poetry project. She is the poetry editor for *Confrontation*, a literary journal of LIU.

Mindy Kronenberg teaches writing and literature at SUNY, Empire State College and in community workshops for P&W and BOCES. Her poems, reviews, and essays have appeared in over 300 periodicals and anthologies in the USA and abroad. She is the author of *Dismantling the Playground,* a poetry collection, and is the editor of *Book/Mark Quarterly Review.* She has an interview featured online in "What Makes Poets Tick?".

Herbert Kuhner was born in Vienna in 1935, emigrated in 1939, and grew up and was educated in the USA living in Locust Valley, LI from 1944 to 1949. He has resided in Vienna since 1963. He is the author of novels, poetry, and plays and has published numerous volumes of poetry in translation, which include *Austrian Poetry Today* and *If the Walls Between Us Were Made of Glass: Austrian Jewish Poetry*. He plays the drums and is author of a collection of jazz poems, *Swing Men and Women*. His papers are archived at Boston University Library.

Phillip Levine is a poet, editor and performer. He is Poetry Editor for the *Mid-Hudson Valley* magazine and *Chronogram*. He is the president of the Woodstock Poetry Society & Festival, and hosts a weekly reading series and open-mike in Woodstock, NY. He is a five-year alumnus and invited reader of the Chenango Valley Writers' Conference. He was a featured poet at Woodstock Poetry Festival and coordinated a workshop for young poets at the festival. He has led numerous poetry workshops in local area middle and high schools, and taught an 11-week poetry class to incarcerated youth at the Highland Correctional Facility in Highland, NY through a grant from P&W and Incisions, Inc.

Maria Lisella was a finalist in the competition for Poet Laureate of Queens in 2007. Her poetry has been published in numerous literary journals and anthologies. She is a member of the online poetry circle, *Brevitas*. She co-hosts the IAWA readings and is co-editing an anthology based on those readings.

Wes Magee was born within sight of the River Clyde, Scotland. He worked as a primary school teacher and head teacher before resigning to become a fulltime author. He has published 5 poetry collections for adults - *No Man's Land* was a Poetry Book Society Recommendation, and over 80 books for young readers - fiction, poetry, picture books, plays, and anthologies. *The Very Best of Wes Magee* won the Children's Poetry Bookshelf Award. He lives in a cottage in Rosedale, a remote part of the North York Moors in England, UK.

Rita Malhotra is a Mathematician at The University of Delhi, India, and is a poet, essayist, and translator. She has been a Post-Doctoral Fellow at The University of Paris IX, on a French Government Fellowship. Her algorithm on Bi-criteria network problem is included in the Bibliography of Algorithm / Software in ZENTRALBLATT FOR MATHEMATIK HARDENBERGSTRABE, BERLIN. She was awarded a Michael Madhusudan Millennium award for poetry and education. Her poems are widely published in literary journals and translated. She has initiated a program called *Poetry Across Cultures* with support from the respective Embassies.

Mankh (Walter E. Harris III) is a writer, small press publisher, and Turtle Islander. He teaches haiku workshops, hosts the Locust Valley Library Poetry Society Series, and co-hosts a PPA reading at Smithtown Library.

Maria Manobianco is a member of the LIPC, LPS, LIWG, PPA, TNSPS, FCWG and FPG. Maria's first book of poetry is *Between Ashes and Flame*. She has an MA in Studio Art and a BS in Fine Arts Education. She resides in Farmingdale with her husband.

Joan Marg while growing up, her favorite pastime involved a chair, a window, and a book. Now she is a member of the FCWG and FPG. Her poetry has been published in numerous literary journals and anthologies.

Maria Matthiessen was born and brought up in Tanzania, East Africa, and now lives with her husband on Eastern Long Island. She was nominated for a Pushcart Prize.

JB McGeever's stories have appeared in numerous literary journals and anthologies. He's received consecutive IPPIE awards for best editorial from The Independent Press Association, as well as a full scholarship to attend The Southampton Writers Conference.

Sandy McIntosh's collections of poetry include *Forty-Nine Guaranteed Ways To Escape Death* and five others. His poetry has been published in numerous literary journals and anthologies.

Tom McManus teaches ethics in the MBA program at Hofstra University, and has been lead guest editor for three special issues of the international management journal, *Journal of Management Development*. He is President of the *World Water Rescue Foundation*, a member of the *NYC Friends of Clearwater*, and is on the organizing committee for the *NYC First Annual Water Festival*. He has a BA in History from Boston College, and a JD from The Vermont Law School. He is admitted to the bar in NY. He is a life-long sailor and lives on Eastern LI with his brother's cat, Louie.

D. H. Melhem is the author of seven books of poetry, including *New York Poems, Conversation with a Stonemason, Country*, and *Rest in Love*. She is also the author of *Heroism in the New Black Poetry, Stigma & The Cave*, and two short novels completing the trilogy *Patrimonies*, begun with *Blight*, currently in development as a feature film. Among awards for poetry and prose: an American Book Award, a National Endowment for the Humanities Fellowship, and three Pushcart Prize nominations. Part-time resident of Springs, she serves as VP of the International Women's Writing Guild.

Robin Metz has received the Rainer Maria Rilke International Poetry Prize for his book *Unbidden Angel*, the Literal Latté International Poetry Prize, the Marshall Frankel American Fiction Prize, and 14 additional international awards. His play Anung's First American Christmas received four "Top Ten" citations for its 2009 Chicago premiere. His poetry, fiction, and nonfiction have appeared in numerous national and international journals. He has presented his work in more than 70 US cities and in 23 nations. He is Director of Creative Writing, Knox College.

Edmund Miller, Chairman of the English Department at the C W Post Campus of LIU, is the author of several books of poetry, most recently *The Go-Go Boy Sonnets: Men of the New York Club Scene.* His stories were recently collected as *Night Times.* He is also the author of scholarly books about seventeenth-century British literature.

Jesse Miller is currently a student at Oberlin College in Ohio where he is learning to read minds. He has successfully read his own on several occasions and can sometimes guess the weather report.

Greg Moglia has had poems in over 100 journals in the USA, Canada, and England, as well as five anthologies. He has been nominated for a Pushcart Prize, as well as the University of Virginia anthology *Best New Poets Of 2006.* He lives in Huntington, NY.

Eliza Jo Morgan has been writing poetry for many of her seventeen years and has been nominated for a Pushcart Prize. She plays softball and was the first female wrestler for her high school. She will be attending SUNY Brockport with a double major in Education and ASL in the fall of 2009.

Annabelle Moseley's most recent published chapbook is *Artifacts of Sound.* She is Founder of the June Gallery of Poetry at The Stevenson Academy of Fine Arts.

Gloria g. Murray's works have been published in various journals and online including Ted Kooser's column. She has been nominated for a Pushcart Prize and is a member of P&W. Her new chapbook is *In My Mother's House.*

Melanie Myers is a native Californian living in the Bay Area for the last 33 years. Her passion for writing began at a young age; she has participated in poetry competitions through her college years. She has a BA in Mass Communications and she's a reporter/contributing writer for *The Spectrum Redwood City Magazine.*

Paddy Noble is an award-winning poet and has been published in numerous literary journals and anthologies. She has two chapbooks, *Kitchen Privileges* and *From The Outside In.* She co-hosts bi-annual poetry readings with Tammy Nuzzo-Morgan through TNSPS and the Bridgehampton Library.

George H. Northrup is President of the Fresh Meadows Poets. His poetry has been published in numerous literary journals and anthologies. He has also been featured on TNSPS's Arts Forum, poetryvlog, and QPTV.

Barbara Novack is Writer-in-Residence at Molloy College and a member of the English Department. She has written historical biographies, three collections of poetry, and novels, one of which was a finalist in Pushcart Press's Editor's Book Award competition. She is a member of The Authors Guild and is listed in the *Directory of American Poets and Fiction Writers*, *Who's Who,* and *Who's Who of American Women.*

Tammy Nuzzo-Morgan is the current and first female Suffolk County Poet Laureate and founder/president of TNSPS. She has her BS in Accounting & Business Administration from LIU, her MBA in Banking/Finance & Management from CW Post and is pursuing her MFA in Creative Writing & Literature from Stony Brook- Southampton. In 2006 her poetry book, *Let Me Tell You Something* was nominated for a Pulitzer Prize. She has penned 4 books, her latest is *For Michael.* She is Editor of *Long Island Sounds* and host of ***TNSPS's Arts Forum*** TV Show on CH. 20 on Cablevision in Riverhead. She is Chairperson for the Poetry Panel for the EEAC and is endeavoring to create an archival/arts center for LI poetry.

Thaddeus O'Neil's poems from his collections, *Thousand of Beautiful Girls and Three Ugly Ones* and *Oblivion Poems - Hunting Naked in the Green Mouth of the Swan,* have been featured in numerous publications. He recently collaborated with fashion photographer Bruce Weber for Weber's new clothing line, Weberbilt, producing garments which feature his poetry. He lives in NY with his wife/model, Pania Rose, two cats, dog, vintage surfboard collection, and a beloved 1960 Morris Minor Woody Traveler.

Linda Opyr is the author of six collections of poetry, including *If We Are What We Remember*: *New and Selected Poems.* All of her books have been published by Long Island presses. Her poems have appeared in numerous journals.

Alicia Ostriker has published eleven books of poetry, most recently *No Heaven.* Her anti-war sequence *The Mother/Child Papers* has just been reissued. She has been twice nominated for a national Book Award, and teaches in the Low-Residency MFA Poetry Program of Drew University.

Jim Papa, poet and essayist, is an associate professor of English at York College, CUNY where he teaches creative writing and literature. His poetry, essays, and literary criticism have appeared in journals around the country and locally, as well as in several anthologies. A sailor and surfer, he's a native Long Islander who grew up and still lives on Suffolk's south shore.

Joanne Pateman is a graduate of the MFA Writing program at Stony Brook – Southampton, and has been published in numerous local presses and anthologies. She has taken poetry classes with Julie Sheehan, Gerald Donovan, and Vince Clemente.

Simon Perchik is an attorney whose poems have appeared in prestigious presses and his most recent collection is *Family of Man.*

Russell Cameron Perry is an engineer, inventor, photographer, poet, wood craftsman, naturalist, and metaphysical philosopher, living in Nissequogue. He has been published in several journals. His love of nature leads him to Nature Conservancy sites all over the Island, to comb their beaches, fish and clam, and paddle his kayak in our rivers, bays, and harbors.

Nancy Picone has been published in several journals. She has participated in open mike events throughout Eastern LI and has given poetry performances in NYC.

Susan Pilewski is a graduate of the MFA program at Sarah Lawrence College. She teaches English at SCCC and SUNY Farmingdale. She was a radio co-host on WUSB along with poet George Wallace on the show, *Poetrybrook. Fetish* is her first full-length collection of poetry.

Allen Planz is the author of seven books of poetry, and has won numerous awards including two NEAs, two New York State fellowships, and one from the poetry society of Great Britain. He was poetry editor of *The Nation* and directed the LI division of the NYS Poets-in-the-Schools Program in the 1970s. He has been Poet-in-Residence at the Walt Whitman Birthplace. As a licensed captain, he has piloted both commercial and sport fishing vessels on the East End of LI, and has written extensively about the sea. He was the 2005 Recipient of **TNSPS Recognition Award.**

Anthony Policano is a poet who writes in order to free the dove hiding under the hat of springtime. He lives in Oyster Bay, LI, with his wife, daughter and King Charles Cavalier Spaniel (also, a female).

Philip J. Postiglione graduated from Dowling College, with a BA in Accounting. He is currently finishing a MA in Creative Writing at Warnborough College via their distance program.

Kelly Powell graduated from SUNY Binghamton's Creative Writing Program. She is a bookkeeper, living on LI with a couple of black cats, doing a little white witchcraft. She hopes someday all poets will drive Mercedes.

Elaine Preston is Assistant Academic Chair/English at SCCC/Grant Campus. She is listed in P&W. Her poetry has been published in numerous national journals. She is the author of *Look for a Field to Land* and *Fishing Underground*: *A Poet's Guide to Creating, Publishing, and Beyond.*

Tara Propper is an MFA student at Stony Brook - Southampton. She is an editor and featured writer for *Studio Photography* and *PTN* magazine. She also writes exhibition and book reviews.

JoAnn Proscia lives in Northport, NY with her husband. They have two sons. She loves poetry.

Dominick Quartuccio is a poet, fiction-writer, artist, and Christopher Walken impressionist. He lives on LI in a large tree with a gorilla that cooks for him.

Barbara Reiher-Meyers is a board member of the LIPC and TNSPS. Barbara curates a poetry calendar for www.poetz.com/longisland, and sends weekly emails of local poetry events. She has coordinated events for the NAC and Smithtown Township Arts Council. Her poetry has been published in journals and online. Barbara facilitates monthly workshops, and has edited several volumes of poetry. *Sounds Familiar* is the title of her first book of poems. She is one of the 2009 honorees of **TNSPS's Recognition Award.**

Marie Emmons Wayne Reinstein rediscovered writing poetry after a 30 year interval which included a career as a critical care nurse and the raising of 3 children. Her poetry book is *Old Poems*. Her poetry has been published in the PPA Literary Review. We are sad to say that Marie has passed on; we will miss her greatly.

Phil Reinstein with the untimely passing of his wife Marie has gotten involved in the poetry world through his adoration of her work, sharing her poetry at various LI venues. Encouraged by a few wonderful poets, he began writing as well.

Tom Romeo is a writer/storyteller. He performs as a solo artist and as one half of the storytelling duo, *Old Friends*, along with noted musician and songwriter, Judith Zweiman. He has a recording of his collection of poems entitled *Memorial Da*y.

Ruth Sabath Rosenthal has been published in many literary journals and has been nominated for a Pushcart Prize.

Andrea Rowen is a LI poet. Her work has been included on poetryvlog.com and in the anthology, *primal sanities: A Tribute to Walt Whitman.* She has been a featured poet at LI and NYC locations. Her BA is in Writing and Literature.

Paul Rubin is the nephew of Tammy Nuzzo-Morgan. This is the first time he has been published. He entered the Army in January 2009.

Alexander Russo requested assignment aboard a transport that landed troops in Sicily and he volunteered to make a graphic record of invasion activities in Normandy. He went aboard a landing craft that reached Omaha Beach on D+2 where he made drawings of invasion activities depicting Allied Forces activities, some of which were later reproduced in two of John Mason Brown's books, *To All Hands, An Amphibious Adventure* (McGraw Hill, 1943) *Many A Watchful Night* (McGraw Hill, 1944). His book of poems, *Vignettes,* is among the books in the LI Poetry Archival collection. Alex is a member of the EEPW.

Thaddeus Rutkowski is the author of the books *Roughhouse* and *Tetched.* Both were finalists for an Asian American Literary Award. He has been published in Walt's Corner in *The Long Islander*. He teaches fiction writing at the Writer's Voice of the West Side YMCA in Manhattan.

Wendy Salinger is the author of *Listen*, a memoir. Her book, *Folly River,* won the first Open Competition of The National Poetry Series. A Guggenheim Fellow, she has directed The Schools Project at the Unterberg Poetry Center of the 92nd St. Y in NYC for the past 20 years.

Darren Sardelli is an award-winning poet and children's book author. He has visited hundreds of schools and libraries.

Robert J. Savino is a native LI poet. His poems have been published widely. Robert was a long-standing Board Member of Island Poets. He new book of poems is, *Inside a Turtle Shell.*

Steven Schmidt is a software developer. He has a B Math from the University of Waterloo (Ontario) and an interest in modal & relevance logic and self-referential paradoxes. He was active in the Great South Bay Poetry Cooperative. He has participated in the LIPC peer workshop for 11 years. He hosts the Northport Arts Coalition's Poets-in-Port readings.

Mary McGrath Schwartz is a native Long Islander. She shared her love of reading and writing poetry with young children in the public schools as a teacher. Mary kayaks creeks and bays, hikes throughout the Pine Barrens, and swims in the ocean and sound.

Ron Scott is a native of Brooklyn, NY. He is an avid sportsman, dedicated to the preservation of outdoor life in all capacities. A veteran of the Vietnam War, he

496

credits his military experience for his introduction to the trials and rewards of the writer's life.

Alan Semerdjian is a multi-disciplinary artist. He released a chapbook of poems entitled *An Improvised Device*. His songs have appeared on television and film and charted on CMJ. He currently teaches at Herricks High School in New Hyde Park, NY.

Jackie Sheeler is a poet, performer, blogger, and producer with one full-length CD and three books. Once named the Poet Laureate of Riker's Island, she has performed widely and founded both the poetz.com website and the Pink Pony reading series.

Neil Shepard has published three books of poetry: *Scavenging the Country for a Heartbeat, I'm Here Because I Lost My Way,* and *This Far from the Source*. His poems appear in literary magazines as well as online. He founded the Writers Program at the Vermont Studio Center and directed it for eight years. He now teaches in the low-residency MFA Writing Program at Wilkes University, as well as in the BFA Writing Program at Johnson State College where he edits *Green Mountains Review*.

John L. Silver grew up on LI near Cold Spring Harbor. He was persuaded to do covers for *Tamarind Found* and was host of *Tamarind Collation* magazine for 10 years. He published his first book of poems, *Poems From a Trembling Road*.

Cathy Silverstein is a poet who lives in Wading River, NY. She says maybe someday she'll get her act together. The rest she leaves up to your imagination. Hint: she doesn't intentionally date Republicans.

Hal Sirowitz is the former Poet Laureate of Queens. His latest book, *Father Said*, was just translated into Icelandic. He is a former teacher; he got his Masters at Hofstra University.

Marcia Slatkin's most recent book is *A Woman Milking*. A chapbook about her relationship with her mother, an Alzheimer patient, is entitled *I Kidnap My Mother*. Her full-length volume of poems, *My Hollowed Mother*, includes 6 poems were accepted for publication by Ars Medica, School of Psychiatry, Toronto School of Medicine, Ontario, Canada.

Justin Slone while at NCC, was VP of the Creative Writing Club. He recruited members and coordinated special events, such as poetry slams. He was Editorial Assistant for *Luna*.

Callie Jean Slusser is a senior at SUNY Brockport. She is currently working on finishing a Theatre Degree and a Creative Writing Degree. She plans to move to CA after graduating to pursue an acting career as well as earn an MA in English and Fine Arts.

Barbara Southard starting out as a painter and printmaker; her work evolved over the years into combining word and image. Her poetry is a continuum of a lifelong process. A number of her poems have been published in recent years in various journals and anthologies.

Cassian Maria Spiridon is a poet and essayist, born in Iași. He has been editor-in-chief of the magazine *Convorbiri literare*, founder and editor-in-chief of the magazine *Poezia – Poetical Culture*, and director of *Timpul* Publishing House. He has published about thirty volumes of poetry, journalism, and essays. He is the recipient of many prizes for poetry and the prize for essay conferred by The Writers' Union. He is member of the Writers' Union of Romania, of the Romanian Journalists' Society, the Romanian Journalists' Association, and of the European PEN-Club.

Ed Stever is a poet, a playwright, an actor, and a director. His poems have been widely published, and his one-act plays have enjoyed productions in six festivals in Manhattan. He has appeared in approximately twenty-five to thirty plays.

Carole Stone's most recent book of poems is *Traveling with the Dead*. An essay "David Shapiro: New Jersey as Trope" was published in *Burning Interior David Shapiro's Poetry and Poetics*.

Mario Suško holds a PhD from SUNY Stony Brook and is currently an Associate Professor in the English Department at NCC. He is the author of twenty-five poetry collections, five of which were originally published in English. His new book of poems is *Closing Time*.

Douglas G. Swezey received his BA in English and Art History at Stony Brook University. He has since worked at the Walt Whitman Birthplace State Historic Site and Interpretive Center and written as a journalist for many weekly newspapers throughout Suffolk County. He is the author of *Stony Brook University: Off The Record*.

Patti Tana is Professor of English at NCC and the author of seven books of poetry, most recently *This Is Why You Flew Ten Thousand Miles*. She is Associate Editor of the *Long Island Quarterly* and Editor of *Songs of Seasoned Women*.

Gayl Teller is the current and first female Nassau County Poet Laureate and author of four collections, most recently *One Small Kindness*. She is founder/director of the Poetry Reading Series at the Mid-Island Y JCC, Plainview, NY, now in its 14th year; teaches at Hofstra University; and won the Edgar Allan Poe Prize for Literature; a National League of American PEN Women Poetry Prize; and First Prize in the Peninsula Library Poetry Competition.

Peter Thabit-Jones was born in Swansea, Wales. His latest book of poems is *The Lizard Catchers*. His poem "Kilvey Hill" has been incorporated into a permanent stained-glass window by the leading Welsh artist Catrin Jones in the new Saint Thomas Community School built in Swansea. He has tutored Drama, Children's Literature and Adult Literature for the Adult Education Department at Swansea University for fifteen years. He is founder/editor of THE SEVENTH QUARRY Swansea Poetry Magazine. His poem "Peace" has been awarded First Prize in the first International Festival of Peace Poetry. In 2008 he undertook a tour of the USA with Aeronwy Thomas.

Aeronwy Thomas born in London and brought up in Laugharne, South Wales, the town that inspired her father's play for voices, "Under Milk Wood." She is the daughter of Dylan and Caitlin Thomas and has inherited an interest in words, any shape or form. She is President of the Dylan Thomas Society, Swansea; Patron of the EDS Dylan Thomas Literary Award; President of the Alliance of Literary Societies; and was awarded an Honorary Fellowship from the University of Wales, Swansea. In 2008 she undertook a tour of the USA with Peter Thabit Jones. Her book of poetry, *Shadows and Shades* and a Memoir entitled, *My Father's Places,* were recently published. As well as publishing in many literary magazines and anthologies, she has several published books: *Later than Laugharne, Poems and Memories, Rooks and Poems, A Daughter Remembers Dylan,* and *Burning Bridges.* We are sad to say Aeronwy passed away during the production of this anthology; we will miss her greatly.

Juanita Torrence-Thompson is a poet, speaker, columnist, instructor and Editor-in-Chief/Publisher of 27-year old international *MOBIUS.* Her poetry book, *NEW YORK AND AFRICAN TAPESTRIES* was a *Small Press Review* best pick. Her award-winning work has been published in numerous US newspapers and magazines.

Edilberto González-Trejos was born in Santiago de Veraguas, Republic of Panama. He currently lives in Panama City. He is a writer, translator, attorney-at-law, and member of the Board of Directors of the Writers' Association of Panama. His poems have been published in several anthologies both in English and Spanish, as well as in North American and Latin American poetry magazines. He has published one poetry book, *Balanceo.*

499

Jack Tricarico is a NYC painter, poet, and T'ai Chi instructor who has been published in numerous poetry journals and anthologies based in NYC and in upstate NY. He has written 7 chapbooks of poetry and he lives in the East Village with his dog, Blanca.

Martin Tucker is the author of four volumes of poetry, the latest *PLENTY OF EXITS*. He is the author of five volumes of literary criticism, among them the widely-praised *LITERARY EXILE IN THE TWENTIETH CENTURY*, and the editor of more than 20 volumes of literary encyclopedia. He is Editor-in-Chief of the prize-winning literary journal, *CONFRONTATION*, and Professor Emeritus of Long Island University.

J R (Judy) Turek is the 1st Associate Editor for *Long Island Sounds*. She was awarded 1st place in 2009 The North Sea Poetry Contest and recipient of a 2008 Special Recognition for Years of Service Award from TNSPS. J R is the editor of *Young Voices An Anthology of Poetry by Nassau County Students* and Chairperson of the Nassau County Poet Laureate School Poetry Project. She is an award-winning poet whose poetry has been published in numerous literary journals and anthologies. She is in her 11th year as Moderator of the Farmingdale Creative Writing Group, and the author of *They Come And They Go*. She lives in East Meadow, NY with her soul-mate husband and their dogs.

Kempton B. Van Hoff is a lover of the ocean, reluctant human, interdisciplinarian, friend, educator, bipedal voyager, kung-fu disco warrior, eternalist and Hyperboreal. He presently dwells in a barn in Amityville, near the Great South Bay, where he writes, smiles, works on classic boats, makes art and love and fire and food, and generally enjoys his existence.

Kausalya Venkateswaran is a voracious reader of Tamil literature, both classical and contemporary. She lives in Chennai, India, and participates in poetry readings with her daughter, Pramila Venkateswaran, whenever she visits the USA.

Pramila Venkateswaran is the author of *Thirtha*. She has performed her poetry nationally, including the Geraldine R. Dodge Poetry Festival. She is currently doing multimedia performances that include dance, poetry and music. She teaches English and women's studies at NCC.

George Vulturescu was born on in Tireac, a hamlet in Satu Mare county. He graduated from the Faculty of Philology of Babeş-Bolyai University in Cluj-Napoca. He worked for the culture authority in Satu Mare: the Bookshop Department, the "G. M. Zamfirescu" House of Culture of Satu Mare. He has been chief counsellor at the Culture, Cults and National Culture Patrimony Inspectorate of Satu Mare. He is the founder, editor-in-chief, and producer of the literary review *Poesis, Satu Mare*, which was awarded several prizes.

Lois V. Walker has just brought out a collection of her poems, *Pandora's Box,* and continues to write and paint. She has served recently as an editor for two books of poetry. She continues to work with older writers for Taproot.
George Wallace is an award-winning poet and journalist from NY who has performed his work across America and in Europe. Author of sixteen chapbooks of poetry, he is Editor of *Poetrybay*, an online poetry magazine archived and distributed worldwide by Stanford University through its LOCKSS program. In addition, to he is Editor of *Long Island Quarterly*, *Polarity,* and *Poetryvlog.* In 2003, George Wallace was named first Poet Laureate of Suffolk County, NY. He was the 2008 honoree of **TNSPS's Recognition Award.**

Richard Walsh has a MA from LIU in English and is currently an adjunct professor at LIU as well as at SCC and Five Towns College.

Muriel Harris Weinstein has a children's picture book, *When Louis Armstrong Taught Me Scat,* and she penned a biography of Louis Armstrong, *Play Louis, Play!* She has had poems published in several anthologies.

Daniel Weissbort for many years edited the journal *Modern Poetry in Translation*, with leading British poet Ted Hughes. His recent book, *Historical Reader in Translation Theory*, was co-edited with Astradur Eyteinsson. He is an honorary professor in The Centre for Translation at the University of Warwick.

Mark Wells has been living on LI for most of his life. Mark has returned to his love of poetry and the musical arts after an absence of nearly a decade, during which he continued to earn certifications both at the Audio Recording Tech Institute. He works as a computer repair technician and personal tutor and also mans the tech department at Access Highway. He resides in Mastic with his two cool jazz cats, where he occasionally serenades his nice neighbors with medieval overtures on his ukulele.

Maxwell Corydon Wheat, Jr., Freeport, NY, first Poet Laureate of Nassau County by acclamation of poets, 2007 – 2009, was honored with **The North Sea Poetry Scene's Recognition Award in 2007**. He is a teacher for Taproot Workshops, providing writing instruction for people 55 and older.

Claire Nicholas White was born 1925 in the Netherlands and is a poet, translator, and art critic. She has lived in St. James, LI since 1947, except for four years at the Academy in Rome, Italy. She is the author of a novel, a biography, a memoir, a family history and of one volume and six chapbooks of poetry. She is the Editor of *Oberon*.

Jamie White is a graduate of Colgate University where he studied with novelist/short story writer Fred Busch and Anne Sexton.

Sandy Wicker has been writing poetry since childhood. She enjoys her participation in various poetry groups and has had her work included in several Long Island anthologies among other publications. She is a retired reading teacher and she has published two books, *The Tennessee Waltz and Other Dances* and *Finding My Jewish Self.*

Ginger Williams is a retired elementary teacher from the Three Village Schools. She co-facilitates a reading at the Cool Beanz Café in St James, NY with Gladys Henderson for PPA. She is the author of *Restringing the Beads*.

John A. Williams was educated at the University of Wisconsin and the University of California, Berkeley. He is the author of *Classroom in Conflict*.

Robert Windorf born and raised in Brooklyn, lives in Williston Park. He worked in the financial and non-profit industries for many years and obtained degrees in Russian language and literature, economics, Middle Eastern area studies, and adolescent education. A former college professor and lecturer, he is at present an EdD degree candidate. He is a middle school teacher, which ironically allows him more time to devote to writing poetry.

Jack Barrett Wohl was born in Vienna, Austria. Left Europe as a baby on the last American boat out of La Havre, France; attended orphanage; runaway; participated in gang wars; graduated City University with honors.

Walter C. Wojcik III was born and raised on LI's south shore where he developed a strong relationship to the land. He studied English at Stony Brook University and earned a degree in Secondary Education. His first chapbook of poetry is *Chasing Clouds Away*. He currently resides in West Bayshore and teaches English and poetry in the Copiague School.

J. Barrett (Bear) Wolf was born in Jamaica, Queens and raised in Freeport, LI, He has won numerous awards for his poetry, including first prize in the Stamford Festival of the Arts. His credits include *Rubber Side Down: The Biker Poet Anthology, Passing,* and *The Limestone Dust Poetry Festival Anthology, 2007 & 2008*. He is also a long-time member of the Highway Poets Motorcycle Club. He is editor of RoadPoet-NY.com, an online biker literary magazine. He is a decorated former police officer and a current volunteer fireman in upstate NY.